# ARCHAEOLOGIES

B

# Social Archaeology

**General Editor**
Ian Hodder, University of Cambridge

**Advisory Editors**
Margaret Conkey, University of California at Berkeley
Mark Leone, University of Maryland
Alain Schnapp, UER d'Art et d'Archeologie, Paris
Stephen Shennan, University College London
Bruce Trigger, McGill University, Montreal

**Titles in Print**

ARCHAEOLOGIES OF LANDSCAPE: CONTEMPORARY PERSPECTIVES
*Edited by Wendy Ashmore and A. Bernard Knapp*

ENGENDERING ARCHAEOLOGY: WOMEN IN PREHISTORY
*Edited by Joan M. Gero and Margaret W. Conkey*

SOCIAL BEING AND TIME
*Christopher Gosden*

IRON-AGE SOCIETIES
*Lotte Hedeager*

THE ARCHAEOLOGY OF ISLAM
*Timothy Insoll*

AN ARCHAEOLOGY OF CAPITALISM
*Matthew Johnson*

ARCHAEOLOGIES OF SOCIAL LIFE:
AGE, SEX, CLASS *ET CETERA* IN ANCIENT EGYPT
*Lynn Meskell*

CONTEMPORARY ARCHAEOLOGY IN THEORY
*Robert W. Preucel and Ian Hodder*

BEREAVEMENT AND COMMEMORATION: AN ARCHAEOLOGY OF
MORTALITY
*Sarah Tarlow*

METAPHOR AND MATERIAL CULTURE
*Christopher W. Tilley*

**In preparation**

THE RISE OF MESO-AMERICA
*Elizabeth Brumfiel*

TECHNOLOGY AND SOCIAL AGENCY
*Marcia-Anne Dobres*

ARCHAEOLOGY AS CULTURAL HISTORY
*Ian Morris*

ARCHAEOLOGICAL INTERPRETATIONS
*Robert W. Preucel*

# Archaeologies of Social Life

## Age, Sex, Class *et cetera* in Ancient Egypt

Lynn Meskell

BLACKWELL
*Publishers*

First published 1999

Transferred to digital print 2004

2  4  6  8  10  9  7  5  3  1

Blackwell Publishers Ltd
108 Cowley Road
Oxford OX4 1JF
UK

Blackwell Publishers Inc.
350 Main Street
Malden, Massachusetts 02148
USA

*British Library Cataloguing in Publication Data*
A CIP catalogue record for this book is available from the British Library.

*Library of Congress Cataloging-in-Publication Data*
Meskell, Lynn.
    Archaeologies of social life: age, sex, class et cetera in ancient Egypt/Lynn Meskell.
        p.   cm. – (Social archaeology)
    Includes bibliographical references and index.
    ISBN 0-631-21298-1 (hb:alk. paper). – ISBN 0-631-21299-X (pb:alk. paper)
        1. Egypt–Social life and customs–To 332 B.C.   2. Egypt–Antiquities.   I. Title.
    II. Series.
    DT61.M57   1999                                                  99-27890
    306'.0932–dc21                                                   CIP

Typeset in 11 on 13 pt Stemple Garamond
by Best-set Typesetter Ltd, Hong Kong
Printed and bound in Great Britain by
Marston Book Services Limited, Oxford

This book is printed on acid-free paper

*For Ian*

Les historiens, s'ils n'ont pas eu tort de renoncer à expliquer les actes du peuples par la volonté des rois, doivent la remplacer par la psychologie de l'individu, l'individu médiocre.

Marcel Proust, *A la recherche de temps perdu*

# Contents

# Figures

# Acknowledgements

This book would not have been possible without the constant support and inspiration of a great many people, foremost among them being John Baines, Ian Hodder and Dominic Montserrat. Throughout my time at Cambridge and Oxford they have been incredibly kind and generous with their time and their ideas. They heroically read the book in various stages, made valuable contributions and inspired me by their example. I owe them everything.

I have been especially lucky to have friends who have been there throughout my research and writing, making this a better project at every step of the way. My time at Cambridge would not have been the same without Emma Blake and Victor Buchli. Their close reading of the text has been an invaluable help, as have their companionship and sense of humour. Other friends have provided great inspiration and have shown me the personal and political virtues of feminism: Zainab Bahrani, Roberta Gilchrist, Rosemary Joyce and Susan Kus. Each took great time and care in looking over this manuscript and I have learnt a great deal in the process. They are the best role models a girl could ask for.

In the past few years I have been fortunate enough to establish a network of friends and colleagues who have generously read sections of the book at various stages and provided unpublished manuscripts and references: Kate Chedgzoy, Chris Gosden, Sandra Hollimon, Bernard Knapp, Andrea McDowell, Stephanie Moser, Stephen Mulhall, Jonathan Patrick, Diane Purkiss, Sarah Tarlow. Richard Parkinson, Gay Robins and Terry Wilfong kindly read the entire book and made valuable suggestions. Special thanks to Bruce Trigger who supported the project when it was proposed and then read the book in the final stages. I am very grateful for his many good humoured e-mails and his encouragement.

My research in Cambridge and fieldwork in Egypt was funded by a King's College scholarship between 1994 and 1997. King's was the perfect place to consider issues of identity and difference in an interdisciplinary environment. I will always be grateful for those three precious years. I am fortunate enough to have written this book while I was Salvesen Research Fellow at New College, Oxford, and I want to thank the Warden and Fellows of New College warmly for providing a wonderfully friendly and scholarly environment. They have been a source of daily inspiration. The Oriental Faculty in Oxford generously provided additional financial support, and has been a particularly positive place to be associated with. And, finally, I want to acknowledge Nick Dirks and the Department of Anthropology at Columbia University who patiently waited another year for me while I completed this book and many other projects – I hope it will have been worth the wait.

Many people and institutions have been extremely kind and generous. I owe an enormous debt of gratitude to the Institut Français d'Archéologie Orientale (IFAO) in Cairo, particularly Nicholas Grimal and Anne Gout for their help with the Bruyère archives and photographic material. Richard Parkinson helped with material from the British Museum, as did Elizabetta Valtz from the Egyptian Museum in Turin, and Catharine Roehrig from the Metropolitan Museum of Art. Other material was provided by Stuart Swiny. Lastly, I need to acknowledge Blackwell, but more particularly Tessa Harvey, for supporting an unorthodox project to link social theory with the archaeology of Egypt. She has proved to be a great editor and friend.

# Prologue

> Society is a very complex structure, and therefore the study of it cannot be simple. In any country at one time there are many varieties of it in different classes, and probably the contemporary differences are as great as those of many centuries in any one class. In different lands under different climates, with different ancestries and different religions, and still more different modes of life, the diversity far exceeds our power of realisation . . . It is not too much to say that the discoverer is the maker of society. Each step of discovery or invention reacts on the structure of social relations.
>
> W. M. Flinders Petrie, *Social Life in Ancient Egypt*

Flinders Petrie, acclaimed as the father of Egyptian archaeology, was perhaps a greater theoretician than has previously been thought. He saw the un-realized potentials of variability and difference in archaeology, especially Egyptian archaeology, and the importance of a contextual approach. Perhaps more importantly, he acknowledged that we make our own history in a very real sense. These issues are central concerns of this book. Difference and individuality are key concepts throughout this volume since they are indelibly linked to the fundamental social factors of sex, sexuality, class, status, ethnicity and age. Some might feel that these issues are very much of our time and perhaps not relevant to antiquity: they say more about us than them. Countering this I would suggest that for many groups, such as Egyptians of the New Kingdom (c.550–1070 BC), these identity issues were also pressing, although they may have been played out in very different ways. However, I also agree that we are writing our own history as we write the past. Questions of difference have a particular valency for me at the time of writing. Being Australian, female and coming from a social position which has no correlate in the British class system has subsequently reinforced my own variant position within the Oxbridge system over the past five years. When I was interviewed for the fellowship at Oxford, the first question posed by the panel concerned my place of birth, a small seaside town in northern New South Wales. They asked simply: how did *you* get here? Somehow I had transgressed my expected role in the scheme of things. Identity issues are always political ones: recognizing the valency of difference in the contemporary setting prompts us to consider the power of such machinations in the past. And the personal is always political, yet that measure of rebalancing the scales – past and present – should be viewed as a vehicle for positive re-evaluation.

It is for these reasons that I embrace a third wave feminist approach and apply it throughout this volume. While issues of sex are central to this approach, other salient identity issues are given prominence, be they class, sexuality, ethnicity or age. For many feminists these other vectors are just as important, if not more so. Simply being female has never proved substantive grounds for unity, and experience in the academic world serves to reinforce this. So while it is true that applying a third wave feminist approach is part of a personal project, I would argue that it is similarly a closer fit to the ancient evidence. Unsurprisingly, social life for women of the Egyptian elite classes was very different from that of domestic servants and slaves, and this is conclusively borne out by the Egyptian material data. Social experience also changed radically over the course of one's life and that recognition of temporality is something we might share with the ancients. In view of this, one could argue that the traditional woman-centred approach of gender archaeology, while valuable, cannot completely encompass the range of social relations experienced in the village of Deir el Medina (*c.*1500–1100 BC), the subject of this volume. I hope to have gone beyond finding or adding women (Wylie 1991: 34), although perhaps the *stirring* remains.

For many reasons this is an unorthodox project. It is not often that social theory is applied to Egyptian material and even less often that archaeologists are faced with the archaeology of Egypt – a *rapprochement* between fields could only be a productive step forward. Here I realize that my research falls outside many traditional categorizations. An interest in the archaeology of village life and of ordinary people is not always seen as the usual domain of Egyptologists. According to Andrén (1998: 41), '[t]heir focus on texts, pictures, and architecture has led to a concentration on philology, art history, and to a certain extent political history.' I hope to present another face of Egyptian scholarship to a wider archaeological audience who often deride the field for its inherent conservatism and general irrelevance. As an archaeologist primarily, I am always aware of the aura Egypt

holds, especially when surrounded in the UK with colleagues interested specifically in prehistoric Europe. Many consider Egyptian
material too exemplary and too different to bear on other research.
But Egypt does offer a viable data set, perhaps comparable to the
complex societies of Meso-America, and one which cannot be ignored
simply because of the wealth of its data. It is also one of the most convincing test cases for the application of social theory in archaeology,
as I hope the current work will demonstrate.

In the first two chapters I attempt to set the theoretical scene in
terms of individuals, bodies and personhood, as well as clarifying
many of the new issues surrounding sex, sexuality and difference. The
following chapters attempt to demonstrate how they are to be put
into practice with a substantive data set, the village of Deir el Medina.
These are complex themes and the reader might ask 'why Egypt?' or,
more specifically, 'why this village?' For me, Deir el Medina is the
Montaillou of the East (Le Roy Ladurie 1980), and there are many
stories to tell. Its history begins early in the New Kingdom, probably
under the reign of pharaoh Tuthmosis I (c.1504–1492 BC). At that time
the settlement was known as the *Place of Truth*, or simply *the village*
by its occupants. The inhabitants formed a rather special community,
specifically assembled by pharaoh and the state and placed in a
purpose-built village surrounded by an enclosure wall. Their *raison
d'être* was clear, they were the architects and workmen who created
the royal tombs in the adjacent Valley of the Kings. These men constructed the rock-cut tombs, decorated them lavishly and were
involved in the final burial of pharaoh. The team was drawn from a
number of locations and permanently housed, with their families, in
regularly constructed dwellings (Gutgesell 1989). The state also provided for them, sending rations on a monthly basis (Černý 1973; Valbelle 1985). They also supplied slaves or servants to each household
to assist with domestic duties. It appears to have been a unique existence, closely intertwined with and even monitored by the state. It
would seem to be the perfect exemplar for a top-down approach to
social history, ripe for studies of structuration or habitus, of inculcation and emulation. The village should have functioned in a more
structured way, as opposed to other settlements that were free to
develop more fluid, organic social and material trajectories. But *the
village* has challenged many of our preconceptions and the villagers
themselves led extraordinary lives. Of their many stories are tales of
murder, assault, bribery, robbery, private enterprise, legal battles,
adoptions, illicit pregnancies, social climbing, seductions and affairs,
and a surfeit of family problems. It renders a colourful tapestry of

social and anti-social behaviour in which individuals manoeuvred rather freely. As for the state, the workmen liberally took days off, some stole from the royal tombs, many went on strike due to slow payments and engaged in private enterprise at the state's expense. But there were also more routine incidents, such as the constant modification and expansion of village houses, trading state-supplied servants for other services, taking female slaves as partners, and so on. The possibilities were wide open. If we imagine that the villagers led a constrained life, perpetuating views and practices sanctioned by the state, leading the lives of dupes – we are creating a misleading fiction and selling short their vivid life experiences.

The village provides a perfect scenario to explore the tensions of society and self. In one of the most state-oriented contexts of the New Kingdom we can observe the desires and practices of people who stand outside the system, impelling us to question what constituted Egyptian experience, what counted as representative or normative? But the story does not end there. The richness of the material presents a vast social mosaic, which is comprised of the experiences of many individuals: elite men and women, servants and slaves, children of various ages, foreigners, the disabled, the elderly and outcast. Each presents a different picture of life in the village, challenging the nomothetic analyses one might ordinarily proffer. They catch us up, making our narratives more complex and messy, and potentially closer to ancient realities. Many of the issues surrounding these social relationships find a resonance in our own society: love and desire, the fluidity of relationships, family tensions, domestic violence, loss and betrayal. Irrespective of these familiar themes, the villagers experienced such issues through their own cultural lens and sought to resolve the disjunctures of social life in different and distinct ways. We might draw from this that social life is immensely varied and contingent and that what we take as essential or normative is predicated solely on recent experience: 'sexuality' is one such sphere, the construction of 'childhood' is another. It is not simply that the theoretical arguments bear upon modern social experience, but that the actual evidence of ancient encounters might open up a horizon of possibilities – another 'etc.' in the spectrum of cultural potentials.

Sourcing these fragments of social life, we find much evidence embedded in the substantial materiality of Deir el Medina. Today the site has some 68 well-preserved houses within an enclosure wall. From the archaeological remains we know that the 18th Dynasty village (c.1500–1307 BC) was smaller, some 40 houses, and the burials reveal a markedly ranked community. The wealthier cemetery was situated on the western escarpment, while the poorer cemetery was on the eastern slope. The Ramesside Period (c.1295–1069 BC) was marked by a larger, more cosmopolitan village with inter-related families and larger, more complex generational tombs. Many family members, including women and children, were incorporated into the tombs of the Western Necropolis, while the Eastern cemetery fell out of use. These tomb complexes show much greater wealth in terms of construction and decoration and suggest a less ranked community than in earlier times. The enclosed village was surrounded by almost 400 tombs containing burials dating from the 18th Dynasty to Graeco-Roman and Christian times. Those bodies have extraordinary histories, imparting knowledge about concepts of the self and embodiment, cultural trends, social difference, age/sex/class/ethnicity issues and, ultimately, personal histories. In addition, Deir el Medina is the most literate extant village in pharaonic history, yielding thousands of ostraca (inscribed potsherds or limestone flakes) and fragments of papyri, presenting yet another important corpus of evidence to draw upon and to use dialectically with material sources. John Baines (1988: 209) eloquently said of this dialectic that 'archaeology and writing complement each other's silences.' Despite the richness of the textual data, specifically in gleaning social information, we must be critical of its elite production, its canonical styles and specific genres. The archaeological remains may not always reveal the specificities of social interactions, yet they can offer more concrete evidence of social inequalities and differences, for example, which may be smoothed over in textual accounts. These are methodological issues not specific to studies of Egypt, but to many archaeological cases where texts are implicated (see Andrén 1998), be they Near Eastern, Mediterranean, classical, Mayan, medieval or historical archaeologies.

Many apologies have been made by Egyptologists for the particular nature and differential preservation of the Deir el Medina material, one result being that no complete, systematic research has been undertaken for the house or tomb assemblages *in toto*: this current research represents a first attempt at quantifying the extant data. While many qualifications need to be made, the Deir el Medina data still represent our best evidence for a New Kingdom settlement and associated cemeteries. Some years ago a rather unorthodox Egyptologist also attempted to uncover the people of Deir el Medina. John Romer (1984: xi) prefaced his book *Ancient Lives* by saying:

This is the biography of a 3000-year-old village – a village whose life is preserved in rich and often eccentric detail. Of one of its people, for example, there might remain a comb with some hair around it, a fragment of a letter, a receipt or two; of another, a legal document . . . I have aimed to make these ancient villagers walk through their own landscape once again. Nothing of the merely typical has been loaded upon an individual back: these villagers are *real* people . . . my descriptions of their homes, their belongings and their lives . . . are drawn from a mixture of scientific research and my own experience of the places where they lived and the work that they did there.

This is a sentiment with which I concur. The villagers of Deir el Medina were *real* people and many of their stories and life experiences are recoverable from the rich body of archaeological data from the New Kingdom site. They are more than simply *people*, they are individuals who can be teased from their historical milieu, as the textual experts have demonstrated for some seventy years. Nor are they the result of historical fiction, since they left tangible imprints in both the documentary and material record. Yet it must be said that Romer created his own embellished narrative and the result is a kind of popularist script for various outstanding village *men* in the Ramesside Period. While Romer's methodology was questionable, his intent to restore the individuality of the villagers and their lives, as represented materially, is perhaps in keeping with a postprocessual archaeology. In the 1990s attention has shifted towards an archaeology of the individual and identity, inspiration for which stems from developments in the social sciences. Finding suitable case studies to exemplify this approach has not been easy for archaeologists and there have been few publications in which theory and practice meet. Here I attempt to address the significant 'need for theory to stay rather closer to the ground' (Geertz 1973: 24).

In this volume I aim to mesh developments in social theory with substantive archaeological data to produce a social archaeology, in which society and self are seen as constantly constituting one another. Deir el Medina demonstrates that relationship in vivid detail. But this should not be seen as a strident programme for a contemporary individualism. I argue that both levels, society and selves, are necessary to produce a truly representative picture of the past. Each of the following chapters attempts to link large-scale social process with individual variation and choice, and to look at how the two levels interact with each other – a concept which can be traced back to Malinowski and Leach. These chapters illustrate that interdisciplinary contributions can truly stimulate archaeological theorizing, making social archaeology more rigorous and positioning archaeology as a relevant social science. Although archaeologists are not yet in a position to influence related fields by developing our own theoretical models, this goal may not be far off. We should not be suspicious of *outside* theory, nor should such theory be applied when clearly inappropriate. Theoretical insights from anthropology, sociology and feminist, masculinist and queer theory should prompt archaeologists to question some false foundational claims about the nature of sex and gender, the significance of the body and the individual and the fictional search for 'representative' data at the expense of variation and contingency. Each of these assertions has a palpable impact on archaeological research, specifically the undertaking of a social archaeology at Deir el Medina.

I hope that the project represents the people of Deir el Medina and portrays some measure of their complex social relations as they were played out through the centuries. Yet we can never truly *know* the people of the past, a lesson learned from our sister discipline, anthropology. In this endeavour we should not aim to present a unified narrative of life, since all data sets provide varying vignettes, whether it be textual, iconographic, domestic or mortuary archaeology. There is considerable slippage between what we say and what we do. And given Petrie's reminder that the 'discoverer is the maker of society', we should expect our constructions of the past to be multivocal and multivalent. The multi-dimensional analysis advocated here might present a range of different representations, yet this complex picture of life may be closer to the elaborate contradictions of reality, both in the past and present. In sum, an archaeology of individuals and their social relations is possible, if the questions we ask, and the interpretations we offer, allow the people of the past intention, volition and agency.

# 1

# Individuals, Selves and Bodies

The individuality of the individual does not consist in the autonomy of a singular set of powers and a singular sensibility within him or her. Nor does it consist in signifying a transcendental referent – an ideal category to which he or she would belong, or an ideal individual that his or her own individuality would reflect, in the measure that he or she participates through his or her own function in the scope of power of that ideal individual. For him or her to identify himself or herself is not to declare that he or she is a priest of a great God or a knight or servant of a great lord.

Alphonso Lingis, *Foreign Bodies*

Part of any investigation of social life involves an understanding of individuals, their social networks and socio-cultural context. However, all such terminology is loaded due to the pervasiveness of a particular Western historical narrative. Before embarking on an archaeology of the individual and providing alternative visions, those terms and associations require clarification. This also leads into discussions of personhood and culturally specific experiences of the self. While all societies recognize 'persons', each has different ways of transforming persons into individuals. Constructs of identity and selfhood are crucial in the steps towards that process of individuation. Personhood is similarly linked with the concept of the body, a core issue in interpretive archaeology, and a major theme of this volume. Egyptian data are particularly rich in this regard and the Egyptians themselves had much to say about personhood, the self and the body and its various constituents. Apart from their myriad writings on the topic, we are fortunate that many hundreds of bodies uncovered from Deir el Medina have their own material histories to reveal, specifically in terms of changing cultural traditions, social difference and inequalities, and personal predilections. The village offers one of the most fertile testing grounds to explore such themes and how they impacted upon the lives of specific people. Throughout this chapter I explore three inter-related issues: what are the existential grounds of individuality – its temporal and cultural specificities; how can we reconcile the individual with the multiplicity of social factors operative; and how can we recast the individual as an active agent within a social milieu? In considering these questions, I hope to demonstrate that social theory gleaned from sociology, anthropology and feminist theory can be successfully applied to a variety of archaeological contexts, bringing to fruition an archaeology of individuals, persons and bodies.

## Why Individuals Matter

Most theorizing about individuals has, quite understandably, come from outside archaeology, from fields such as philosophy, sociology, anthropology and the social sciences. Many social anthropologists now propose that it is in individuality that the roots of the social and cultural lie, so that a study of the individual is ontologically necessary. Except for the conscious individual, there is no social mover, no possibility of social progress or organization, of structured relations, routinized interactions or institutionalized behaviours. As Oscar Wilde (1913: 123) said, there can be 'no unity without individuals', i.e. no society. Even Margaret Thatcher had cause to comment, famously saying that there is 'no such thing as society, only individuals and families'. Because of the extrinsic nature of social theory, many archaeologists feel that accessing the individual in antiquity is an unattainable project and an inappropriate category of analysis. I believe that this is due to a disciplinary time lag and a definitional confusion. I use the terms 'individual' or 'individuality' to refer to a single person as the fount of agency, consciousness, interpretation and creativity in cultural and social life, by virtue of his or her sole ownership of discrete, corporeal, sense-making apparatuses. The term refers to a unique embodiment, both being and becoming each individual body (Rapport 1997: 6). Moreover, individual consciousness is responsible for animating social practices with energy, intentionality and meaningfulness. This 'single' identity is made up of a multiplicity of social variables – age, sex, class, status, religion, ethnicity *et cetera* – embedded within a matrix of social relations. The problem for archaeologists rests with the term 'individual', which is often conflated with the concept of 'individualism'. Put simply, an *individual* can be a single person, whose identity is made up of a host of social variables, whereas *individualism* is a particular historico-cultural conception of the person – the social actor as ostentatiously distinct, sovereign and autonomous. Individualism refers to independence of thought and action and is linked to notions of church and state, political philosophy and law, liberalism and so on. As such, this term has a very specific definition rooted in time and space, so that to deploy the concept of individualism is to set up a circular logic which excludes ancient societies by nature of their cultural and temporal circumscription.

This terminological conflation has prompted great debate in anthropology over the concept of the individual, and when the rise of the individual (as we know it) actually occurred: a debate initiated by Marcel Mauss's evolutionary position (Mauss 1938/1985). He claimed 'that there has never existed a human being who has not been aware not only of his body, but also of his individuality, both spiritual and physical' (quoted in Carrithers 1985: 234). This was reiterated 60 years later by Rom Harré, who argues that everyone has a sense of themselves as occupying a point of view from which they perceive the world around them and the state of their bodies (Harré 1998: 8). Yet concepts of selfhood only moved to centre stage for anthropology in the late 1970s and 1980s in tandem with developments in 'reflexivity' and the critique of writing, broadly inspired by the postmodern turn (Cohen 1994: 3). Prior to that time anthropology was in the grip of modernist theories of social determinism and was divided among Marxism, structural functionalism and positivistic functionalism. This was followed by symbolic interactionism with an attendant interest in hermeneutics, phenomenology and agency theory, each focusing upon the self and the symbolic links between individual and society (Cohen 1994: 69). Given the slow development in anthropology, a sister discipline, it is not surprising that archaeology has been remiss in taking up the challenge.

There have been sustained debates in anthropology over the term 'individual' and its application. Anthropologists have often made ethnocentric claims that 'primitives' have no real concept of the individual separate from their social roles and no morally universal idea of the person (Strathern 1996: 89). Others have posited that the rise of the individual was a result of Christianity (Dumont 1986), and have been duly criticized for this narrow circumscription (Cohen 1994: 14). Many still see the individual as a bourgeois post-Enlightenment concept, deeply embedded in the nation-state. But it would seem that even this recent notion of the individual is on the

decline (Turner 1996: 20). The rise of philosophizing about the individual might be highly topical today, but this does not negate the fact
that the concept of the individual existed in the past and in other cultures – in one form or another (see Geertz 1973, 1983). For instance,
why cannot *a* concept of the individual have been operative in ancient
Egypt? According to Midgley (1984: 51), the 'whole idea of a free,
independent, enquiring, choosing individual, an idea central to European thought, has always been essentially the idea of a male...taking
for granted the love and service of non-autonomous females (and
indeed often the less enlightened males as well).' The concept of the
autonomous individual is central to modern ideology, though as
Midgley and Melhuus point out, the definitions themselves are logically incompatible. Individuals are perceived as being of the same
kind, irrespective of race, sex, *et cetera*, each having equal value and
rights. To *read* autonomy here is to *read* male, with all other aspects
of difference being subsumed and glossed (Melhuus 1993: 238–9). In
fact, I would argue that concepts of individuals have always been in
flux, and in changing societies they continually take on new forms.
Bryan Turner (1996: 20) suggests that while we are still individualistic in terms of being knowing cognitive subjects, much of this cognitive rationalism has been replaced by an emphasis on emotionality,
sensibility and sensuality. According to writers such as Shilling,
Giddens and Synott, theories of the individual have been transposed
into the body project: focusing upon bodily image, presentation
of self, intimate relationships, sexual identity and so on. So that
even the popular construction of the post-Enlightenment individual
must now be tempered by socio-cultural changes at the end of the
twentieth century.

At present there are two positions on the rise of the individual.
There are the *universalists* who believe that there could never have
been a culture without concern for the human individual, and *rela-
tivists* who believe traditional societies thought of people as an undif-
ferentiated mass. It may be best to talk in terms of culturally specific
constructions of the individual, rather than prioritizing our own
Western precept. Psychologies of the individual in various cultures
are not simply structures of abstract thought, but should be seen as
functional realities operating within society and playing a key role
in establishing the boundaries of human nature, of which they are
supposed to be a model (Lukes 1985: 292). Again there is a recursive
process in place between self and society. Perhaps Mauss was correct
in stating that concepts of personhood are neither universal, nor
immutable: 'it is formulated only for us, among us' (Mauss 1938/1985:

22). There is no doubt that our current Western fascination with *individualism* is culturally specific, and at no other time has there been a stronger emphasis on self, with an intense focus on personal relations, personal feelings, privacy and bodily fixations. That this exists now in a highly articulated form is not to negate earlier forms of individual identities.

Employing an archaeological metaphor, we might consider that accessing the individual in antiquity relies on three related layers of interpretation. The interpretative bedrock is certainly the idea of experiencing oneself as an individual entity and this is connected to the body's materiality. Layered upon this is the culturally specific determination of what it is to be a person, in a given time and place, with specific thoughts and beliefs about one's body, mind, self, soul and so on. Thus an individual in New Kingdom Egypt will not have the same perceptions as ourselves: the concept of hermeneutics would verify this. This second stratum is overlain with a third, finer layer of interpretation – that of individually determined experience which depends on one's age, status, sex, class, life history, ethnicity, religious orientation, sexual preference *et cetera*, all of which produce individual difference and variation. No two people will experience themselves in exactly the same manner. Obviously this interpretative framework is itself conditioned by the modern Western mode of thought, which we cannot ultimately escape, though attention to anthropological and archaeological sources may assist in producing some necessary distance.

At this juncture, it is important to summarize briefly the pervasive historical views on the rise of the individual because it is this intellectual history that colours all contemporary interpretations about individuals both cross-culturally and in antiquity. I do not suggest that this narrative is correct, but it is the theoretical template from which we have previously patterned the past. Lastly, I want to challenge the grand sweep of history with some early examples from outside the Western *koine*.

## Historical Trajectories

I would like to outline Roy Porter's (1997) narrative for the rise of the individual. It is explicitly Western in orientation and, as Porter would recognize, presents a very ethnocentric, circumscribed and teleological account. The Western historical narrative begins with the 'dawn of consciousness': so called 'primitive societies' are assumed to have had a sort of tribal/group mentality, when all thought processes were collective and all activities communal. The traditional view was that the savage mind was in the grip of ritual and supernatural spheres, precluding any genuine individuality. The first real stirrings of indi-vidual consciousness came with the Golden Age of Greece (the great Oriental cultures of Egypt and Mesopotamia are excluded from this historical narrative, presumably because they were not European). In Greece, philosophers such as Socrates spoke of inner goodness and conscience, while the plays of Aeschylus, Sophocles and Euripides showed that the struggles between the individual and fate could only end in tragedy (see Williams 1993). And later, under the iron rule of the Roman emperors, stoic philosophers like Seneca were to find the ultimate expression of self-determination in suicide. This was followed by the age of Faith, which asserted the sovereignty of the inner self. The core doctrine of Christian belief was based on a unique, eternal soul, housed within the individual body. But while the individual had a choice between good and evil (remember Adam, Eve and the Devil himself), self-denial was the supreme good as demonstrated by saints and martyrs. Christian ideals sought to stamp down pride and vanity and, coupled with the feudal doctrine that everyone has his or her ordained place in the hierarchical order of lords, serfs, masters and men, the whole was greater than the parts.

In Darwinian terms, the ascent of man began in the Renaissance – and it is man alone who is the subject of analysis; women existed outside these discursive boundaries. According to traditional narratives, the Renaissance signalled a truly decisive breakthrough for individualism. According to Peter Burke (1997: 28), leading historians and art critics have always told us that Renaissance Italy was the time and place when mankind – meaning literate, gifted, elite males – began to liberate itself from the chains of custom, conformity and the church, leading to self-discovery and self-fulfilment. The literary movement of humanism rejected the dogma that man was a sinner and began to take delight in man himself, the apex of creation, master of nature, the wonder of the world. This is the time of the portrait, particularly the self-portrait, and of the diary and the biography. I will argue later that all such discourses were present in antiquity and that only cultural chauvinism stands in the way of our recognizing this.

From the sixteenth century onwards, the narrative continues, there was a new sense of personal singularity and distinctiveness. Michel de Montaigne (1533–1592) spoke eloquently of a 'room behind the shop all of our own', which referred to a distinctive store-room of consciousness which lay in each individual mind – a new personal world.

Some would call this the psyche. The seventeenth century formed the great divide in this evolutionary story. It was the point where rationality could serve as the foundation stone of the self-determining individual. According to this reading of the pysche's progress, it was René Descartes (1596–1650) who staked out a new role for the individual based on *cogito ergo sum* (I think, therefore I am). Man rethought the universe, against the notion of microcosm:macrocosm correspondences, seen so clearly in Shakespeare's writings. Descartes dreamt of the uniqueness of human interiority and invited later philosophers to probe the mechanisms of the mind. The question of who we were now hinged upon how our thinking processes worked and identity became a matter of intellect (Sawday 1997). John Locke (1632–1704) followed, claiming that the self is a product of experience and education; we are what we become. By implication, Locke gave his blessing to human diversity, change and progress. This was a bold vision where man became both the *producer* but also the *product* of social development (Porter 1997: 4). Other influential thinkers of the time, Hobbes, Spinoza and Leibniz, also grappled with issues of God and man (Morris 1991). The new Enlightenment myths favoured the model of the self-made man, and thinkers such as Francis Bacon spoke of man as the author of his own destiny. However, as Porter notes, this supposed evolutionary trajectory was to have its own sub-plots and complications. Consider Rousseau, and later the Marquis de Sade, who discovered that the anatomy of the psyche involved considerable psychopathology, a heart of darkness, that might have been better left unexplored or unsaid. Baring the soul acquired a seemingly inexhaustible fascination and one which has continued unabated.

In the eighteenth century the novel became the vehicle for such explorations of intense inner consciousness (Williams 1997). The individual also moved centre stage in a variety of other domains: political liberalism, the fundamental rights of life, liberty and property (if you were male), economic theories surrounding private property, and the market place. David Hume (1711–1776) and other rational hedonists contended that *homo economicus* was good for both the individual and society. New Enlightenment individualism reached its apex in the American constitution and in the liberty, equality and fraternity of the French Revolution. Romanticism pushed the individual to even higher planes, the sentiment being that life must be a journey of self-discovery (Porter 1997: 6). Such a journey attained almost a religious ethos and this notion of self-awareness as spiritual destiny fused in the philosophy of Hegel. Conversely, bleak philosophers such as

Schopenhauer and Nietzsche centred their tragic visions on the lone individual, isolated from society.

According to Porter, the quest for the ultimate self made a crucial breakthrough with the 'discovery of the unconscious' in the work of Freud, Jung and later Klein and Lacan. Psychoanalysis argued that the rational understanding espoused by Renaissance humanists was not, after all, master of its own house, and so not the real thing. What really mattered was the unconscious, repressed feelings expressed in illness, hysteria and nightmare. Thus, Freud opened new horizons of self-hood (or multiple selves), delving into the depths of dark desires and dangerous drives. And at the heart of this alien realm was sex and sexuality. The journey into inner space led to the single truth that the self's ultimate secret was sexuality. Our present century is one which has spawned scores of creeds and cults, building on Freud and similar experts, and claiming to help people understand themselves, maximize their potential, like themselves, express themselves and, of course, be themselves (Porter 1997). Giddens also (1991, 1992) posits this as a time of the intimate self where the self is a project we work on and improve, whether it be our relationships or our bodily image. Relationships and emotional integrity have become key concepts for contemporary individualism, and this was clearly seen in modern British society with the death of Princess Diana and its surrounding phenomena (Merck 1998). This highlights how the concepts of *individualism* and emotionality have changed within a matter of decades: all such terms are flexible, fluid and highly contextual. Indeed, Marilyn Strathern (1992) has even taken issue with this view of a progressive increase in individualism, suggesting rather that what we term *individualism* has merely changed.

I have presented an overview of a singular, popular Western narrative of the individual from the Greeks to the Renaissance, from humanism to Romanticism and from the Enlightenment to psychoanalysis. Other theorists who might have figured in Porter's narrative, such as Wittgenstein, Hegel, Lukács, Durkheim, Husserl, Heidegger and Merleau-Ponty, have been summarized elsewhere (Morris 1991). This is simply one story, but it is the evolutionary paradigm in which most current theorists are steeped and which accordingly constructs their views of modern and pre-modern individuals, as well as those from other cultural contexts. Significantly, the story began with the Greeks, our supposed intellectual ancestors, and not with non-European cultures. Western interpreters cast the latter as 'primitive', 'exotic' and 'other' in a host of intellectual spheres from anthropology through psychoanalysis to fine art. The narrative does not take into account the civilizations of Asia, Africa, the Americas or the Middle East from which there is certainly evidence of self-conscious individuals: they too wrote biographies and painted portraits.

Archaeological evidence provides examples of this alternative history. As a case study I have chosen the mummy portraits from Roman Egypt, which clearly depict individuals and are rather tantalizing in terms of biographies. I describe briefly their contexts of production and use them to challenge explicitly the traditional Western narrative outlined above. The portraits derive from a mortuary context and clearly convey a sense of the individual, although whether they were completely realistic is debated. The portrait as a record of an individual's personal appearance in his or her lifetime has long been regarded as one of the most successful and enduring genres of Roman art.

The mummy portraits began in the mid-first century AD and stayed in vogue for some 200 years. In Egypt they were made for a local purpose: to cover the head of the mummified person represented in the portrait. They were there to serve as a record of the deceased as he or she appeared in life. They can be dated according to stylistic analysis and by careful assessment of hairstyles, clothes and jewellery worn by the subjects (Walker 1997: 14). The physical appearance seems to tell us something of their subjects and their familial relationships with others: scholars have proposed identification of parents and offspring, for example, on the basis of apparent familial resemblance. Most do not have accompanying inscriptions, but some tell us names, ages, professions, date of death, parentage, place of residence. According to Walker (1997: 16), one woman is known as a teacher of Greek grammar. These portraits also convey a keen sense of individuality: skin tone, facial hair, bone structure are meticulously recorded. When studied in context, some portraits do seem to reflect the age and sex of the individual body under the portrait and mummy wrappings. Various scholars have argued that these portraits were commissioned during their lives and hung in houses before death. Others may have been painted at death, especially in the case of young children. Dominic Montserrat (1996) claims that the portraits also tell us something about ethnicity, status and sexuality. Several show youths with varying degrees of facial hair, often crowned with gold garlands – it is likely that they represent boys who had a traditional Greek education. Many are shown tanned, reflecting the fashion for tanned male beauty in imperial times. According to Montserrat (1993), tanning also had well-documented homoerotic overtones at the time. The young male is a well known and widely attested type in the portraits and they were usually post-pubertal. Given the cultural background of Greek and Roman sexuality, we know that there was considerable interest in same-sex relations between men. Consider the portrait of the young boy, named Eutyches, who lived around AD 100–150 (figure 1.1). From the Greek text we know that he was a freedman of

**Figure 1.1** Mummy portrait of Eutyches, freed slave of Cassianus, from the Fayum (courtesy of the Metropolitan Museum of Art, New York, Inv. 18.9.2)

Cassianus Heraclides and it is possible that the latter commissioned the costly portrait. The fact that Cassianus cared enough for Eutyches to liberate him, pay for an expensive funeral and record this on a funerary docket so that he might be reborn as a free man in the next life suggests a close emotional tie, possibly even a sexual relationship, between the two (Montserrat 1996: 156). Irrespective of the intimate details, it should be clear that neither the concept of the portrait, nor that of the individual, is a recent or Western invention. Moreover, we should question the teleological construction that frames the question of individuality in terms of genres like portraiture or biography.

## Why is the Individual Ontologically Necessary?

In moving away from this historical scene-setting it is important to examine why the individual has become such a key concept in the social sciences, of which archaeology is part. Many contemporary disciplines are now focusing on reinstating the individual, and I believe that part of the reason for this new fascination is a backlash against structuralism and post-structuralism, first developed in France and then imported into British scholarship. This theoretical tradition involved writers as diverse as Durkheim, Foucault and Giddens. In their writings, it is social actors, rather than individuals, that are the initial point of reference which are then subsequently dissolved, decentred and deconstructed. And they see them as products and pawns of social structures or social relations or systems of signification (Rapport 1997: 7). The holistic tradition, so strong among American sociologists and British structural anthropologists, stressed the need for society to impose itself over individuals and imprint itself upon their consciousness (Cohen 1994: 15). This led to a burgeoning growth of discourse theories, best illustrated in the work of Ricoeur, Bourdieu, Foucault and Giddens (see below). Foucault is perhaps the best-known example of a theorist who placed great importance on discourse at the expense of the individual. He said 'it is a matter of depriving the subject of its role as originator, and of analysing the subject as a variable and complex function of discourse' (quoted in Rapport 1997: 171). Foucault has rightly been charged with writing unpeopled histories. Reacting against Foucault's position, anthropologists such as Nigel Rapport have written in defence of methodological individualism:

While it is certainly true that human life is lived in personal relationships, and while individuals depend on others (living and dead, real and
imagined, particularised and generalised) for all matter of securities,
physical, emotional, intellectual – while human individuals contextu-
alise one another – nevertheless, they begin from different points
(bodies, brains, consciousness) and, ultimately, they end there too. The
personal relations in which individuals live may eventuate in sharing
and intimacy of a variety of levels and kinds, but not necessarily in a
common or even consistent knowledge of the relations that are being
practised. (Rapport 1997: 25)

Individuality does not entail individualism. The latter connotes
a particularistic vision of the individual fashioned especially by
Enlightenment thinkers and their followers, a supreme, autonomous
and consciously self-made 'man', whereas individuality refers to
human agency, intentionality and creativity. Expressions of individuality vary greatly according to context: from hunter-gatherers
to pastoralists to subsistence agriculturalists to peasants to villagers to city-dwellers, new intellectualizations are always being
offered. As Victor Turner cautioned, 'there were never any innocent, unconscious savages, living in a time of unreflective and instinc-
tive harmony. We human beings are all and always capable of
laughter at our own institutions' (cited in Rapport 1997: 46). Other
astute observers such as Clifford Geertz still argue that 'becoming
human is becoming individual' (1973: 52). But in the past it was
customary for anthropologists to make generalizing statements
about the societies that they studied and to perpetuate the top-
down approach. They have in turn affected the way in which
archaeologists have sought to identify cultures and representative
social units.

Anthropologists, and by extension archaeologists, have read
culture as a constant. Durkheim's influence has been pervasive
through the traditions of structural-functionalism and British structuralism. As such, the individual was consigned to membership of the
structural elements of society: lineage, village, caste or another collectivity (Cohen 1994: 14). We have come to see society as something
objective – 'out there' – a cohesive unity, a set of structures and rules
that will, if we are fortunate, leave tangible patterns in the archaeological record. What we primarily strive for in our quantitative analses
is representativeness or the core of a communal culture. We are asked
regularly to identify a type-site, a typical settlement or tomb, and
this is something we have shared with anthropology. But, recently,

anthropologists such as Anthony Cohen (1994: 20) have realized that such accounts of cultures and communities have resulted in narrative fictions often prefaced by 'the Bemba think that...; the Bedouin believe...'. And, again:

> [t]here is no essential opposition between the consideration of the self and the description and analysis of social relations, indeed, quite the contrary. In the past, our concern with groups and categories, that is with the social bases of social relations, has largely ignored the dimensions of the self and self consciousness, and may therefore be regarded as having dealt with bogus entities ... which focuses wholly on what a person *does* socially to the exclusion of who the person *is*. (Cohen 1994: 7)

In our unconscious ethnocentrism, we accord the possibilities of self-awareness or detachment to ourselves, but seldom to others.

The fundamental premiss of anthropology, and by default of archaeology, is that society imposes itself on its members and thus reproduces itself with each generation, albeit with some modification. So the self is merely a reflex of superordinate determining forces. If one follows that outline, one can then be satisfied with a notion of representativeness leading to observable patterning. I would suggest we need a more nuanced approach, in which large-scale social process, individual response and creative transformation are all acknowledged. Historically, archaeological formulations have tended to deal with classes or groups of peoples (*women* being a classic example) at the expense of the individual. Such an approach can be insightful for the general societal level upon which the individual is constituted. The category of the individual is a social construction, and it cannot be mutually exclusive from society. The individual is always situated relationally and relationships with the social and material environ-ment are always in a state of flux. Additionally, we must consider the temporal dimension since one's attitudes, for example, are rarely stable throughout life (Harré 1998: 7).

Archaeology has tended to ignore the relationship of the individ-ual to society in favour of treating individuals simply as micro ver-sions of larger social entities. This is achieved by extrapolating from the supposedly representative sample of *society* to the assumption that subjects are the normative constituents which aggregate to make the whole (Meskell 1996a, 1998a). Kirsten Hastrup (1995) has referred to this as the 'fax-model' of the internalization of culture, suggesting that the individual simply copies a set of shared notions about the world; socialization is reduced to a process of getting the original through the fax machine! While many cultural notions are shared, social practice cannot be studied without reference to choice or individual creativity. Western social science tends to proceed from the top downwards, from society to the individual (for example, Thomas 1996: 96), deriving individuals from social structures to which they belong: nationality, state, religion, generation and so on (Cohen 1994: 6). For instance, processual archaeology has been stridently critiqued for being 'acutely unsatisfactory about social phenomena . . . because it is excessively materialist and drastically underconceptualizes the individual actors from whose behavior large-scale social phenomena emerge' (Cowgill 1993: 551). We cannot continue to privilege society and treat individuals as merely socially or culturally driven, ignoring the authorial or self-driven aspects of behaviour. My work on New Kingdom Egypt provides numerous instances of individuals as authors of their own destinies, from female slaves enhancing their status by becoming pregnant to elite men of the household (Meskell 1997a), adopted children rising through the ranks, and high-status men falling from grace. Yet these incidents are generally considered idiosyncratic and unworthy of study, whereas collective behaviour alone is deemed worthy and meaningful.

Part of the explanation for this focus on society, especially in anthropology, is that it was and is much easier to deal with structures and institutions and to make inferences from them to people. Social anthropology began as encyclopaedic comparisons of systems of law, kinship, ritual and so on. In contrast to the classic view, which defines culture as a self-contained whole made up of coherent patterns, culture should be viewed as a more porous array of intersections where distinct processes criss-cross. These heterogeneous processes often derive from differences of age, sex, class, race and sexual orientation (Rosaldo 1989: 21). Influenced by anthropology, the concept of culture has taken prominence, yet it has often been formulated as a monolithic, implacable and somewhat abstract entity. Nigel Rapport (1997), in sardonic tone, has implied that 'society', 'culture', 'ritual and religion' have become autonomous entities of their own determination, orientation and evolution. They have a life of their own in both anthropological and archaeological accounts. As Clive Gamble (1998: 428) has persuasively argued:

> The study of social archaeology traditionally depends on definitions of institutions, be they bands, tribes, chiefs and states, sodalities, kingroups, alliance networks, connubia, peer-polities, élites, craft specialists, theocracies, cores and peripheries or world systems. The procedure

is then to identify, usually by means of a checklist (Gamble 1986), these institutions through their component parts. Hence, we recover temples, palaces, villas, exchange systems, status burials, writing, monumental sculpture, storage, defences and production centres. Then we work towards definitions within a well-ordered social framework. The institutions thus defined are seen as *preceding* the individual who is born into them and grows within them. Very often they are presented as adaptive where culture and society become synonymous.

But individuals are more than their membership and participation in collectivities and these collectivities are themselves the creations of individuals (Cohen 1994: 133). A salient example of individual innovation towards material culture is evidenced in the work of Helen Cordero, a Cochiti woman, who created a genre of 'storyteller' ceramics in the Southwest which reinvented and revolutionized a moribund tradition of pueblo pottery. As a result she reshaped cultural life in her own community as well as in many others (Babcock 1993). The importance of imagination and creativity, while slowly coming to the fore in anthropology, has yet to make a substantive impact in archaeological theorizing.

Archaeologists need to discuss both levels of data, the social and the individual, where possible. Not all archaeological contexts, however, will have illuminating information on both. Many archaeologists feel that they cannot access the individual, especially in prehistoric contexts. Despite this reticence or lack, most of us could in our analyses work back and forth between these two levels. We need the general social and cultural information to set the background, to provide knowledge on general trends and social patterning. This is the context in which individuals are embedded and to which they can respond, changing and creating the social matrix. But they are never free from society, or the networks of social relationships that link them to other people. Alternatively, we need to recognize the individual level – that archaeologists actually uncover individual houses and tombs and we often extrapolate from them in the attempt to make generalized statements. But in the end they remain single entities and they are necessary to demonstrate human diversity and variability. If we fail to recognize the complexities of self and society we end up with two potential extremes: complete glossing or complete idiosyncrasy. Anthony Cohen (1994: 71) puts it neatly when he refers to the relationship between society and self as a:

*pas de deux*: each tries to cover the moves of the other, sometimes they merge, at others they separate. Their combination may be harmonious or awkward in the extreme. Society creates the illusion (which social science has perpetuated) that it controls the dance, because it sets the music and the stage. But, to coin a phrase, it takes two to tango!

At issue here is the acknowledgement of individual agency. This stresses the 'active involvement of individuals in the creation and performance of social life' (Gamble 1998: 430). Agents initiate causal sequences of a particular type: 'events caused by the acts of mind or will or intention, rather than the mere concatenation of physical events' (Gell 1998: 16). But, as Gamble reminds us, such a stress does not mean that the individual is unfettered either by historical circumstance or by other individuals. In 1989 Matthew Johnson called for a socially aware archaeology, which took account of individuals, agency and human intentionality. He suggested that this would 'fill a gap in our understanding of the cause of material culture variability . . . we cannot understand such variability without reference to active agency' (1989: 190). This he separated from the project of identifying 'real people,' as one can in historical archaeology. I would suggest that both propositions, as distinct lines of enquiry, are possible and desirable. At the close, Johnson was still left with problems arising from the dualism of structure and agency. Yet the encounter between society and self doesn't have to be pitched in micro : macro terms or even at the level of structural dualism. Emma Blake (1999) has suggested that we dispel that other dualism, structure : agency in favour of a dynamic nominalism. This follows from Ian Hacking's (1995: 247) idea that 'categories of people come into existence at the same time as kinds of people come into being to fit those categories, and there is a two-way interaction between these processes.' Following Hacking, Blake suggests that self-categorization influences not only what one chooses to do, but also the behavioural possibilities available. This might seem at first glance to be no more than agency theory in a new guise, but Blake cautions that there is a significant difference. Self-categorization is not merely a type of agency, in the sense of it being an agent's way of negotiating through the structural framework, but is itself a structuring device. As discussed below, agency theory posits that these two principles, though enmeshed and recursively informing each other, are distinct. The example of self-categorization makes sense only if the concepts are in fact one and the same: structures are no more than ingrained practices. This may prove to be a much more nuanced and realistic way of conceptualizing social process as well as social relations.

## Discourse Theories

> I do not want to risk dissolving the lived experience of the subject into the anonymous field of discourse, allowing Episteme or Language or Mind to take on the epistemological privileges denied to consciousness and subjectivity.
>
> Michael Jackson, *Paths Toward a Clearing*

Georg Simmel (1971: 27) once said that 'society exists where a number of individuals enter into interaction; society is interaction.' But individuals and interaction have often been downplayed, perhaps understandably, for the sake of uncovering larger-scale cultural patterning, often under the rubric of 'discourse'. Agency is often eschewed in these narratives. While it is easy to acknowledge that to be human is to be a differentiating entity, this presents problems in recovery for social theorists and archaeologists alike. Not surprisingly, individual accounts cannot always be extrapolated out to *society* at large, and it is *society* which most major thinkers aim to understand and explain. This is, after all, what sells books, and what challenges us to rethink our own position in the scheme of things – a point not lost on Michel Foucault in *The Archaeology of Knowledge* (Foucault 1972). Foucault was one of the pre-eminent writers of discourse theory. He was famously to say: '[d]iscourse is not life; its time is not your time; in it, you will not be reconciled to death' (1972: 211).

The broad label of 'discourse theory' has been deployed to cover some of the most influential social theorists of the twentieth century: Ricoeur, Bourdieu, Derrida, Foucault and Giddens. As Foucault, Derrida and Lacan have argued, the notion of a self-contained, authentic subject conceived by humanism to be discoverable beneath the veil of cultural and ideological overlay is, in reality, a construct of humanist discourse itself. Following Alcoff's critique (1997: 337), the subject itself is not a locus of authorial intentions or natural attributes or even a privileged, separate consciousness. Lacan uses psychoanalysis, Derrida uses grammar, and Foucault uses the history of discourses to deconstruct the notion that the subject has an essential identity which is natural to us. Many now challenge the views of Foucault, who depicted the individual as having no motivation, intentions or agency at all. Moreover, post-structuralists have denied the individual the ability to reflect on social discourse or to challenge its determinations. What has proved so appealing about this movement is its capacity to encompass a multiplicity of differences, suggesting an inherent contradiction in the aims and outcomes of the work.

Because discourse theories have been so pervasive in archaeological writings in the past two decades, it is necessary to examine briefly their impact and discuss the rationale for their popularity.

Ignoring chronology, I wish to examine Anthony Giddens's work first since his writings have perhaps had the greatest impact on archaeology in the 1980s and 1990s (for example, Barrett 1988, 1994; Thomas 1996; Gamble 1998; Lyons 1998). Despite the fact that much of this work is now under scrutiny (Shilling and Mellor 1996: 1), or has been surpassed, it remains an important source for questions concerning *society* and *self* in archaeology (see Last 1995: 148–53). In an early paper John Barrett employed Giddensian structuration to construct a scenario of 'knowledgeable agents' who were 'constrained by the very world of their creation' (Barrett 1988: 8), yet he only ever alluded to how this applied to material contexts. Oddly, Barrett's major contribution in this short paper was to propose that gender was constructed as a relationship rather than an activity zone (1988: 13): a far-sighted disclosure that long remained unexplored and seems rather distanced from structuration theory. The problem with theories like structuration (Giddens 1984), which are widely cited in the archaeological literature, is that they treat society as an ontology which is somehow independent of its members (Meskell 1998a: 157). The agency Giddens allows individuals gives them the power of reflexivity, but not of motivation: they are doomed to be perpetrators rather than architects of action. While he recognizes that selves are reflexively made and individuals do contribute to social influences (Giddens 1991: 2–3), this is rarely demonstrated in his over-arching theories. His individuals are over-rationalized and over-socialized (Craib 1992). As stated in the Prologue, we might imagine that the state-initiated village of Deir el Medina, existing within the framework of a hierarchically ordered society like New Kingdom Egypt, might readily conform to Giddensian structuration. Yet all the evidence points to a minimum interventionist model, where individual villagers exercised a remarkable amount of social mobility and manoeuvring, ignoring the sanctions of the state to their own personal benefit and profit. Individuals subvert the system, and customarily rise through the ranks by mechanisms such as bribery and corruption, adoption or even fortuitous pregnancy. Under the force of such data it is difficult to subscribe to his more reductive theories of social life.

For Giddens, selfhood might be a reflexive project, but his agents take for granted the existential foundations of that selfhood and parameters of activity, along with philosophical analysis and so on (Giddens 1991: 37). Moreover, he posits that people are *essentially* minds for most of their lives, rarely shaped by the sensual experiences of the body. He fails to reconcile structuration theory with the phenomenological experience of embodiment. The body might represent a core feature of structuration theory, but 'it exerts a predominantly constraining influence on both the exercise of human agency and on the reproduction of structures' (Shilling and Mellor 1996: 3). Although Giddens seems eager to jettison the structure : agency dualism, he erases notions of irrationality, contingency and sensuality in the process. He displays a certain amnesia to the sociological tradition – to Marx, Weber and Durkheim who stressed the 'rational' and 'emotional' dimensions of human action (Shilling and Mellor 1996: 6, 12). His bodies are there to be managed and moulded according to the dictates of the mind. It is the mind which is reflexively activated, rendering the sensual and embodied nature of individual agency absent.

However, my real point of contention is Giddens's temporal chauvinism, which accords modern society certain freedoms and self-construction, set against the narrow confines of traditional or non-modern societies. For Giddens, tradition structured action and ontological frameworks in non-modern societies (1991: 48), which is simplistic and reductive in the main. In terms of the individual, he quotes Baumeister's notion (1986) that the 'idea that each person has a unique character and social potentialities that may or may not be fulfilled is alien to pre-modern culture' (Giddens 1991: 74). While Giddens wants to temper this to some degree, I think the general tenet continues to colour his work. His position is formulated from ignorance of rather than any specific reference to *other* cultures or ancient ones. And this is a key point for Giddens, since much of his argument is based on the positioning of high modernity as essentially different from its precursors. In fact, his volume *Modernity and Self-identity* is laced with these pre-modern : modern dichotomies. Here I am not suggesting that this work is not valuable in a contemporary context, rather that the application of such theories to non-modern and non-Western contexts is considerably problematic (see chapter 3).

But was 'structuration theory' simply Bourdieu's theory of habitus a decade later? According to Bourdieu (1977: 79–80), 'subjects do not, strictly speaking, know what they are doing, [and] that what they do has more meaning than they know.' He defines habitus as the 'universalising mediation which causes an individual agent's practices, without explicit reason or signifying intent, to be none the less "sensible" and "reasonable" '. A common-sense world is constructed, imbued with *objectivity*, secured by a consensus of meaning and reiterated by ongoing practices, eschewing individual agency in the process. Habitus is the product of history which generates individual and collective practices in accordance with the schemas engendered by history (Bourdieu 1977: 82). As with structuration theory, Bourdieu's habitus is another over-arching discourse theory which leaves little room to manoeuvre in individual terms. Class habitus, for example, means that interpersonal relations are never, except in appearance, *individual-to-individual* relationships, and that such interactions are not bounded to the event itself. He goes so far as to say that 'the history of the individual is never anything other than a certain specification of the collective history of *his* [my italics] class or group' (Bourdieu 1977: 86). While it is true that individuals, past and present, recognize the marks of their social position, this does not necessarily constrain their opportunities for innovation and self-fashioning. A more radical view might posit that 'culture does not impose meaning on individuals. It provides *form* which individuals substantiate themselves' (Cohen 1994: 50). Where Bourdieu appears to be more flexible is in his concept of bodily *hexis*, allowing for individual and systemic interactions (Meskell 1998a: 153). Although he acknowledges the hierarchies set up between things, persons and practices, his primary focus is upon generative schemes. And though he pays lip service to contradiction and contingency, these important transformational practices remain side-lined.

So why has habitus been so influential a model for archaeology? First, it is an explanatory model for large-scale social practices that focuses on reproduction/inculcation on a grand scale, rather than on individualizing strategies. So it is broad and general, seemingly attainable from the long-term record, as well as being socially determined. Secondly, Bourdieu describes habitus as a system of dispositions – a past which survives in the present and then perpetuates itself in the future. This is certainly the subject of any historical discipline, particularly archaeology. Habitus might then be used in areas as diverse as the phenomenology of landscape approach to the study of distinct groups or classes of people. For example, it would be possible to argue for an application of habitus to Deir el Medina since the village provides sufficient data to represent certain patterning among age and class groups. We might be able adequately to characterize the 'system of dispositions' operative in the elite sphere, although this would be more difficult for other social groups. Additionally, there would be significant overlap at both upper and lower ends of the elite spectrum. However, such a structure would have to be modified according to rather short time-spans, say, for example, from the 18th to the 19th

Dynasty where there is significant change in the representation of social relationships. This pattern is borne out in the cemetery data, and while it may not exactly mirror social *life*, such material is after all what most archaeologists have to work with. Here I suggest that habitus could be a useful model, but only on a rather small and circumscribed scale.

Perhaps the most successful deployment of Bourdieu's theory in archaeology is Gilchrist's *Gender and Material Culture* (1994). In her eloquent study of medieval monasticism, Gilchrist concludes that the 'hegemony of medieval religion conspired to create a habitus for women, in which their own desire for spiritual salvation caused them to reproduce the structural gender relations of medieval society through their own agency. And it is particularly through material culture that *habitus* constitutes gender' (Gilchrist 1994: 15). What is innovative here is her reading of gender as habitus itself, coupled with the recognition that religious women were active agents in the processes of socialization and enculturation: they were not structural dupes. Additionally, her data set seems particularly pertinent to the concept of habitus: it is socially circumscribed, with a well-developed attendant ideology, explicitly disciplinary and regulated, and historically documented. It is a concrete illustration of theory meshing with data (Meskell 1998b: 183–4).

Decades after his original writings on habitus, Bourdieu has produced a series of essays under the title of *Practical Reason* (Bourdieu 1998), in which he hopes to clarify his original intent. His theoretical position seems to be essentially unchanged. Right from the outset he posits a two-way relationship between the social field, which he defines as 'objective structures', and incorporated structures, defined as habitus. And, as he makes clear, habitus is all about generalizing strategies and remains unconcerned with contemporary issues of difference. He goes as far as saying that he wants to be divorced from anthropological accounts of practice. Whether in his discussions of class, education, sport or politics, his view is invariably from the top down. His over-arching patterns are deterministic and ultimately serve to reinforce the status quo. Perhaps this is simply the world view of a French intellectual. Yet anyone reading this who fails to conform to their predicted class, status or educational niche, who perhaps doesn't care for opera or football, will see the limitations of such a rigid, deterministic and somewhat gloomy view of life's myriad possibilities.

Most influential of all the deconstructionists and a strident advocate of discourse theory, Michel Foucault spent some 25 years writing

books that challenged the liberal belief in human agency and popu-
larizing Barthes's concept of 'death of the author'. Writers of subjectivity were simply deluded, in his view, because, as Porter reflects
(1997: 11), 'Foucault argued for the primacy of the semantic sign
systems, cognitive structures and texts. We don't think our thoughts,
they think us; we are but the bearers of discourse, our selves are discursively constructed.' In attempting to survey Foucault's corpus of
writings, two elements of his theory of discourse are striking. First,
he suggested that discourse creates subjects as well as objects and, secondly, knowledge and power are inextricably linked in discourse
(Hekman 1990: 18). It is not surprising, then, that his main subjects
of analysis were the prison, the clinic, the madhouse and, memorably,
the scaffold (Foucault 1977a, 1978, 1985, 1986, 1989a,b). His interests
coalesced around sexuality, madness, illness and deviance and their
concomitant discourses of discipline, domination, bodily regimes,
surveillance and power. Underlying this was a real fascination with
the corporeal and the visceral, and many of his works are dramatic
evocations of bodily torture, disease, medicalization: 'the malign
effluvium that exudes from the bodies of the sick, from gangrenous
limbs, decayed bones, contagious ulcers, and putrid fevers' (Foucault
1989a: 17). He was primarily interested in re-thinking history, rather
than attempting to theorize for its own sake. This was summarily
illustrated in *The Birth of the Clinic* (1989a: xix), where he aimed to
'disentangle the conditions of its history from the destiny of discourse, as do others of my works'.

Perhaps his most famous work was the influential trilogy, *The
History of Sexuality* (1978, 1985, 1986), although here his contribution to history has been largely questioned. Throughout, Foucault
explored power relations over the social body, although I would argue
that he adopts a more moderate position than that expressed in *Discipline and Punish* (1977a). In the latter volume, he detailed the historical emergence of complex social practices that regulate human
behaviour, moulding and forcing individuals through historical
inscription (Crossley 1996: 102). The human body is a passive receptacle for historical interventions. He once commented that 'One needs
to study what kind of body the current society needs' (Foucault 1980:
58). In his over-inscriptional fashion, he described bodily investment
as the 'insistent, persistent, meticulous work of power on the bodies
of children or soldiers' (Foucault 1980: 56). Similarly, his history of
sexuality is analogous to the historical relationships of power and discourse on sex, which is ultimately a self-recursive process (1978: 90).
He does not situate power as an institution, structure or strength we

are endowed with. Rather, it is the name given to a complex strategic situation in a particular society (1978: 93). Power is not an abstraction that can be acquired or seized: it is exercised within a scheme of asymmetrical relationships that include interactions of a social, economic, sexual or knowledge-based nature. He adhered to the notions of domination and resistance, though neither can be in a position of exteriority. There is a plurality of resistance which is irregular and dispersed temporally and spatially, and which may even cut across social stratifications and individual unities (Foucault 1978: 96). For Foucault, bodies are 'broken down by a great many distinct regimes' and as such are 'totally imprinted by history' (1977b: 153). Finally, he seeks to cast off the preoccupation with rationality within such processes, since power relations can be both intentional and non-discursive or non-subjective. Foucault's descriptions of power have been duly criticized for delimiting the possibilities for individuals to have power or agency. Moreover, late in Foucault's career *power* was endowed with enough theoretical gloss to encompass many qualities within social relations (Anderson 1995: 71).

It is important to contextualize Foucault's work, since it both informs and is challenged throughout this volume. One must also recognize its fluidity, that there is neither a uniform programme throughout his *oeuvre* nor uniformity in style. His work should not be read as history, but as combative intellectual challenges to re-figure normative assumptions and complacency. His meta-narratives and sweeping histories are intended sensationally to shake us from the belief that all is right with the world and that we have arrived at some logical outcome of the historical process. Like everyone, I have different responses to his different writings. His studies of the clinic, prison and madhouse, while providing evocative reading, are too reductive and power-based, whereas his studies of sexuality find important contemporary resonances and have been very influential in my own work on Egypt. His ideas on difference and history are also deeply relevant to archaeology. Indeed, much of his work suffuses this volume, although it operates in a dialogic manner. Many of my criticisms are more forcefully directed at what I term Foucauldian archaeology, especially with regard to power and the body, than to Foucault himself (Meskell 1996a). Archaeology once readily adopted Foucault's canons, although major adherents such as Shanks and Tilley (1987a: 129–30; 1987b: 70–3) gave primacy to a narrow and rigid concept of hegemonic power, exploitation, domination and resistance that presents a simplistic and formulaic binary equation. For a time, Foucauldian regimes of power took hold in archaeological theorizing (see the contributions in Miller and Tilley 1984; Shanks and Tilley 1987a,b; Miller et al. 1989; Thomas 1989, 1993; Tilley 1990). There is an inherent danger in dealing with issues such as class and sex since the picture presented is one that highlights a model of oppressor versus oppressed, which is in itself a form of temporal/cultural chauvinism which reinforces those relations – whether or not they existed in reality. At present, the firm grip Foucault held on archaeological theories of agency and power seems to be on the decline, possibly to be replaced by more nuanced theories of difference.

I would suggest that these narratives, albeit briefly outlined, were formulated somewhat earlier than in the major works of Bourdieu, Foucault and Giddens by Paul Ricoeur. Writing since the 1940s, the appeal of Ricoeur's approach lies in his acknowledgement of distanciation, which allows for the critique and transformation of social structures, rather than viewing them as the implacable structures described by later writers. Many of these ideas are developed in his *Hermeneutics and the Human Sciences* (Ricoeur 1981). He sets up a dialectic between ideology and individual critique, which is always historically embedded. He argues that we are sufficiently distanced from our history to appreciate that we belong. Distanciation is an essential part of understanding ourselves as historically constructed beings, so that it is literally the condition of understanding (Ricoeur 1981: 131; Moore 1990: 101). This suggests that self-awareness and reflexivity are part of the transformative process and integral to Ricoeur's thesis. Distanciation and belonging operate in dialogue, a vision that seems more progressive than the imposition of structuration or habitus. Drawing on the work of Austin and Searle, Ricoeur posits that discourse should be seen as an internal dialectic between event and meaning (1981: 11). Thus discourse is always seen through an interpretive lens. As Henrietta Moore (1990: 111) notes, 'the social world is made up of individuals who speak and act in meaningful ways; these individuals create the social world which gives them their identity and being, and their creations can only be understood through a process of interpretation.' Action can never be interpreted objectively, so that every aspect is a reading, a re-reading and so on. This is not to deny structure, but rather to underscore its imaginative and interpretative elements. Unlike later writers on social structure and action, Ricoeur affords the individual the necessary agency, intentionality and meaningfulness. The sadly attenuated self presented in structuration theory was a later development, perhaps even a step backwards from Ricoeur's theorizing. Lastly, in his analysis of history, he proposes that we 'recognise the values of the past in their differences', leading to the acknowledgement that 'there is only a history of the potentialities of the present' (Ricoeur 1981: 295). This is a potent theme taken up by later scholars such as Foucault in his notion of history (see chapter 6).

## An Archaeology of Persons and Selves

Leaving aside theories of the individual and society, I want now to move to the level of personhood. There are complex concepts layered around terms such as 'person' or 'individual', and in many writings (within and outside archaeology) it is easy to conflate terms. In teasing these out, there appear to be four critical terms: *individual, person, identity* and *self*. In most discussions, archaeologists are either targeting individuals or concepts of the person. As previously outlined, the individual is the skin-bound mortal human being, and the primary object of observation (Alexander 1998). Personhood endows the 'culturally recognized individual as a social being with those powers or capacities upon which agency depends' (Poole 1994: 842). In Western culture a person is a 'spatially bounded organism', and what individuality does, in effect, is to transform the person, a social someone, into a real social agent with intention and volition. Persons are 'to be understood as the result of ascribing subject status or selfhood to those sites of narration and expression which we call human bodies' (Rapport 1997: 75). Identity is what is draped over a person by the group of which he or she is part. Identity is subject to change and is multiple. The person is constituted from a host of identities, all relying on social attitudes to age, sex, class, marital status, ethnicity, nationality, religion *et cetera* (see chapter 4). Not surprisingly, none of these terms – individual, person, identity or self – is fixed and all are interconnected in lived experience.

Even in cultures that place great emphasis on membership of a collective as the basis for personal being, the groundwork is still the singularity and ultimate uniqueness of every person. At the same time, each unique human being is a complicated network of ever-changing personal attributes and relations. Alfred Gell (1998: 137), in his discussion of Pacific societies, has referred to the 'fractal person'. Each is enmeshed in a series of networks with other individuals: partners, family members, friends, community, state and so on. Rom Harré has elegantly argued that 'each human being is a person, a unique, embodied centre of consciousness' (1998: 72) and that each is 'rich in attributes and powers of many kinds, having a distinct history. According to the Kantian principle, people should not be treated as means to an end, but ends in themselves' (Harré 1998: 71). When people refer to personhood, they are referring to discursive productions; that is, in dialogue and other forms of joint action with real and imagined others. Persons are not simply entities, but evanescent properties of the flow of public and private action (Harré 1998: 68). This is clearly demonstrated in Marilyn Strathern's work on gendered persons in Papua New Guinea. The Hagen person is seen as an embodied set of internal relations, and rather than being unitary, as in the West, each person is part of a plural, multiple or partible composition: 'In the partibility of its extensions into relations beyond itself and in the internal relations that compose its substance, the body consequently appears as a result of people's actions' (Strathern 1988: 208). As such, society does not operate like a unitary code over individuals, and human achievements do not culminate in culture. She remarks of the Sambia, '[p]ersons composed of one kind of relation subsequently appear to be composed of another, as Hagen men transform their identities from spouse into male, and from male into one of two types – clansman or exchange partner' (1988: 220). Likewise, she recalls work on the Kanak of Caledonia, which similarly shows that social reality is not centred in the body; rather, it is the place where they have their names and it corresponds to a relationship. Drawing on Leenhardt's ethnography, the name can never cover the whole person since the Kanak are obliged to have a different name for every relationship domain (Strathern 1988: 269). Personhood is a relational state: the 'person is construed from the vantage points of the relations that constitute him or her; she or he objectifies and is thus revealed in those relations' (1988: 273). As a corollary, the agent is conceived as the one who acts because of those relationships and is revealed in his or her actions. Here Strathern is describing multiple selves which are aspects of individual persons. Each person is a narrator of selves. Obviously, language inscribes these discourses and the language of the ancients is not commensurate with our own, and thus our constructions and categories are fundamentally different. However limited we are in our pursuits, the desire to enable them to give voice to their own experiences where possible should not be devalued because of the hermeneutic pitfalls.

Moving to the level of selfhood, Rom Harré has argued that the self is not an entity, but the site from which a person perceives the world and a place from which to act. To have a sense of self is to have a sense of one's location, as a person, in a culturally constructed context of personhood. The self is the collected attributes of a person.

But the self in ancient Egypt would not correspond with selfhood in ancient Mayan culture, contemporary Papua New Guinea or Anglo-America. According to Harré (1998: 4–5), there are three fundamental layers of the self. First, there is the point of view from which one perceives the material world and acts upon it, which is indispensable to the management of human life. Secondly, there is the concept of the self as the shifting totality of personal characteristics and these attributes might be fairly permanent or evanescent, some intrinsic, others existing only in relation to aspects of the human and material environment. And, thirdly, we should consider the personal impressions we make on other people. None of these operate in isolation. The self could be described as the inner, subjective sense of being. The presentation of the self is thus the negotiation between this inner self and an outer layer modified by social expectation, role and setting. From bodily change to psychosocial behavioural alterations, the process of being is one of constant renegotiation.

> If we regard social groups as a collection of complex selves (complex, because any individual must be regarded as a cluster of selves or as a multi-dimensional self) we are clearly acknowledging that they are more complicated and require more subtle and sensitive description and explanation than if we treat them simply as a combination of roles. (Cohen 1994: 7)

We all have to juggle the contradictions within our selves to cohere neatly with others in groups and in society at large. People constantly change to accommodate families, peer groups, colleagues and so on. These finer-grained dimensions of the individual are not easily retrieved from the archaeological record, especially in prehistoric cases. Obviously, historical contexts will prove more fruitful.

Given this rich sociological framework, it is possible to tease out several dimensions of the individual that archaeologists, in fact, regularly pursue. First, there is the cultural concept of what constitutes a person. How do people in specific cultures perceive themselves, from ancient Egyptians (see chapter 3) to classical Greeks, or from Papua New Guineans to urban Westerners? A second dimension is a focus upon the anonymous individual or individual bodies. This occurs most frequently in mortuary contexts (for example, Morris 1987; Bietti Sestieri 1992; Bard 1994; Carr 1995; Last 1998) or the phenomenology and landscape approach (Thomas 1989, 1995; Barrett 1994; Gosden 1994; Tilley 1994). A third might be individuals and their actions: this is most likely an approach borrowed from art history, referred to as attribution, which seeks to identify the artist's hand (Hill and Gunn 1977; Keller 1984; Morris 1993). Fourthly, there is the representation of individuals in texts (McDowell 1999), iconography (Bailey 1994; Lesure 1997) or architecture (Johnson 1989; Gilchrist 1994) which gives an intimate sense of self. And, fifthly, the most complex study is probably the historically known individuals (Černý 1973; Bierbrier 1982, 1990), individuals like those from Ur (Pollock 1991) or the villagers of Deir el Medina (Meskell 1996a, 1997a, 1998c). These archaeological studies are usually bolstered by documentary details. It is these individuals that we *feel* that we can *know* more fully and talk about more confidently. None the less, I am not suggesting that this is tantamount to contemporary *individualism*, with its intense focus on personal relations, personal feelings, privacy and bodily fixations.

It is perhaps timely that archaeology recognize the potentials of locating the ancient individual, given the contemporary interest in social studies generally. The narrative of the self and its concomitant reflexivity cannot be avoided in the postmodern setting. As a corollary, we are also currently engaged in the democratization of personhood, where women, children, ethnic minorities and homosexuals can claim their rights to the category. Drawing on the insights of feminist theory (De Lauretis 1984, 1986), we might aim to formulate a subjectivity which gives agency to individuals while simultaneously placing them within their particular discursive configurations. Subjectivity may thus become imbued with gender, race and class without being subject to an over-determination which erases agency (Alcoff 1997: 343). Given society's reluctance to recognize these persons in modern times, it is no wonder that we deny similar possibilities for ancient individuals. We are similarly in a position to interpolate difference and identity issues into archaeological dialogues, providing a space from which we might (re)consider individuals in the past. As Joyce and Claassen (1997: 7) remind us:

> [d]ifference between individuals is not simply noise to be factored out of general propositions that can hold true for all members of past societies that created sites we attempt to understand. Difference is, instead, at the heart of the creation of distinctive settings for action, and distinctive kinds of action, that we can perceive archaeologically.

A significant dimension of the individual, personhood and identity is surely the locus of the body itself: at times a somatic grounding for the self and at other times merely a linked entity. Experiences and constructions of the body provide an important existential grounding for individuality and for the processes of individuation in any given culture. Sociological debates revolving around the self and the individual are fundamentally connected with the recent emergence of a sociology of the body (Turner 1996: 190). This is a domain which archaeology has eagerly seized upon, but given its wealth of related data – whether textual, iconographic or material – the success of archaeology's project has been variable. Some have deemed it easier to uncover cultural concepts of the body, than to identify individuals, in the past. Previously the body has been cast as an object, a thing, a metaphor for society or a product of semantics (Jackson 1989: 123). Such isomorphic relationships might be compelling, but these reductive elisions cannot be epistemologically sustained. Following Grosz (1995: 104), the body is a concrete, material, animate organization of flesh, organs, nerves, skeletal structure and substances, which are given a unity and cohesiveness through psychical and social inscription of the body's surface. But the *body* is not tantamount to embodiment. I have previously argued (Meskell 1996a, 1997b, 1998a) that embodied individuals constitute the site of intersection for a host of social factors and determinants. An embodied body represents, and is, a lived experience where the interplay of natural, social, cultural and psychical phenomena are brought to fruition through each individual's resolution of external structures, embodied experience and choice (Berthelot 1991: 395–8). It represents the nexus of several different irreducible domains: the biological and the social, the collective and the individual, structure and agent, cause and meaning, constraint and free will. But, as the following sections demonstrate, it is 'not enough to reformulate the body in non-dualist and non-essentialist terms. It must also be reconceived in specifically *sexed* terms. Bodies are never simply *human* bodies or *social* bodies' (Grosz 1995: 84). In the following section new readings of the body and corporeal philosophy are offered, specifically the materiality of embodiment rather than a reductionist treatment of representation and exteriority. Here I draw predominantly upon anthropology and feminist theory to rethink the archaeological body, illustrating these formulations with relevant ancient examples.

## Bodies Matter

This section takes its title from a key work written by Judith Butler, *Bodies that Matter: on the Discursive Limits of 'Sex'* (1993). As she makes clear from the outset, writing the body is not a matter of writing a single subject, but rather of incorporating a number of discourses on materiality, sex/gender, sexuality, identity, embodiment and discourse itself. A central question for Butler is how the performativity of gender relates to the materiality of the body – or to sex, for that matter. Hers is a new, perhaps not unproblematic, position (Hughes and Witz 1997: 47). She has been criticized for eliding the body altogether in her attempts to privilege gender performativity. In fact, a division has formed in the social theory of the body: on one side, corporeality is depicted as a lived experience (Butler 1990a,b, 1993; Grosz 1994, 1995; Gatens 1996); on the other, we are presented with the Foucauldian body which is historically inscribed, externally. Superficially, the first sees the body operating as subject in a phenomenological sense, whereas the second positions the body in an object-like system. While these positions appear irreconcilable, Nick Crossley (1996: 102–3) argues that the difference between writers such as Merleau-Ponty and Foucault is simply one of emphasis or ethos and that both positions aim to understand being-in-the-world. For Foucault, it is a matter of political history and functions; for Merleau-Ponty, it is feelings and passional conduct. This difference is central in the debate between social constructionism and experiential embodiment, a major theme which will be explored in this section.

What I would like to suggest is that embodiment is made up of a number of related experiences. First, there is the materiality of the body: the way we eat, sleep, bleed, menstruate, feel pain and so on. Although we might experience these incidents in variant ways, we always start within a single type of body, to be human is to be embodied. Secondly, there are the elements of construction, the social setting and constitution of the body, depending largely on cultural context, whether it be the Sambia or classical Greece. Each society has a corporeal style. For some the body is not skin-bound, but may connect to other bodies, ancestors, spirits and so on. Bodies cannot be considered as ahistorical or non-cultural. Thirdly, there are the operations of sex and/or gender upon the body plus all the other identity markers of sexuality, age, race, ethnicity, disability *et cetera* – these issues are also echoed in the previous section devoted to individuals. But to imagine that we simply 'acquire' a particular gender is to be mistaken about the significance of gender and its intimate relation to biology-as-lived in a social and historical context (Gatens 1996: 14). And, lastly, there is the individual dimension: what is uniquely our experience of living in and through our own specific bodies. As Harré explains (1998: 72) '[t]he concepts of identity, singularity and uniqueness are logically tied up with the embodiment of a human being as a thing among things in a world laid out in space and time.' I would like to re-centre the materiality of the body, not in terms of the nature : culture paradigm which Julian Thomas (1998) reads into my work, but in a simple and grounded way. Like Kus (1998) and Jackson (1989: 148), I believe our studies would benefit from a *radical empiricism* that posits an 'inseparability of conceptual and bodily activity'. We experience the world from the position of one body, no matter how the specificity of our cultural context names or forms that experience. It is a multi-dimensional project, but it must surely start in the experience of being-in-the-body.

The tripartite project of interrogating the foundational categories of the body, sex and gender have become central to feminist theorizing. These projects are inextricably related, yet each achieved different intensities of significance depending on the theorist, whether it be de Beauvoir, Butler, Grosz or Gatens. Judith Butler has become a buzz name in archaeology – a reference that is dropped without any necessary understanding or application of her work. Similarly, she has received little criticism from the field, despite the fact that she undermines the materiality of the body to push for the complete dominance of gender performativity. While she is sensationally useful in impelling us to rethink the sex : gender dichotomy and for re-evaluating a heterosexual economy, she elides the materiality of the body, the being-in-the-body which is determined to some extent by one's specific physicality. In *Gender Trouble*, Butler (1990a) attempted to 'reassociate the categories of gender and sex via the third notion of bodily performativity, or corporeal enactment/stylization' (Hughes and Witz 1997: 53). Here she moves away from the notion that the sexed body has more fixity than the gendered one to a position where the body represents that which gender works through and indeed constitutes. In *Bodies that Matter*, she adopts a more Foucauldian stance which considers 'the matter of bodies as the effect of a dynamic of power' (1993: 2). It represents a 'return to the notion of matter, not as a site or surface, but as *a process of materialization that stabilizes over time to produce the effect of boundary, fixity, and surface we call matter*' (1993: 9). Surely there are sexed modes of bodily materiality as well – relating to the experiences of menstruation, conception, contraception and the colonization and control of female bodies, for instance (Hughes and Witz 1997: 56). These are issues of female specificity taken up primarily by the Australian feminists Elizabeth Grosz and Moira Gatens, although in different modes. Grosz (1995) applauds the demise of 'gender' as a wholly redundant category in a post-Foucauldian age, whereas Gatens (1996) wants to renegotiate analyses of corporeality taking into account the experience of female and male embodiment. This is a 'phenomenologically inflected under-standing of embodiment as a lived, gendered materiality' (Hughes and Witz 1997: 58). Both positions impel us to rethink Butler's influential proposals.

It is already clear that two fields have dominated the recent dis-course on bodies: sociology and feminist theory. The theoretical influences present in my current work stem mainly from the latter, and I would argue that, rather than simply providing a heuristic framework, feminist challenges offer concrete ways of conceptualiz-ing real bodies, past and present. By critiquing the predominant Western paradigm, feminist theorists have presented us with other ways of being-in-the-body. Moira Gatens argues that '[t]he distinc-tion between the sexes is taken to be a fundamental feature of nature that could only be represented in culture in this dichotomous way. The notion that culture constructs nature or that cultural practices construct bodies as dichotomously sexed is theoretically *inadmissible* in the modern account' (Gatens 1996: 51). In many cultural contexts, both past and present, it is also likely to be inadmissible. Given the value of this contribution, I want first to situate recent trends in the feminist refiguring of corporeality, then to consider archaeology's engagement with the body.

## Feminism, Bodies and Selves

[T]here is no one experience of being a woman, there is even no one experience of biological sex. We are, of course, sexed beings, but that biological fact is always understood socially and culturally.

Susan Hekman, *Gender and Knowledge*

Following Elizabeth Grosz (1994), I argue that there are three groups of feminists engaged in the issues surrounding the body and embodi-ment. First, there are those who elevate and bestow primacy upon the body, specifically the female body, as the critical metaphor and motif exemplifying not only *our* strengths but our seemingly timeless strug-gles. Simone de Beauvoir was the leading exponent, famously saying that '[o]ne is not born but rather one becomes a woman. No biologi-cal, psychological or economic fate determines the figure that the human being presents in society: it is civilization as a whole that pro-duces this creature indeterminate between male and eunuch which is

described as feminine' (de Beauvoir 1972: 295). There was the suggestion of a unified female experience by virtue of being in a sexed
body. The body offers feminists a voice, yet it often appears to be
an ahistorical, essentialist, unitary voice. It assumes a commonality
between women which is precultural and transhistorical. There are
inherent problems for feminists who uncritically adopt the body as
an icon for their pro-active political position. Some radical feminist
epistemologists and ecofeminists (see Meskell 1995: 83) attempt to
privilege the female body, a stance which in itself relies on dangerous
assumptions of biologism and naturalism. Consider the different
types of female body – the differences between women on the bases
of race, class and sexuality alone. Women's corporeal specificity is
used to explain and justify the different, and unequal, social positions
and cognitive abilities of the two sexes (Grosz 1994: 14). This
universalist, over-riding preoccupation does not represent the entirety
of all women's experience and continues to be a totalizing, oppressive meta-narrative.

A second group of feminist theorists are social constructionists,
Marxist and psychoanalytic feminists such as Mitchell, Barrett, Kris-
teva and Chodorow, who are committed to the notion of the social
construction of subjectivity. They, too, see the body as biologically
determined and fixed, adhere to ahistorical notions of the body and
retain the mind : body dualism. Bodies provide the raw material base
for the inculcation of and interpolation into ideology but are merely
media of communication rather than the object or focus of ideological (re)production (Grosz 1994: 16–17). Presuming that biology or sex
is fixed, feminists have tended to focus on transformations at the level
of gender and its corresponding cultural meanings and values.

A third group situates itself in terms of sexual difference, including Irigaray, Spivak, Gatens, Butler, Cixous, Schor and Wittig.
Notably, the French feminists' work on the body has enabled us to
reinscribe the body as the site of production of new modes of subjectivity, while de Beauvoir prompted our understanding of the body
as a situation (Bordo 1993). For them, the body is crucial to women's
psychical and social existence, though it is no longer understood as
an ahistorical, biologically given, acultural object. They are concerned
with the *lived body* so far as it is specifically represented and used
in particular cultures. The body is not passively mapped, but is inter-
woven with, and constitutive of, systems of meaning, signification
and representation. On the one hand, it is a signifying and signified
body; on the other, it is an object of systems of social coercion, legal
inscription, and sexual and economic exchange (Grosz 1994: 18).

The body is thus regarded as the political, social and cultural object *par excellence*, not the raw, passive body which is overlaid and inscribed with culture. If we are to engage in the body dialogue, we must regard it not only as a site of social, political, cultural and geographical mapping but as recursively engaged in production or constitution.

Part of the problem of confronting corporeality is this tacit link between *women* and the *body*. In all this theorizing, one could argue that what underlies the body project is the antique belief that women are well situated within the flesh zone as designated by men. What is doubly disconcerting is that some feminists are actively pursuing and claiming this site as their own forum of expertise without recognizing the undesirable heritage. Feminists such as Cixous see a direct connection between feminine writing and the body and she claims that women must bring themselves into the text (Hekman 1990: 45). In short, women must 'write the body' and since 'woman is body more than man is . . . more body, hence more writing' (Cixous and Clement 1986: 94–5). This connotes a form of essentialism more akin to second wave feminism (see chapter 2). The female sex is restricted to its body, while the male, fully disavowed, becomes the incorporeal instrument of freedom and philosophical formulation (Butler 1990a: 12). According to Moira Gatens (1996: 23), '[a]t different times, different kinds of beings have been excluded from the pact, often simply by virtue of their corporeal specificity. Slaves, foreigners, women, the conquered, children, the working classes have all been excluded from political participation, at one time or another, by their bodily specificity.' Embodied subjects have not been portrayed as equal or analogous in any way. Yet feminism has sought its political foundation in the unity of the female body and its intrinsicness. Reclamation of *individual* bodies, rather than universalist collectives, may be our way out of the dilemma. Grosz argues (1994: 22) that if corporeality can no longer be linked with one sex, then women can no longer take on the function of being *the body* for men, who are left free to soar the heights of theoretical reflection and cultural production, just as people of colour, indigenous people or slaves can no longer fulfil the role of the *working body* for white elites, who are free to create values, morality and knowledges. In view of this assertion, the central dilemma for gender studies within our field is that gender and feminist archaeologists have cast the body as their own area of speciality and positioned themselves as privileged in these discourses. In retrospect, by claiming or reclaiming the body, scholars have failed to produce any radical perspectives or alternatives, but have simply

adhered to the dichotomous structures already established by elite
Western males since the time of Plato. Some feminists have failed to
see the lineage of their current position or to realize that they have
simply subscribed to a subordinating and deterministic paradigm.
This has serious implications for gender theorists in archaeology
whose project it has been radically to alter the discipline, and to offer
fresh insights and an altogether different framework through which
to conduct archaeological interpretation. The above assertions would
suggest that these objectives have been impeded and that the way
forward does not lie with further analyses of the body in any natu-
ralistic, biological or extreme social constructionist sense.

## Archaeological Bodies

It is now expedient to examine the way in which our own discipline
has appropriated the body motif, since chapters 3, 4 and 5 are concerned with Egyptian notions of embodiment and treatment of
bodies. I have argued (Meskell 1996a, 1998a; Knapp and Meskell 1997)
that archaeology has adopted the body as somewhat of a latecomer,
via developments in the social sciences, and has not yet developed a
significant corpus of theories applicable to our specific data. Instead,
we have been too easily seduced by the body's overt aesthetic possibilities, the promise of new avenues to ancient sexualities, and the
straightforward power dynamics of a Foucauldian *body politic*.
Archaeology tends to align itself with an inscriptive model. Emphasis is upon the 'processes by which the subject is marked, scarred,
transformed and written upon or constructed by the various regimes
of institutional, discursive, and nondiscursive power' (Grosz 1995:
33). Counterpoising this approach, psychoanalysis and phenomenology focus more productively on the body as it is experienced and rendered meaningful: these traditions have had lesser impact upon the
archaeology of the body.

Archaeological engagement with the body has taken two divergent
paths. One clear trend exists, primarily in the literature of British and
European prehistory, of a predilection for the body as artefact (see
Shanks and Tilley 1982; Thomas 1993, 1995; Yates 1993; Barrett 1994;
Tilley 1994). Archaeologists of the Neolithic, whose evidence often
consists of disarticulated bones and ceramic fragments, stemming
from mixed contexts, usually tend towards artefact-oriented views of
the body. They posit that human remains are manipulated in ways

similar to objects of material culture, yet this does not mean that such categories were commensurate. Cynically, one might ask in the depths of prehistory who can tell what groups or individuals were manipulating these remains? They might represent secondary or even tertiary burials, suggesting that we may have missed the crucial social dimensions following death. This begs the question of how much information about the meanings of bodies can be derived from such contexts? Moreover, we cannot assume that the treatment of the body in death is tacitly commensurate with experiencing the body during life in any given cultural context. This suggests we have to be inherently careful with our extrapolations.

There are other more theoretically nuanced ways of accessing the prehistoric body, yet sophisticated theory does not always cohere with the limitations of the data. Recently, Julian Thomas (1996: 11–18) has attempted to overthrow the tyranny of Cartesianism, the pervasive dualisms of mind : body, nature : culture and so on, through the lens of Neolithic culture. The aim of his project is certainly admirable, yet after reading his entire volume one never actually gets the sense of *any* body in particular: it is perhaps a theoretical template rather than a compelling illustration of uncovering the body. Here again the desire for sophisticated theory sits uneasily beside a fairly unconducive data set. Another type of social body popular in British prehistory is that described in relation to the landscape or spatially experiencing ancient monuments (see Barrett 1994: 15, 18, 23; Thomas 1995), without any corporeal, lived or individual identity. Each set of bodies consists of social players, normative representatives of larger social entities fulfilling their negotiated roles circumscribed by powerful social forces. Most archaeologists still bypass the embodied individual in favour of a body which is a passive reflector of large-scale social processes – or what I term the society-in-microcosm model. Bodies do not operate in space as things, they inhabit and haunt space. And when we wish to move, we do not move as an object, since it is our body and because, through it, we have access to space (Merleau-Ponty 1962: 5). The corporeal phenomenology of Merleau-Ponty challenges the notion of body as object. Only I can live my body; it is a phenomenon experienced by me and thus provides a perspectival point which places me in the world enabling relations between me and other subjects and objects (Grosz 1994: 86; see Kus 1992). Consciousness is not only an awareness of the environment or state of one's body, but an awareness of being aware. We are not only conscious, but self-conscious. An exception to this trend in

British prehistory can be found in the recent work of Jonathan Last (1998), who focuses upon the unique identities of buried individuals at Barnack, Cambridgeshire. Combining both landscape and embodied approaches, he manages to uncover narratives of difference in a Bronze Age context. British archaeologists have presented interesting insights and alternative perspectives on antiquity, but one has to question whether such grand theories (for example, those of Heidegger, Foucault, Giddens, Derrida, Lacan) usefully serve the limited scale of the data from the Neolithic? Post-structuralism's interests are often at odds with archaeology's, in terms of subject matter and scale, particularly given its application to prehistoric contexts (Gosden 1992: 808).

The other trend, which is evidently more relevant for this study, is the body as the scene of display. This view is more prevalent in Mediterranean, Near Eastern and Egyptian contexts, and follows indirectly from the work of social constructionists like Foucault, though this lineage is seldom acknowledged. Foucauldian fascination can be seen in recent general developments within Egyptian, Near Eastern and Mediterranean archaeologies, where the adoption of engendered analyses has been construed as the identification of women, sexuality and the feminization of specific groups (duBois 1988; Marcus 1993; Robins 1994a, 1996; Winter 1996; Wright 1996). The data employed are generally visually evocative, namely wall paintings, iconography, motifs, jewellery and ornamentation. In these examples, scholars are concerned with posture, gesture, costume, sexuality and representation in preference to the construction of individual identities, bodily experience or *lived bodies* in any corporeal sense. In a series of Slade lectures in Cambridge several years ago, Irene Winter likened the body of Naram-Sin to contemporary body-builders and male icons such as Arnold Schwarzenegger. Images of both modern and ancient men were juxtaposed in an attempt to draw out the sexual and sensual messages imbued in the famous stele (Winter 1996). This might have been a misplaced effort to 'do the body' in the ancient Near East, yet may also have been part of the normative trope of Orientalism which sees the Orient and all things in it tinged with a powerful and 'other' sexuality. Here race and sexuality cross-cut, being singled out as the salient markers for the Mesopotamian cultural sphere. Whether this was representative in reality, or simply a product of Western construction, is open to interpretation. As Zainab Bahrani questions (1996), why is Greek statuary referred to in more neutral ways as opposed to the sexually loaded descriptions of their Mesopotamian counterparts? Sexual differences, like those of race and class, are *bodily* differences (Grosz 1995: 32), both in ancient experience and modern reading.

Both archaeological trends outlined above could be seen as derivative of social constructionism which was once exceedingly popular and is now heavily critiqued by sociologists, anthropologists and feminists alike (McNay 1992). To map the historical landscape of the body and social constructionism in archaeology, we must acknowledge our substantive debt to Foucault. Archaeology has been seduced by Foucauldian notions of control (Meskell 1996a, 1998a), where power relations are mapped on the body as a surface which can be analysed as a forum for display. Despite the eager and enthusiastic adoption in archaeology of these ideas, replete with postmodern posturing and sanctioned by feminist practitioners, there is still the implicit adoption of binary, dichotomous and essentially Cartesian notions of rigid sex-typing. It could be argued that the current preoccupation with control and elaboration is a typically androcentric, externalized separation of mind, body and emotions which forms an essentialist duality through its own mode of discourse and retrodicts that perspective into the past as if temporal and cultural stasis were tenable. The result is that an upsurge in theorizing has prompted a new desire for groundedness, whereby we regard the body as a material, physical and biological phenomenon which is irreducible to immediate social processes or classifications. Bodies cannot simply be explained away (Shilling 1993: 10). In contrast to social constructionists like Foucault, it is important to recognize that the body is not merely constrained by or invested with social relations, but also forms a basis for and contributes towards these relations. All this mapping and elaborated treatment of the body may reflect the postmodern predilection for surface, but it still represents a separation from our bodies as lived and our identities as individuals.

## Libidinal Economies

Many contemporary studies of the body, and almost all those within archaeology, concentrate on the exterior body as if internal corporeality, or the transitory fluids which accompany it, do not constitute the bodily self. Westerners are threatened by the leaky body, its permeability, its dependence on an outside and the perilous divisions between the internal and external body (Grosz 1994: 193). Intensities are concentrated around the bodily borders – orifices, fluids and visceral depths. Deleuze and Guattari (1987: 160–1), following Artaud, speak of a *body without organs*, as a way of rupturing our views of the body as a bounded organism and a fixed, stratified entity. Customarily we privilege the surface and deny our internal organs and substances as confronting or repulsive, an ethnocentric perspective not necessarily shared by others.

> In our conception, body fluids flow, quite outside of, and beneath, our political economy – fluids enter our bodies naturally, unnoticed by our conscious surveillance and uncoded by our social codes, and evaporate or are discharged in the extreme privacy of our closed-door bathrooms and our dark bed-sheets as we retire alone, an emission outside of social laws unmentionable in our socially significant discourse. (Lingis 1994: 140).

Are not blood, sweat and tears the stuff of bodies too? As an alternative reading of the body, I draw on the work of anthropologist Alphonso Lingis (1994) who has examined the fluid economies of Melanesia. Lingis has many analytical projects and a provocative narrative style. He is interested in how cultures code their sensuality; the susceptibility of the body; how power produces diversity and incites a multiplicity of bodies; and how we experience the fluidity of the body and our various identities. The Melanesian data are particularly rich in these respects.

In Melanesia the body is personified along with its physical parts (Strathern 1988: 208). Many groups attribute great significance to the transmission and circulation of semen. An inherent difference between these groups and ourselves is that '[t]he fluids in our bodies ... their seepings into it and evaporations and discharges from it are neither regulated by our public codes nor valued in our politico-economic discourse' (Lingis 1994: xi). For the Sambia, the person is essentially perceived as a conduit for fluids – blood, semen, milk. The transmissions of fluids are meted out as social transactions. In such systems men create men, and women's role in reproduction is mystified and devalued. Inequality between men relies on age and kin status, who is male and who is in the process of being made male (Strathern 1988; Herdt 1993; Lingis 1994). In fact, the gender of one's sexual organs is reliant on the acts one performs with them. So that the creation of men and women (and their corresponding bodies) occurs through repeated ritual practices. Bodily difference is constructed rather than biologically given at birth. Fluids literally 'coagulate into the bones, organs and flesh of [the] child' (Lingis 1994: 137): the womb is a container and transformer, but it is semen that creates the baby. Boys are initiated from ages 7–10, 11–13 and 14–16 years old, when they break with their mother and receive the penis-milk of older men. Semen is a scarce resource of life, growth, strength and spirituality of the individual and the group.

Melanesian fluid economies create the materiality of gendered bodies. In ancient Egypt, bodily fluids also had transformative power, but in the magical world. Thus in Melanesia they operated in the terrestrial sphere, and in Egypt in the psychical. Fluids transubstantiate in both cultures in sexual ways, but with very different outcomes. New Kingdom Egypt had a libidinal economy in its ritual superstructure, evidenced by the well-documented discourse pertaining to bodily fluids and boundaries. Magic coalesced in the body of the magician, but it required conscious manipulation through spells and rituals. Many of these practices relied on the materiality of the body and particularly its bodily substances – saliva, blood, excrement. Magic was 'on the mouth' and this oral dimension involved spitting, licking and swallowing. There were over 20 words for spit/spittle: it was a generative force which could create gods, kings, demons, plants and animals (Ritner 1993: 75). Saliva was creative and sexualized. There was a psychological pairing of spittle with semen and the mouth with the vulva. It had both positive and negative connotations: it conveyed purification and healing, conducting evil away from the body, but also viewed as waste and corruption. Medico-magical spells were written on the flesh then licked off, other texts were written on papyri then burnt, ground up, dissolved in water and drunk (Ritner 1993: 96) so that the power of the spell was ingested. Deities such as Maat, goddess and personification of cosmic order, could also be painted on the tongue. Power was transmitted through fluids, they became animated and empowered substances, becoming efficacious around bodily boundaries, orifices and surfaces. Eating and ritual were linked through mythological discourse and the consumption of food was paralleled with consuming the god Horus himself. Consuming magic is illustrated in the so-called Cannibal Spell:

> *The King is the one who eats men and lives on the gods . . .*
> *The King eats their magic, swallows their spirits:*
> *The big ones are for his morning meal,*
> *Their middle ones are for his evening meal,*
> *Their little ones are for his night meal . . .*
> *He has smashed bones and marrow,*
> *He has seized the hearts of the gods . . .*
> *The King feeds on the lungs of the wise,*
> *and likes to live on hearts and their magic.*[1]

Bodily fluids retain the powerful essence of the gods, and even of pharaoh. Yet certain fluids were dangerous: semen and blood were considered unclean and thus menstruating women were ritually impure. Menstrual blood might thus be used as a repellent. The *tyet* amulet was probably linked to menstruation, resembling a girdle or sanitary towel, and made from red stone. Like saliva, urine was considered as both cleansing and destructive. Following Mary Douglas (1966: 3), some pollutants may be perceived as expressing general views of the social order. This suggests that sexual contact is dangerous through contact with sexual fluids and it is men who are most as risk: reflecting the sexual asymmetry of Egyptian society. The urine of a pregnant woman was especially potent, with life-giving properties. An ancient Egyptian pregnancy test consisted of having the woman urinate on young plants; if they grew, she was pregnant; if they died, she was not. Mother's milk, either human or animal, was positively power-laden. It was regularly used in medical pre-scriptions. If a woman wished to know whether she could conceive, she drank the milk of a woman who had borne a son: if she vomited she either was, or would soon be, pregnant (Pinch 1994: 82). Here fluids are powerful, almost independent, entities which seep from the innermost regions and secret parts of the body (Grosz 1995: 196).

Magical ingredients consisted of menstrual blood, animal blood and animal dung. Human detritus such as saliva, hair or nail clippings could also be used (Pinch 1994: 81). A similar scenario has recently been discussed by Lyons for the Mura of Cameroon (1998: 350). Exuviae are the abject products of the body which exist in a border-line state, signaling danger and vulnerability (see Grosz 1994: 187–210). According to Gell (1998: 104), exuviae sorcery works 'because of the intimate causal nexus between exuviae and the person responsible for them. These exuviae do not stand metonymically for the victim; they are physically detached fragments of the victim's "dis-tributed personhood" ... beyond the body-boundary.' Egyptian pharmacopoeia illustrates an extensive use of blood and excrement: there are 19 different words for excrement cited in the papyri. A sub-stantial portion of the Coffin Texts feature the deceased's denials of drinking urine or eating excrement (Kadish 1979), usually seen as a metaphor for chaos or the world turned upside-down. Following Douglas (1966), Kadish (1979) suggests that it is more than this; it is an explicit statement by each individual about choosing to be part of the moral order of the universe. The deceased states:

*What I doubly detest, I do not eat.*
*What I detest is excrement; I do not eat it.*
*Faeces, it does not enter this mouth of mine.*
*I will not touch it with my fingers;*
*I will not step on it with my toes.*[2]

Perhaps linked to these scatophagus writings, the stomach and digestion were also central concerns: digestion was linked to the putrefaction of the corpse (Pinch 1994: 134). Women also wore amulets across the pelvis and stomach to protect from evil entering the body through the navel or vagina. An archaeological example of this can be found on the body of Merit in tomb 8 at Deir el Medina, who had a gold cowrie-shell girdle, worn across her pelvis (Meskell 1998c; see pp. 180, 185–6). Amulets could be applied to any part or orifice of the body. Such sites of intensity were also dangerous, liminal zones. Douglas famously argued (1966: 115) that the body is a model that can stand for any bounded system and its boundaries can represent any boundary which is threatened or precarious. Yet why should these bodily margins be specifically invested with power and danger? More recently, Judith Butler (1990a: 132) has taken this as a potent metaphor for the representation of AIDS and homosexuality as trespassing the boundaries of the body, sexual practices and hegemonic order. Butler indirectly targets the key issue, something not lost on students of psychoanalysis, the libidinal dimension of body boundaries and orifices. These 'libidinal zones are continually in the process of being produced, renewed, transformed, through experimentation, practices, innovations' (Grosz 1995: 199).

Perhaps the libidinal nature of Egyptian magic has been downplayed by traditional scholars, although it appears to have operated at both subtle and explicit levels. Why is the transmission of semen in Melanesia sexualized and not in Egypt? The Egyptian words for semen and poison were closely related and the semen of some demons was particularly feared. There was even a spell to protect the sleeper against a demon ejaculating in his ear (Pinch 1994: 82). Fluids and orifices feature strongly in Egyptian fears of bodily integrity. Psychoanalytic theory posits that sexuality introduces death into the world, both are inextricably linked, as are lust and horror (see chapter 3). As with the Egyptian linkage between semen and poison, fear, power and revulsion are deeply imbricated. Practices in Egypt and Melanesia belie a sexual antagonism and what Freud would have called a 'death drive'. This is not to argue for commensurate practices or beliefs, but rather to highlight the potency of the body's internal corporeality and its variable expression in specific cultural contexts, whether it be modern Melanesia or ancient Egypt. It is yet another dimension of human embodiment, and of archaeology's body project.

## Conclusion

In this extensive chapter I have sought to explore a number of themes central to contemporary social science theorizing: the individual, the relationship between the individual and society, discourse theories, personhood and the body. Following Jackson (1989: 162), I would argue that the 'human "project" is thus a bringing into being which discloses and conserves the prior conditions of our individual lives, yet at the same time realizes and surpasses these conditions by addressing them as a field of instrumental possibilities'. Throughout I have attempted to clarify terms which commonly obscure debates about the individual and issues of identity, particularly within archaeology. Julian Thomas (1996: 237) has remarked that 'it is important to distinguish between an emphasis on positioning and a belief in "the individual" as a transcendental subject who is context free.' To date, I cannot think of any major theorist, or any archaeologist, who would posit the latter. But it does exemplify the conflation of terms quite neatly. To stress the importance of the individual does not suggest the 'redundancy of categories of collectivity, such as culture, society or ethnic group' (Cohen 1994: 133). Rather, I suggest that we find ways of accommodating social patterns and individual variability within archaeological analyses, by considering various scales of data. We need to accommodate the *multiplicity* of social identities as well as the *singularity* of individual experience. Previously, archaeology has focused too closely upon top-down, discourse theories. They are, by their very nature, over-arching meta-narratives which seek to explain society in broad and general terms, whether it be Foucault's notion of discipline or surveillance, Bourdieu's concept of habitus or Giddens's structuration theory. To fulfil such a role, such theories must have significant elements of stasis embedded within them and this extends to the notion of identities. Those identities are, by virtue of that grand theory, static and resilient to change, whether it be gender, ethnic or class identity. Yet what is intrinsic about identity, or the creation of identity, is its propensity for change and re-alignment as a result of an individual's experience or simply the ageing process. This is certainly true in an Egyptian context. Identity, past and present, should be seen as mutable and multiple, with complexes of meaning and networks of interpretation.

Identity – perhaps the burning question of our time – is certainly a topic of increasing interest to archaeologists in the 1990s. It is now axiomatic that our identities are fluid and mutable, under negotiation as we experience life, and open to manipulation if we have the opportunity. Here we have much to learn from our sister discipline, anthropology. For example, gender identity should be seen as a complex assortment of networks of signifying practices, varying for individuals over time and among individuals, as gender identity intersects with other such networks of signifying practices located in such concepts as class and race (Nicholson 1997: 319–20). The concept of identity politics does not necessarily entail objective needs or political implications, but challenges the connections between identity and politics and interpolates identity as a factor in any political analysis (Alcoff 1997: 348). Thus, we can say that, though gender is not natural, biological, universal or essential, we can still claim that it is relevant because of its political ramifications. Here gender is defined in positional terms. In the past few decades we have been indelibly influenced, both in political and professional terms, by the sexual revolution, gay liberation, feminism and race-minority power (di Leonardo and Lancaster 1997). It must come as no surprise then that much work is suffused with those very concepts or, at the least, contemporary theory has been influenced by those events. This has certainly been part of my own project when interpreting Egyptian social life, not as a means of artificially interpolating such difference for its own sake, but simply in recognizing a horizon of possibilities in the past.

The other major theme introduced here was the body and embodiment, drawing primarily on feminist writings and corporeal philosophies. Their major contribution has been to challenge Cartesian epistemologies and provide ameliorative strategies to acknowledge individual bodily experience. I have attempted to ground that experience as 'a *materialization*, a socially mediated formation, lived individually and in communities as *real effects*' (Zita 1998: 4). The way to bypass the undesirable dualism (mind : body), which has characterized phallocratic Western thought, is to perceive the body as the nexus of many domains. We have to acknowledge the materiality of the body, its corporeality and fluidity, as well as its sexed manifestation. The body can be regarded as the site of social, political, cultural and geographical inscriptions, production and constitutions (Grosz 1994: 23). Similarly, we must factor in the social construction of bodily experience and categorizations, relying on the rich matrix of cultural specificities. Individual experience of sexuality, of one's age, sex, ethnic or racial group and the psychical dimension of the subject's lived body have all been brought to the fore through feminist theory. These contributions form the theoretical underpinnings of the next chapter.

# 2

# Feminisms, Gender Trouble and Sexuality

But individuals are not only male and female, they are also hermaphrodites, transsexuals, Siamese twins, lacking or with nonfunctional
reproductive organs. They are not only masculine or feminine, they
are transgendered, multigendered, nongendered, cyborgs, werewolves,
angels; they elaborate a semiotics and culture coupling their organisms
and their sensuality across species, with animals, with hermaphroditic
organisms, with plants and rivers, with machines, and with spirits
and death.

Alphonso Lingis, *Foreign Bodies*

In this broad chapter I discuss the burgeoning, but related, fields of
feminist theory, gender studies and approach the newly constituted
field of sexuality. Arguably, in the current academic and political
climate, one cannot study these topics in isolation from each other.
While they are inextricably imbricated, they have often been conflated
or elided in archaeological discourse, evidenced most clearly in recent
citings of sex and gender. Most often the study of gender has been
speciously construed as the study of women. Clearly we have not
been in a position to theory build and have been impelled to borrow
from the other social sciences: thus it is imperative to clarify our terminologies. The chapter begins with an excursus into feminism and
its various formulations, as well as masculinist theory with relevant
case studies. I then consider recent developments in theories of
gender, particularly the important work of Judith Butler, and how
this translates into archaeological theorizing. This is followed by a
discussion of sexuality and its specific constructions in ancient contexts, suggesting that archaeology could benefit from the more inter-
rogative readings of queer theory. Throughout, I suggest that
archaeology might contribute to the contemporary interest in issues
of identity and alterity by providing swathes of evidence from long-
term historical settings. Archaeological contexts might prove to be

more than a heuristic arena for test cases since their historical depth can also provide a significant contribution to the theoretical sources.

## Wave Theory

It may prove expedient to outline briefly the various *waves* feminism has experienced, though any such periodization will have cross-overs and continuities, so can only provide a historical sketch. I should also point out that there is no consensus on the historical setting. For instance, what Linda Nicholson (1997) refers to as *The Second Wave* in her volume conflates both second and third wave feminists to my mind. To begin, she views the first wave as emerging in the early 1960s with the women's rights movement and the new left. The second wave, which began in the 1970s, had then to account for the oppression of women and respond to Marxism. She sees this movement continuing with the gradual recognition of difference in the process, culminating in debates over essentialism in the 1990s (Nicholson 1997: 4). I would suggest that more radical shifts have occurred since the 1980s onwards and that these are too divergent to be encompassed usefully under the rubric of second wave.

Instead, I argue that feminism has undergone three major movements with their own specific epistemological and ontological breakthroughs. Briefly, first wave feminism emerged in the 1960s and endeavoured to allow women into the sphere of rationality as defined by men, to allow them political, economic, social and sexual equality and liberation. First wave feminism has come to represent the most well-known, and derided, movement in the popular psyche. It was the first instance, in a Western context, when many women explicitly unified for personal and political freedoms and the resultant movement treated women as a single group. It should be noted that a significant women's movement existed in the Middle East, particularly Egypt, at the turn of the century. I tend to separate modern feminism from the suffragette movement (1860–1930) because the application of such a specific term – feminism – seems retrospective. Yet for many American commentators suffrage does implicitly represent the first wave (di Leonardo 1991: 2).

Second wave feminism emphasizes the 'inherent' differences between men and women, plus women's link to the natural world through reproduction, and harks back to the nineteenth century, so that later feminists argue that it was far from new (Hekman 1990: 138). This broad movement took shape in the 1980s and still continues in attempting to find women's voices: under its umbrella are women's studies, sexual difference, radical lesbian feminism, ecofeminism, women's spirituality and so on (Humm 1992), which has led to an upsurge in gynocentric feminism. Archaeology has been firmly situated in the second wave throughout most of the 1980s and 1990s. Second wave scholars, while not denying the significance of the body, were eager to escape its confines. The distinction between sex and gender seemed one way of doing that (McDowell and Sharp 1997: 201), and this also characterized the epistemic framework of engendered archaeology for the most part. The second wave has been primarily concerned with *finding* women and reinstating their position in long-term history; or, as Nicholson (1997) argues, responding to long-term oppression (for example, Simone de Beauvoir). Other strands of feminism sought to produce an account of oppression as compelling as Marx's and similarly to establish a link between their theories and Marxism (for example, Gayle Rubin, Shulamith Firestone, Michèle Barrett). Some retained the idea of 'historical materialism' as a way of focusing on women's oppression while responding to Marxism (Nicholson 1997: 2). Whatever their particular preoccupation(s), second wave feminism should be seen as radically divergent from the third wave project.

Third wave feminism, emerging in the 1980s, has been led by women of colour, lesbian feminists, queer theorists and postcolonial feminists (for example, Judith Butler, Michaela di Leonardo, Gaytari Chakravorty Spivak, Lila Abu-Lughod). They argue that it is not enough to claim unity on the basis of biology; given the other powerful axes of difference (Moore 1988: 10; 1994), women must be seen as multiply constituted. There is not one feminist viewpoint, but many, depending on sexuality, class, ethnicity, religious affiliation and geopolitical locale. The third wave does not seek to be a unified, coherent front and has been known to attack other feminist positions: Judith Butler attacks Catherine MacKinnon over queer politics (Butler 1997a); black feminists point to the racism of white feminists (Collins 1997; Combahee River Collective 1997); and women from developing countries like Uma Narayan (1997) argue that feminism itself is a Western construction. Post-structuralist feminists would suggest that there is no such thing as 'woman' at all (Alcoff 1997: 331), but this seems to be over-stretching the point. Some feminists see this destabilized category of *woman* as problematic for the political aims of feminism (Tanesini 1994: 203). Yet one could argue that it simply represents a more realistic, aware and relevant discipline which is in keeping with other important and influential social movements which rail against racial, ethnic or religious inequalities. This is not a single-issue doctrine; rather, it recognizes the inter-relatedness of a host of social issues. If archaeology recognizes the importance of this new, complex picture it will not only be in step with the social sciences, for once, but in the process it will finally do justice to ancient social lives.

In the following sections I want to examine briefly two contemporary, but very different, strands of feminism operating today, which are of particular importance to archaeology. The first is firmly situated in the second wave, whereas the second is more aligned to the third wave project. The first is *ecofeminism*, which draws heavily on archaeological narratives and many archaeologists (and their work) have been deeply imbricated in the movement. The second concerns the question of subjectivity, now a significant and well-charted issue in feminist theorizing and one which should be central to archaeological aims of engendering the past. Throughout I hope to demonstrate that there is a significant difference between feminist texts, feminine texts and women's texts (Grosz 1995: 11).

## Ecofeminism, Essentialism and Desire

Modern goddess worship and ecofeminism represent two sides of the same essentialist position, which has been labelled a form of cultural feminism (Alcoff 1997: 332). I take *essentialism* to have two definitions which are relevant for the examination of social dynamics: first, that particular things have intrinsic essences which serve to identify them as particular; and, secondly, that abstract entities or universals exist across time and space. In this instance, the ideology of a female nature or female essence has been reappropriated by certain feminists in an effort to revalidate undervalued female attributes (for example, Getty 1990; Eisler 1991, 1995; Mutén 1994; Merchant 1995), although what constitutes a female attribute equates to an essentialist argument from the outset (see Fuss 1989). Previously, I have written on the archaeological underpinnings of the goddess movement and its concerted efforts to create what I term an *archaeology of desire* (Meskell 1995, 1996b, 1998d), whereby narratives are formed in which women of the past enjoyed supreme status and led powerful, harmonious and artistic lives. This vision of the past remains unsupported by the evidence, and employs foundational claims which, I have also argued, are patriarchal and anti-feminist at heart (Meskell 1998e: 127). They rely on three Cartesian and dualistic constructions where women assume the inferior position;

namely, culture:nature, mind:body, reason:emotion. Through goddess veneration and its manufacture of the past, women are more natural, more embodied and more emotional. This stands in direct contradistinction to much feminist theory today and, as Wittig remarks (1980), it constructs *woman* as a normative category, used in the service of compulsory heterosexuality. She has gone as far as critiquing the myth of matriarchy as a negative invention which simply replaces one form of oppression with another heterosexist regime: it is only the sex of the oppressor which has changed. This presents an interesting twist for gynocentric feminists. Despite such theorizing, gynocracy continues to be a powerful ideology which has mobilized countless people across the globe (Bamberger 1974; Talalay 1994; Conkey and Tringham 1995; Haaland and Haaland 1995): the current burgeoning interest in Çatalhöyük is only one example of the powerful connection between gynocentric feminism, archaeology and politics (Meskell 1998e).

In a similar vein, the ecofeminist movement has drawn on ancient pasts to infer that a utopian society, once lived and lost, can once again be regained. While the desire is a largely positive one (Meskell 1998e: 134), it too relies on assumptions which can be critiqued for the essentialist stereotyping of both men and women. This is illustrated in the creation of the Mother Earth concept, that the planet represents the female body, personified even by the scientific *Gaia* theory. But as Joni Seager argues: 'The earth is *not* our mother. There is no warm, nurturing, anthropomorphized earth that will take care of us if only we treat her nicely. The complex, emotion-laden, quasi-sexualized, quasi-dependent mother relationship . . . is not an effective metaphor for environmental action' (1994: 219). According to Seager, such a metaphor – a sex-typing of the planet – only serves to obfuscate power relations. This is yet another instance of the essentialism with which ecofeminism is riddled. In this form, ecofeminism actually suggests a necessary causal relationship between sexual difference and its expression in the ecologically destructive culture of patriarchy (New 1996). Here ecofeminism lands in what Rosi Braidotti (1991: 89) describes as the 'double trap which threatens feminism . . . on the one hand a sociologizing reductivism which, on the binary model of the class struggle, sets the female individual in opposition to the male patriarchal system', i.e. oppression, and 'on the other the utopian model which makes "women" an entity (on the) outside, foreign to the dominant system and not contaminated by it'. This concept of an abstract masculinity against which all *we* women must struggle is perhaps just as offensive as blatant androcentrism has been for women, and suggests ironically that things have failed to move on.

## Subjectivity

Both postmodern and third wave feminist discourses have been instrumental in deconstructing any master subject location by highlighting and deploying a politics of difference. Both these movements have attempted to reconfigure the concept of social subjectivity in their associated writings. In the process the notion of a coherent masterful subjectivity has collapsed, and in its place a plethora of sexed/raced/colonized voices have taken centre stage (Haraway 1991). The coherence of the subject, now rendered fictive, has given way to discourses of marginality, alterity and difference which were once seen as 'unmarked' positions in Western theory. As such, we now recognize that both collective and personal identities are precariously and contingently constituted and that they are constantly renegotiated. Prominent theorists, such as Butler, see subjectivity in terms of the wider tensions between power and agency emergent in current debate. To suture this divide she considers that the 'subject is itself a site of this ambivalence in which the subject emerges both as the *effect* of a prior power and as the *condition of possibility* for a radically conditioned form of agency' (Butler 1997b: 14–15). The terms 'individual' and 'subject' are not interchangeable; the latter she describes as a linguistic category, a place-holder or a structure. For Butler, '[i]ndividuals come to occupy the site of the subject (the subject simultaneously emerges as a "site", and they enjoy intelligibility only to the extent that they are, as it were, first established in language' (1997b: 10–11). No individual becomes a subject without becoming subjected or undergoing 'subjectivication' – both categories are interlaced. Understandably, the recent emphasis on subjectivity has had a profound impact on feminist (and queer) theorizing, particularly its constant questioning of what constitutes female subjectivity. For centuries, men have occupied the privileged position of subject while women assumed the lesser role of object: through feminist interventions women are now pursuing their own subjectivities.

Teresa De Lauretis's influential work *Alice Doesn't* (1984) revolves around discussions of conceptualizing woman as a subject. She views gender as the social construction of 'woman' and 'man' and the semiotic production of subjectivity which is itself embedded in 'history, practices and the imbrication of meaning and experience', that is, with the 'mutually constitutive effects in semiosis of the outer world of social reality and the inner world of subjectivity' (De Lauretis 1984: 156–86). She acknowledges that individuals are constructed by 'codes' and social formations, but are still able to renegotiate these influences in individual ways thus avoiding their complete inscription. Each individual retains the capacity to formulate a specific subjective construction from the various ideological formations to which one is subject (De Lauretis 1984: 14; Hekman 1990: 80). Subjectivity is an ongoing, reflexive project 'produced not by external ideas, values or material causes, but by one's personal, subjective engagement in the practices, discourses and institutions that lend significance (value, meaning, affect) to the events of the world' (1984: 159). Importantly, her theorizing attempts to resolve tensions between individual experience and socially specific embeddedness – an issue germane to both feminist and postmodernist sentiments. Here subjectivity should not be read as the rational, autonomous subject of modernity which itself was rife with sexist epistemology. Some would like to see all readings of subjectivity or the individual as embedded in Enlightenment discourse (for example, Thomas 1998), but this is a knee-jerk reaction to the deployment of specific terms without an appreciation of the recent refashioning from within feminist, anthropological and sociological circles.

Much of De Lauretis's project deals with embodiment, experience and the inscriptions of gender in a modern setting: 'woman' as inhabitant in the house of difference (Haraway 1991). In later work she echoed the concerns of third wave feminism, arguing that the 'female subject of feminism is one constructed across a multiplicity of discourses, positions, and meanings, which are often in conflict with one another and inherently (historically) contradictory' (De Lauretis 1987). And this is important for feminist practitioners, especially in a historic discipline, as is her statement that the 'relation between women as historical subjects and the notion of woman as it is produced through hegemonic discourses is neither a direct relation of identity, a one-to-one correspondence, nor a relation of simple implication. Like all other relations expressed in language, it is an arbitrary and symbolic one, that is to say, culturally set up' (1984: 5–6). If this is true, and I imagine that all such formulations of subjectivity are susceptible, then we must acknowledge the fundamental differences and separations between women past and present, and also between the issues which interest us today and those which were operative in the past. This does not entail writing oneself out of archaeology or refraining from feminist analyses of other, or ancient, cultures. But it does mean acknowledging that the patterns we see – for example, interconnections between age, sex and class issues in a given setting – may not have been recognized as such or articulated in analogous ways. Moreover, these are definitely our terms and constructions grounded in our cultural milieu and primarily of interest to us. Yet one factor which makes archaeology both valid and interesting is its potential for asking contemporary social questions of ancient cultures and exploring the horizons of possibility which the data provide.

The idea that archaeologists 'create facts' is not new (Hodder 1984: 27), nor is the concern that archaeologists are 'without any ability to test their reconstructions of the past' (Hodder 1984: 26; Wylie 1992a: 19). Perhaps Fotiadis has highlighted the issue most succinctly (1994: 548). After challenging the 'mitigated objectivism' advocated by Alison Wylie with respect to engendered analyses, he states that 'the new facts recuperated about archaeological gender may from some distance appear neither true nor potentially false but strange indeed.' My point relates to that argument, yet I want to question the very terms and categories at the heart of gender archaeology. In arguing for social structures similar to our own, have we created conflations more serious than, say, whether a piece of flint is humanly modified or not? These interpretations of 'facts' operate at different levels and potentially have variable impacts on archaeological theorizing. Subjectivity is not simply a matter of language and textuality as the locus of meaning, but also involves social practices and habits. For social archaeologists, our questions are posed around many different subject positions: race, class, sex, age, et cetera. Can we assume that we are dealing with the same type of structures, and their results, past and present? The bleak outlook would posit that if we cannot decide on what categorizes female subjectivity in an Euro-American twentieth-century context, how can we extend those definitions to other groups? A more positive position would advocate that we give up the quest for a fictive cohesion altogether, and suggest that theorizing ourselves is almost as problematic as theorizing the ancients. I would opt for the latter, but the key issue is recognizing our position(s) when we think we are *doing* gender. Here again, I'd like to concur with Fotiadis (1994: 551) that we need to resist the idea that archaeology's accounts are fictions, and that one story is as good as the next. Gender archaeology has had a propensity for writings to this effect, both literal (Tringham 1991; Spector 1994) and metaphorical (Brumfiel 1987). While it is another means of presenting archaeology, it too assumes an easy (and isomorphic) familiarity with the past which may well be beyond our scope.

## Theorizing Masculinity

Given that the study of sex, gender and sexuality also extends to men and masculinity, surely this central domain should be of prime importance to archaeological studies of identity and subjectivity. As discussed above, gender archaeology has been reluctant to acknowledge this obvious assertion, despite the prospects of an exciting new area of research. Since the 1990s, there has existed a burgeoning social science literature devoted to the construction of masculinity (for example, Seidler 1989, 1997; Hearn 1990; Haddad 1993; Brod and Kaufman 1994; Cornwall and Lindisfarne 1994; Fenster 1994; Lees 1994; Berger et al. 1995; Connell 1995; Gutmann 1997), inspired by the developments of feminist scholarship. As such, it should not be conflated with androcentrism, since its intellectual lineage is traced to feminism. It has made relatively little impact in archaeology (Knapp 1995; Joyce 1996a; Meskell 1996a; Knapp and Meskell 1997). Recently, it has become a central theme in classics (Foxhall and Salmon 1998a, b; Osborne 1998a), due to its own progressive approaches to gender and sexuality, as well as the wealth of its textual and material corpus. A good example can be found in Robin Osborne's study (1998b) of the shifting representations of 'masculinities' in classical Greek sculpture and its polyvalent messages about power, politics, sexuality and militarism. Indeed, masculinist theory developed in tandem with feminism and should not be seen as *the enemy*. As these studies exemplify, there is not one, monolithic masculinity, and we must recognize the interplay of race, class and sexuality: neither is there *a* single black masculinity or *a* working-class masculinity. But what many feminists have critiqued in the past is more akin to Connell's (1995) concept of 'hegemonic masculinity' which draws on Gramsci's analysis of class relations. Hegemonic masculinity is not a fixed character type, always and everywhere the same – it too is contestable. Rather, it occupies the hegemonic position in a given pattern of gender relations. It simply relates to cultural dominance as a whole, to a specific form of masculinity which is culturally exalted, and to Western feminists this entails the embodiment of patriarchy, which guarantees the dominance of men and the subordination of women (Connell 1995).

It is interesting to see how archaeologists look at men and/or masculinity – if at all. Since the rise of gender archaeology, male scholars have been regularly accused of sexist comments and analyses, yet women have rarely been critiqued for reverse sexism. Consider Naomi Hamilton's discussion (1994) of the ithyphallic figure, the Souskiou 'seated gentleman', from Chalcolithic Cyprus. In attempting to reinterpret the figure, she offers the alternative hypothesis that the figure was created (by women?) as 'part joke-toy, part wry social comment' (Hamilton 1994: 308–9). She suggests that the 'figure is really rather comic with his feet up on a stool and his funny facial expression, and if water were poured in through the head and trickled out of the penis he would be good fun' (1994: 308). Implicitly, this is all at the expense of men – they become the butt of the joke (past and present). I am not suggesting that Cypriot people of the Chalcolithic had no sense of humour; rather, that many feminist archaeologists would not tolerate such a pejorative interpretation if it involved a female. And, as Hamilton herself states, a comparable female figure from which liquid could flow through a genital slit, once interpreted as a toy, is now not generally accepted as such. It is noteworthy that many comments and interpretations made about men in the past can be treated more liberally than those of women in today's political climate. As Seidler reminds us (1997: 14), it has taken time for heterosexual men to appreciate that sexism and gender politics are not simply the domain of women and gay men.

So how do archaeologists tap into the structures and experiences which are constitutive of men's lives, remembering that they too inhabit other constructed worlds rather than a single, unitary one? We could question how the experiences of men were founded around their status, sexuality, ethnic and racial identities, religious persuasions and life stages. How did those experiences vary in New Kingdom Egypt as opposed to ancient Mayan contexts, for example? In Egypt we know that men were castigated if they were unable to father children, as their virility was called into question along with the inability to found a lineage. Such individuals were charged with 'not being a man' (Meskell 1998c: 369). A personal letter found at Deir el Medina from one man to another says exactly this, since he was 'unable to make [his] wives pregnant like [his] fellowmen' (Wente 1990: 149). The man, named Nekhemmut, was further berated for not adopting an orphan son to make up for this apparent lack: significantly, his wife was not blamed. Implicit in this was an assumed heterosexuality and a desire to procreate children, as well as the status quo. The greatness of Ramesses II is emphasized by his claim to have fathered over 90 children, especially in Western eyes. In the artistic repertoire, men of middle and high status were shown with young, aesthetic bodies, as opposed to the completely naked, sometimes scruffy workers who filled the lower registers and represented the place of the lower echelons in the worldly scheme of things. But concepts of beauty were not reserved for women: archaeological findings might suggest that men were the main wearers of jewellery – earrings, bracelets, neck-laces, rings and so on (Meskell 1998c). Aesthetic images of men were created by other men, yet official art did not hint at the possibilities of homoerotic experience. Sensual and sexual images of women were clearly constructed and we know many of the visual puns and erotic motifs that the Egyptians deployed. But a parallel comparandum is sadly missing for the masculine subject, or has yet to be decoded. The optimum existence for a man was a position among the scribal elite, with luck serving pharaoh at court, living a life of ease and leisure. To be a worker in the fields, performing menial tasks was anathema, as set out in many literary texts. The body was not to be subjugated in labour, and Egyptian artists portrayed success, wealth and indolence by carefully rendering discrete rolls of fat around the male, scribal stomach. This trend seems more relevant for middle-aged individuals, and was a representational impossibility for young men, and women of all ages. For modern interpreters there were many contradictory aspects to masculinity which have been recorded in both texts and iconography: aggressive or warlike behaviour was not generally advo-cated in non-royal contexts; men were portrayed aesthetically; as being open about their feelings and emotions with other men and with women (attested in many letters and love poems); men were depicted wearing fine, sensuous clothes and jewellery; they were generally having a sensual existence and being fecund. As a cautionary note, much of this information is gleaned from literate middle and high-ranking sources, and as such it cannot speak for all men.

In looking at an ancient Mayan context, the situation is rather dif-ferent: here the work of Rosemary Joyce is particularly compelling. She argues (Joyce 1998) that the construction of masculinity can be viewed in a number of ways, such as the male-to-male gaze, which included the realization of sexual pleasure, and the aestheticization of the male in terms of a female gaze and experience of desire. Displays of males were inextricably linked to sexualization through evocations of the body – through elaborate costuming which both concealed and drew attention to male genitalia. In fact, the clear depiction of male genitalia is sanctioned in art, particularly the erect penis. Joyce docu-ments (1998) the extensive 'House of the Phalli' at Chichen Itza, aptly named given the three-dimensional phalli projecting from its walls. Another building at the site revealed a large upright stone carving of a penis. Both locations seem suggestive of ritual activity. Phallic imagery is pervasive at the site and other Mayan sites, thus Joyce links them to other male symbolic practices, battle and ceremonial activ-ities such as ballgame playing and dancing, apparently for exclusively male audiences. Iconography revealed examples of naked males embracing and scenes of masturbation. Drawing on the work of Lancaster (1997), Joyce cleverly describes this as 'sensuous practice' offered to 'test the plasticity of the world against the dexterity of the body'. Masculinity and male sexuality are constructed through a male-to-male gaze. In classic Maya texts the penis is used as a metonym for male. Yet much of the structured discourse and citational practices was a recognition of duality and complementarity (Joyce 1996a, b), which positioned male *and* female as central. Not only did representations seek to portray both as necessary referents, some constructions sought to convey the two in a single image. The primordial creators encompassed both genders and in ceremonial contexts mixed-gender costumes were adopted. What is clear from this outstanding corpus of work is the impossibility of teasing apart the related spheres of sex, sexuality and bodily performances and that our continued desire for prediscursive taxonomies is simply a by-product of our own Western fixation on category.

While the Mayan material is very different from Egyptian depictions, there are some interesting overlaps: the stress on male beauty and bodily perfection, the importance of permanent youth, and the depiction of near nakedness with its concomitant sexual suggestiveness. Both feature less formal illustrations of often exaggerated erect penises, and a written language where the penis serves as metonym for male. Classic Maya art stressed ritual setting, warfare, combat and competition, while Egyptian art shows primarily religious and ritual scenes, everyday life and vignettes from the world of death. Large-scale combat was reserved for pharaoh and his military expeditions. In both artistic traditions depictions of men were constituted very differently from those of women, even if they were intended to act as counterparts in life and death. For the Maya, men represented the sexual sex (Joyce 1996b), whereas in Egypt it was predominantly women who were objects of the sexual gaze (see below; Meskell forthcoming a). Too often we assume that women are sexualized objects in a given society, as a result of our own cultural milieu, rather than identifying the varied levels of difference which operate between individuals in the past and between specific societies.

## A Question of Difference

Since difference is crucial to social dynamics in both ancient and modern settings, some understanding of the background, terminology and various readings of the concept will be briefly outlined. Any attempt to construct an archaeology of difference must acknowledge a substantive debt to the early work of Jacques Derrida. However, this section must be prefaced with the acknowledgement that Derrida's 'work is too enormous, too complex, as it intersects with different traditions and disciplines' to be easily apprehended (Yates 1990: 206–7). His work has been both attacked and embraced by feminist scholars (Hekman 1990; Grosz 1995; Feder et al. 1997) and archaeologists (Yates 1990). Many of these 'criticisms apply not so much to what Derrida has written but to what has been written about him by various (mostly American) commentators' (Norris 1992: 173). Some claim that he has re-opened the 'woman' question and re-thought alterity and sexual difference. According to Gallop (1997: 7–9), his paper *Spurs* was a critique of 1970s' essentialist feminism and the second wave, which is now in keeping with third wave feminist theorizing. Through Nietzsche, he criticized the singular concept of woman. Feder and Zakin (1997: 32) suggest that he has produced a new choreography of difference and a new configuration of gender. But another feminist argument can be summarized as follows: just when the subjectivity of women's experience becomes a political force, thinkers like Derrida claim that all identities are fragmented and destabilized, thus robbing women of their hard-won gains. As always, feminist theorists are grappling with the dissonance between theoretical and political/practical issues. Much of the feminist negativity is simply levelled at postmodernism, as an abstract entity, that somehow delimits the impact of feminism. However, postmodern critique operates as an ontological check on feminist thinking and enables a myriad of feminist positions. Postmodernism celebrates difference, fragmentation and multiplicity, and challenges the search for coherence and the desire for singular narratives. Moreover, feminism and postmodernism are the only contemporary theories to critique the Enlightenment legacies of modernism (Hekman 1990: 189). Given that some types of feminism and postmodernism both seek to challenge essentialism and universalism (especially those positions which claim to transcend the boundaries of culture and region), to consider other voices and give credence to difference, diversity and locale, there should be many lines of convergence between the two (Strickland 1994: 266).

To return to Derrida, if we accept part of his body of theoretical work, that dealing with deconstruction and *différance*, it can only help to substantiate the current formulations of third wave feminism and postcolonialism. Derrida links logocentrism with phallocentrism,

cautioning that 'women's studies can't go very far if it does not deconstruct the philosophical framework of this situation, starting with the
notion of subject, of ego, of consciousness, soul and body' (1987: 193).
Derrida's concept of *différance* is premised upon the disjuncture
between writing and speech. *Différance* relies on the English meanings of *differ* and *defer* and, in French, plays upon the fact that *dif-
férence* and *différance* sound the same in speech. In sum, Derrida
argues against the privileging of speech over writing (Derrida 1981: 8;
Hekman 1990: 24). While I am not primarily interested in pursuing
the specific theoretical underpinnings of Derrida's theory of *différance* (and its counterpart, *trace*), there are some central notions to
be gleaned from his writings which are obviously beneficial.

Leaving aside the problematics of Derrida's perceived apolitical
position, he has offered some sound arguments used by feminist and
postcolonial theorists alike (for example, Judith Butler and Homi
Bhabha). Put simply, Derrida is anti-foundational. He explores the
constructions of binaries and Cartesian dualisms (1978: 198), and
advocates pluralism and multiplicities. If every reading is a misread-
ing, then there is no single 'truth' but rather 'truths'. Deconstruction
can lead to 'true interpretations' and thus be a positive force (Hekman
1990: 164), as Derrida himself has recently claimed. In terms of sex,
sexual orientation and identity more generally, this is a particularly
relevant theoretical stance and one in keeping with feminist epistemology. He questions oppositions, such as masculine/feminine, het-
erosexual/homosexual, and the unitary essence of the female, and he
advocates a new pluralistic inscription. While this may resonate with
the third wave, it may be the source of contention for essentialist feminists of the second wave. His position is relevant to notions of the
individual as a hierarchy of fluid identities, based upon lines of age,
sex, social position, ethnicity, religion and life experience. Additionally, *différance* calls into question the limiting binaries that the discourses of sex and gender have perpetuated. Throughout I tend to use
the term *difference*, rather than the Derridean construction *différance*.
The former can cover a larger corpus of identity questions and constitutive inscriptions, while the latter is overtly coloured by the
speech/writing debate.

There are many concepts and constructions which surround the
term 'difference' in the literature, from sexual difference between men
and women (Grosz 1995; Gatens 1996) to difference in terms of sexual
orientation (Humm 1992: 193; Elam 1994: 34). Beyond sex and sexuality, difference can also refer more broadly to concepts of alterity surrounding race and other colonized groups (Haraway 1991: 127–48).

Elizabeth Grosz (1995: 53) has outlined at least two (semantic) versions of difference. Difference, viewed as distinction, implies the pre-evaluation of one term from which the difference of the other is drawn; pure difference refuses to privilege either term. Much of this theorizing has been premised on sexed differences and the feminist aspiration to enhance the position of women. I would like to broaden this term and deploy it in its full potential, extending it to identity markers or social vectors which set people apart from normative constructions. Such indicators have been widely cited in the 1990s: age, sex, class, sexual orientation, ethnicity *et cetera*. Thus, I am not arguing for pure difference, but rather for culturally constructed distinctions that we can deconstruct; this is more in keeping with Haraway's project of alterity. Nor am I advocating the simplistic approach of identity politics whereby individuals are reduced to a list of categories (Elam 1994: 74), of which first wave feminism was perhaps guilty. We should not see identity and difference as simply based on categorical groupings, but rather on processes of identification and differentiation (Moore 1994: 2). Instead, I would hope that people from the past are represented fully as embodied individuals, who consist of many fluid identities which are subject to change over time, and who have the power of agency, choice and volition. As Butler (1993: 168) has argued:

> though there are clearly good historical reasons for keeping 'race' and 'sexuality' and 'sexual difference' as separate analytical spheres, there are also quite pressing and significant historical reasons for asking how and where we might read not only their convergence, but the sites at which the one cannot be constituted save through the other.

## The Trouble with Gender

Judith Butler opened her now famous book, *Gender Trouble: Feminism and the Subversion of Identity* (1990a), by admitting with some trepidation that she had indeed caused some trouble in her analyses of gender. She was at pains to stress that problematizing gender or outlining the indeterminacy of gender would not necessarily culminate in the failure of feminism. But this is exactly the fear that many feminists held and, in fields like archaeology, continue to hold. Gender and feminism have come to be synonymous fields in archaeology which are privileged and held sacred, almost beyond scrutiny. Criticism by men is easily construed as sexism or a continuation of the androcentric ethos, whereas internal criticism by other female practitioners has been limited and considered somewhat of a 'selling out' on the feminist project. Yet Butler was right to cause trouble and as a result has heralded a new epistemic awareness, although archaeology has been rather slow in following her lead. In the following sections I will outline various debates over sex and gender, positioning archaeology's responses in the process and offering insight into the potential of archaeological data for current interests and debates. Here too I'd like to reiterate Butler's desire to 'resist the domestication of gender studies' and to open up the field to a more radical critique.

*Female* no longer appears to be a stable notion and its meaning is as troubled and unfixed as *woman*, since both gain their significations only in relational terms: their relation to man, masculinity, heterosexuality, phallologocentrism and so on. The logical extension is that Western society has tried to enforce discrete and internally coherent gender identities within a heterosexual framework (Butler 1990a: x). It is yet another foundationalist fiction that *woman* connotes a common identity, a stable signifier and a single subject. Just as there is no unitary position for woman, there is no universal basis for feminism: consider the voices of Third World and third wave feminists. The notion that there could be is simply part of Western colonization and appropriation of other cultures, past and present. Drawing on feminist critiques of science, archaeologists such as Erika Engelstad (1991: 504) have drawn similar conclusions, yet there has been a dearth of studies demonstrating variable female experience, most opting rather for a unified narrative of *women's ways of knowing*. This highlights a central tension in current feminism. On the one hand, feminists align themselves with the post-structuralist deconstruction of master narratives; and, on the other, they want to create a feminine voice in opposition to the pre-existing masculine discourse. Feminism and postmodernism remain uneasy bedfellows (see Hekman 1990; Elam 1994; Benhabib 1995; Butler 1995). So in the very action of asking questions about the age-old subordination of women, about possible contexts of resistance in the past, or whether there existed an intrinsic nature in women's practices that set them apart, we have decontextualized individuals from their historical, political and cultural settings and from their other subject positions of race, class, nation, ethnicity and all other power differentials (Butler 1990a: 4–5; Haraway 1997: 28). As Haraway rightly asserts, if a stable notion of gender no longer proves to be the bedrock of feminist politics, perhaps a new sort of feminist politics to contest the reification of gender is desirable, one that accepts the variable construction of identity as a methodological and political goal.

Is unity necessary as a political formula for change? Many third wave feminists would argue that this is no longer the case and would furthermore stress the problems of a false unity, whereby other vectors of difference which structure inequality have been down-played. Some feminists are now attempting to create an alternative topos to work through the dominant dualisms of the mind and the body, nature and culture, biology and psychology, and sex and gender (Gatens 1996: 58). It is no longer possible to ignore the complexities of identity construction where intersections of difference are arranged in various intensities and around specific nodes of power, whether it be age, religion, ethnicity or sex *et cetera* depending on context. While I would stress the importance of the cultural construction of sex as a major variable for many groups and cultures, it cannot always be pivotal as older-style feminists once claimed. To position sex as primary undermines other significant determinants which structure social relations. For example, a man and woman from a similar his-torico-political context may have more in common than two women or two men from radically different contexts. This has been high-lighted by Third World feminists over issues such as adopting the veil in Islamic societies (Delaney 1995) or practising clitoridectomy in specific African ones (Toubia 1985).

## Privileged Categories

The privileging of the category gender over that of sex has been defended in terms of the dangers of biological reductionism. However, this type of gender theory has ignored the role of the body, embodiment and the psyche. We cannot assume *a priori* that the body is a *tabula rasa* at birth (Gatens 1996: 4). I would argue, following Gatens, that the lived experience for an individual in a female body differs from that of a male body, irrespective of the gendered identity that they assume. For example, being gendered male in a female body is greatly at odds with the experience of being gendered female in the corresponding body. Certainly, recent findings through studies of trans-sexuals support this embodied difference (Hausman 1995; Ekins and King 1996; Johnson 1997). The body can no longer be viewed as a passive metaphor or neutral canvas awaiting social elaboration. Here I am simply arguing for embodiment to be fully considered as a factor in social identity, rather than suggesting that it should achieve primacy. This is not to argue for an essentialist feminism or one that posits female difference as central, and I have previously critiqued these positions (Meskell 1996a, 1998a; Knapp and Meskell 1997). One could similarly make a case for the complexities of male embodiment and suggest that this is an under-represented and under-theorized category of analysis. As Gatens reminds us (1996: 9), while we look contextually at the significance of the sexed body and its behaviour, some bodily experiences and events, though lacking in any *fixed* significance, are likely, in all social structures, to be privileged sites of significance. Thus we end in a position where a host of factors – biological, social and contextual – are given prominence.

In the West, sex concerns the body, facts and science (biology), whereas gender concerns the mind, values and ideology (conditioning); both rely on a form of humanism which assumes a fundamental universality across cultures and time periods in terms of what it is to be human or to inhabit a human body (Gatens 1996: 66). But it makes no sense to define gender as the cultural interpretation of sex, if sex too is a gendered category. So that gender is not to culture as sex is to nature – gender is also the discursive and cultural means by which a 'natural sex' is constructed and prediscursive (i.e. prior to culture). It is not a politically neutral surface (Butler 1990a: 7), the *tabula rasa* on which culture acts. The construction and operationalizing of sex and gender is subject to contextually embedded discourses, discourses of the status quo. We need to acknowledge these constructions in our own milieu, and be open to the possibilities of different constructions in the past. Archaeology might consider problematizing the sex/gender system, coined by Rubin (1975), and subsequently overlain on to past cultures and societies. She developed the concept to explain the status quo in our Western society, and the heterosexual economy that was its corollary. It was not explicitly intended to serve as an explanatory model for other groups. As Haraway (1985: 99) reminds us, 'gender might not be a global identity after all.'

Part of the central dilemma in feminist theorizing, and subsequently in archaeological discourse, must be seen as terminological. Few scholars specifically define their terms of reference and thus we cannot assume consensus on even basic designations. The terms *sex, gender, sexuality, gender relations* and *social relations* are wrongly assumed to have common meaning to all groups, but, in fact, are used in a number of quite distinct and different ways (Moore 1994: 6). Hence these terms can never refer to pure concepts. For instance, the term 'sex' is deployed to describe the 'opposite sex', 'biological sex', 'even to have sex' (Weeks 1997: 13). In archaeology, the common view regards the two categories as quite distinct with *sex* representing the externalized manifestation of a biological given and *gender* a socially constituted elaboration which overlays itself upon the former. More progressive research suggests that these fundamental concepts may in fact be similarly constituted (Yates and Nordbladh 1990; Yates 1993), if not one and the same. Elam (1994: 43) argues that if gender is culturally determined, then we must realize that culture is made up of an ensemble of gender determinations. Do we blame culture for gender stereotypes, or gender for cultural ones? Another reaction has been to leave both terms untheorized with *gender* and *sex* collapsed in upon each other so that the resultant examinations are predicated upon predetermined categories of *males* and *females* as broad, but dichotomous, groupings. This suggests that a form of essentialism was operative in the past, and further implies that such a situation exists in contemporary contexts. Such a position regards *woman*, or *man* for that matter, as a given which is transhistorical and transcultural and constant over the trajectories of age, status and/or ethnicity. The contributions of recent feminist and masculinist theory challenge such a stance (for example, Butler 1993; Brod and Kaufman 1994; Cornwall and Lindisfarne 1994; Grosz 1994; Moore 1994; Connell 1995). The sex/gender distinction, 'so crucial to early 1970s feminist theory, also displays this acceptance of the division between bodies on one hand and culture on the other. Sex is understood to be a fact of bodies, gender a socialised addition to sex' (Gatens 1996: 51).

Despite the impact of these political positions, the problem of disembedding *sex* and *gender* remains. Laqueur's (1990) impressive study has shown that sex is a contextual issue and that the notion of two distinct sexes depends very much on the site of knowledge production. Prior to the Enlightenment a one-sex model held prominence, influenced largely by classical authors such as Plato, Aristotle and Galen, who proposed that female biology was merely a variation on the male. Even language marks this view: for example, the ovary was left without a name of its own for two millennia. Galen simply referred to it by the word he used for the male testes, *orcheis*, exemplifying this female-as-male model (Laqueur 1990: 4–5). In fact, Laqueur pushes the issue further by suggesting that in pre-Enlightenment texts *sex* must be understood as the epiphenomenon, while gender (which we would take to be a cultural category) was primary or *real*. Thus, sex before the seventeenth century was still a sociological and not an ontological category (Laqueur 1990: 8; Strathern 1996: 139). It is important to note that by 1800 various writers were arguing that there existed fundamental differences between the male and female sexes. Whatever the setting, the particular construction and understanding of *sex* cannot be isolated from its discursive milieu (see Foucault 1972: 52, 157). Moreover, we should recognize that sex is itself troubled terrain – sex also has a history (Butler 1993: 5).

Both Laqueur (1990) and Butler (1990a) have proposed that sex and gender are socially constructed categories, and thus similarly constituted. Butler exhorts (1990b: 6–9; 1993: 1) that it is no longer tenable to advocate the existence of prediscursive *sex* which acts as the stable referent on top of which the cultural construction of gender proceeds. Rather, the self, sexed or gendered, is knowable through language into which it is subjected and which produces its agency (Lees 1994: xvii). Thus, we cannot assume that biological sex everywhere provides the universalist basis for the cultural categories male and female. Consider the now widely published and theorized case of the Native American 'two-spirit' (Jacobs 1994: 7; Hollimon 1996, 1997). Apart from this well-documented example, several recent anthropological case studies illustrate similar groups in Polynesia, the Balkans, India and New Guinea (Broch-Due et al. 1993; Herdt 1993; Strathern 1996). For many New Guinean groups, such as the Sambia or Etoro, sex is created processually through life, specifically during rites of passage. Gilbert Herdt (1993: 53) believes that this plethora of new studies relates to an opening up of the field, with studies from all sides challenging the assumed structure of sexual dimorphism and the hegemony of the scientific paradigm. These graphic accounts provide invaluable examples of cultural difference and are important indicators of variability. Archaeologists might draw upon such examples to suggest a range of possibilities, where relevant, for ancient sociosexual systems. To reiterate, *sex*, as far as we understand the term within Western discourse, is something which differentiates between bodies, while *gender* has been defined as the set of variable social constructions placed upon those differentiated bodies. Unfortunately, this very formula may obscure rather than clarify when it comes to cross-cultural analyses of sex, sexual difference and gender (Moore 1994: 14). Put simply, we are wrong to approach the symbols of others as we do our own, like reading male and female as generalized gender categories relating to what men and women do (Strathern 1987: 272).

## Sex and Science

Natural evolution produced the orchid. Is our technological history making us into carnal orchids, showy sex-organs, that no longer rise on their own stems, blend their own saps, or impregnate each other?

Alphonso Lingis, *Foreign Bodies*

Conceptions of sex can be discussed from both philosophical and biological perspectives. Archaeologists might be well versed in social science approaches to the issue, yet they are less familiar with the current debates in genetics or biological anthropology over precisely the same issue. It might be helpful, then, briefly to outline some points of convergence between these disciplines.

Beginning with some ideas presented in Deleuze and Guattari (1987), and discussed initially in archaeology by Timothy Yates (1993), it may be possible to circumvent traditional binaries by adopting the notion of rhizomes as a means of conceptualizing sex. This provides an alternative way of viewing sex and sexuality as fluid over the trajectories of time, context, culture, age and so on. From such a standpoint, an individual's sex would not have to conform to a predetermined definition or result in specific behaviours; instead, sex and sexuality are positioned upon a spectrum unbounded by prediscursive categories. The spectrum consists of myriad positions which an individual may assume and live out. 'Sexuality brings into play too great a diversity of conjugated beings; these are like *n* sexes. Sexuality is the production of a thousand sexes' (Deleuze and Guattari 1987: 278). Feminist and geneticist, Anne Fausto-Sterling claims (1993: 21) that 'biologically speaking, there are many gradations running from female to male; and depending on how one calls the shots, one can argue that along the spectrum lie at least five sexes – and perhaps even more.' It has become commonplace for geneticists to talk beyond the binarisms of XX (female) and XY (male); to include XY and XXX females, as well as XX, XXY, XXXY, XXXXY and YYX individuals with a male phenotype, or XXY hermaphrodites; and to use terms like 'intersexuality' (Mittwoch 1992: 471; Schafer 1995: 280). Recent research suggests that chromosomal males can develop fully as females or that chromosomal females may develop as phenotypic males; in some cases, features of both develop partially or wholly, presenting ambiguous genitalia (Schafer 1995: 275). Given this evidence, it is impossible to make a binary genetic classification on the basis of the Y chromosome, since it cannot always explain an individual's set of sexual organs. This imperfect binarization has prompted another set of classifications to account for the range of individual variation.

Genetic sex is dependent upon the presence or absence of a Y chromosome (more precisely, of the Y chromosome SRY). Genetic sex says nothing about the phenotype, or appearance, of the individual: it is simply the chromosomal sex. The type of reproductive organs an individual develops – ovaries or testes – defines phenotypic sex. Abnormal development can occur, usually as a result of hormones, and the reproductive organs can develop as a mixture of male and female, or developmentally somewhere in between. This is the situation termed 'intersex', which is a biological description of the internal and external genitalia, and which has no bearing on chromosomal sex and may or may not be important for 'gender assignment'. If the external genitalia are ambiguous then surgery may be required to create a sex phenotype decided upon medically. That assignment has caused considerable controversy, since those affected often consider themselves to be a third sex. Corrective surgery to eradicate such 'neutrality' is thus seen by intersexed individuals as a form of mutilation. These new genetic studies deal with the variety of distinct sexual phenotypes, which is perhaps the concrete biological manifestation for the metaphor of the spectrum. Sex could be seen as a continuum and bodies as multiple (Gatens 1996: 19). Individuals cannot be divided simply into binary groupings because there are so many variations on this theme, all of which are experienced in living bodies and expressed by individual beings.

The teleological taxonomies separating nature from culture, and the biological from the social, are now being collapsed. It can be demonstrated that social factors may affect the biology of human populations. Again, the body is brought into play because of its privileged position as the nexus of individual and society – one that can be reduced to neither physical autonomy nor social text (Worthman 1995: 600). For example, altered physical activity, fertility patterns and breast-feeding practices related to changing work patterns gender relations and technologies also increase the risk of reproductive cancer (Worthman 1995: 608). Thus, the boundaries between nature and culture, the biological and social sciences, and the individual and society have never been so equivocal.

So what is sex all about? Judith Butler (1993: 4) raised the question and attempted to answer it, questioning our recent fixation on gender in the process. She asks: is sex to gender as feminine is to masculine?

Is it natural, anatomical, chromosomal, or hormonal, and how is a feminist critic to assess the scientific discourses which purport to establish such 'facts' for us? Does sex have a history? Does each sex have a different history, or histories? Is there a history of how the duality of sex was established, a genealogy that might expose the binary oppositions as variable construction? Are the ostensibly natural facts of sex discursively produced by various scientific discourses in the service of other political and social interests? If the immutable character of sex is contested, perhaps this construct called 'sex' is as culturally constructed as gender; indeed, perhaps it was always already gender, with the consequence that the distinction between sex and gender turns out to be no distinction at all. (Butler 1990a: 6–7)

In 1997, Bernard Knapp and I also pondered this question, drawing on the work of Butler and other queer theorists, and attempted an answer which would have some bearing on archaeology which deals with the materiality of dead bodies as well as the cultural dimension of sex, gender, sexuality and embodiment (Knapp and Meskell 1997). It was also an opportunity to develop an archaeology of the body in a prehistoric context. We outlined the complexities of the genetic evidence, to demonstrate that even *science* could not always designate people into XX (female) and XY (male) categories. We then outlined the debates over terminology (sex:gender) and considered the dimension of sexuality and life experience in challenging the restricting binaries created through Western discourse.

When archaeologists refer to sex they in fact refer to a complex constellation of expressions and experiences. On one level there is the social construction of biological sex, with all its variable manifestations. Then there is the matter of how an individual chooses to manifest that defined sex, usually referred to as gender: they may present themselves to society in a number of ways, according to experience, embodiment and socio-cultural factors. Such a 'performance' represents a second level (Morris 1995). However, even this does not always define adequately sexual behaviour and experience. Thus an individual may be an XX female, and may perform in daily contexts as a female, but if she chooses not to conform to a heterosexual lifestyle then there is an added sexual dimension, that of difference, which needs to be considered. Temporality should also be acknowledged, since individual sexual identity is fluid and may change over the course of one's life. To date, the concept of gender has not been adequate to this task. In sum, archaeology needs to account for the range of discourses on offer encompassing biology, socio-cultural studies, feminist and masculinist philosophy, and sexual difference. Sex:gender is no longer a clear-cut paradigm which we are free to overlay onto all archaeological analyses. (Knapp and Meskell 1997: 187)

Debates over sex and gender must now acknowledge the dimension of sexuality because it has too long been assumed to be heterosexual by default. As current research on sexual preference and practice shows, the biological distinction male/female is inadequate in explaining sexuality (Gatens 1996: 16). If gender identity is construed along the lines of sex, gender, sexual practices and desire, and relationships between them, then we must construct more elaborate narratives to encompass the full range of individual identities and experiences – a theme taken up below in the section on 'Sexual Selves'.

In view of the arguments outlined above, I see no reason for using the binary equation, sex:gender, for the Egyptian data and would prefer to use the more nuanced concept of sex as outlined above, since there is no evidence to suggest that the Egyptians employed this construction. The Egyptians were predisposed towards opposites and pairs in mythical and iconographic spheres (see chapter 3). In the hieroglyphic script words might take on female or male determinatives. Only in later history – the Late Period, Greek and Roman times – do we get any concrete sense of sexual ambiguity or *other* categories (see Pinch 1994: 93; Montserrat 1996), although it is possible that the Egyptians had a concept of the eunuch from Middle Kingdom times onwards (Parkinson 1991: 125). Throughout this volume I generally refer to sex, rather than gender. The above discussion also explains why I do not privilege sex as the primary vector of difference. I am not alone in this position; other feminist historians argue that gender identity is a misnomer to the extent that it implies a single vector along which identity could be produced and represented. The concept of positionality (Adelson 1993) allows us to pursue the production of identity as an interplay of many social signifiers: race, nationality, class, ethnicity, sex and other constituents of power. My own work has been informed by third wave feminist and postcolonial scholars who prompt us to rethink those discourses which designate people as one. These writers argue that commitment to a single master signifier, whether it be class, race or sexuality, will prove to be an inadequate paradigm. Homi Bhabha suggests (1994: 1–2) that 'the move away from the singularities of "class" or "gender" as primary conceptual and organisational categories, has resulted in an awareness of the subject positions – of race, gender, generation, institutional location, geopolitical locale, sexual orientation – that inhabit any claim to identity in the modern world.' We need to think beyond these initial subjectivities and focus upon the processes that create cultural differences. Following Bhabha (1994), we can see that these interstices provide the terrain for elaborating strategies of selfhood that initiate new signs of identity and innovative sites of collaboration, and contestation, in the act of defining the idea of society itself.

## Contingencies of Gender

The now weary phrase 'gender as performance' can clearly be attributed to Judith Butler and has become increasingly popular in archaeology. Performativity is not a singular act, or a matter of donning a particular outfit at the beginning of the day and returning it to the closet in the evening. Performativity is always a reiteration of a norm or set of norms (Butler 1993: 12). It is inextricably linked to regulatory sexual regimes, agency conditioned by those regimes, the regime of heterosexuality, the materialization of norms and the limits of constructivism which are exposed at the boundaries of bodily life (Butler 1993: 15). In the process, her project is to destabilize the structural stasis of heterosexuality which has been formative in constructing gender identities. In her earlier work, she also advocated that '[g]ender ought not to be constructed as a stable entity or locus of agency from which various acts follow; rather, gender is an identity tenuously constituted in time, instituted in an exterior space through a *stylized repetition of acts*' (Butler 1990a: 140). This suggests that enactment creates gender categories and that they are contingent and not necessarily rooted in physical specificities. More importantly, there is no single experience of *being* in a female body, for instance, or being a certain biological sex. This has ramifications for our understanding of human societies in both contemporary and ancient settings.

To demonstrate the salience of gender identities, as they are intermingled with other social dimensions, Butler analyses Jennie Livingstone's video documentary *Paris is Burning*, which revolves around drag balls in New York City. It is perhaps the most convincing piece of ethnography I have witnessed which demonstrates how people identify with categories and desire to change their status designations. Butler refers to this phenomenon as *passing* (1993: 129). In the performances which follow, the largely black, gay, 'male' participants walk the catwalk while attempting to *pass* as female, white, straight, rich, successful individuals. There are rigid categorizations and labels: executive, model, university student. They are judged on their realness, their naturalness, their ability to pass. This is concretized by the accompanying soundtrack, *To be Real*. In one poignant scene, an ageing drag queen explains how the ultimate goal is to return from a night out intact, without being beaten or bloodied, or having one's clothes torn. The success of life on the streets is gauged by one's ability to *pass* as a certain gender, class, colour, status and sexual preference. There is an acknowledgement that these categories are mutable and fluid, open to negotiation and reiteration through individual bodies. Here, gender is literally like drag (Butler 1993: 125) since it reflects on the imitative structure by which hegemonic gender is itself produced. Through the course of the film we watch and hear the story of Venus Xtravaganza, who attempts to pass as a white, heterosexual, female, and for a time enjoys local celebrity status until homophobic violence ends her short life. Before her death, she explains how all she has ever wanted to be is a spoilt white girl, a phantasmatic identity she attempts to construct for herself despite her biological sex and sexual identity. It is telling that gender identities cannot neatly be separated from those of other power differentials, in this case race, class, status and sexuality.

Contemporary *ethnographies* are particularly telling in their complexity and contingency. In many societies, like Native American ones, various categories of gender were institutionalized in ways noticeably different from our own. In Butlerian terms, a very different set of norms was reiterated, as opposed to Western constructions. In the 1770s Spanish chroniclers described the Chumash of southern California as having a class of men who adorned themselves with female ornamentation, conducted themselves in the character of women and enjoyed great status among their companions. As Sandra Hollimon (1997) has discussed, the Chumash and their neighbours the Yokuts, Mono and Tubatulabal all had a concept of third gender, known as 'two-spirits', and they were responsible for the undertaking of funerals and associated rituals. These individuals were considered to have supernatural powers, operating liminally between earthly and divine worlds. Recently, these groups have become the focus of a large outpouring of scholarship (Herdt 1993; Jacobs 1994; Hollimon 1996, 1997). According to Hollimon (1997: 177), there is also a confusing conflation of terminology surrounding these individuals who were variously described as homosexuals, transvestites, 'fancy ones', celibate medicine men or gravediggers. Ethnographers and later commentators never escaped the normative language of binarism which significantly impaired their understanding. And, in fact, many ethnographic observers seem to have been confused themselves as to whether they were dealing with men, women, hermaphrodites or another gender category altogether. The common confusion was whether individuals were transvestite males or 'strong women'. Among the Yokuts, it is possible that transvestism lapsed after Western influences and was replaced by homosexuality itself. Moreover, other genders may have been 'performances' constructed for the ceremony of burial, after which an individual returned to his or her 'original' gender (Hollimon 1997: 182). Interestingly, there is no recorded category of female 'two-spirits'. So, despite the lack of a uniform set of practices with attendant socio-sexual categorizations, these remarkable accounts demonstrate the array of possibilities for sexed and gendered categories which were completely accepted and considered 'normative' in Native American societies. Some archaeologists concerned with gender have attempted to apply the third-gender model to cultures for which there is no known cultural correlate, and this analogy might be misplaced. However, it is a concept worth considering, but not necessarily in terms of simply three genders (i.e. a straightforward Western dichotomy plus a variant). As Hollimon (1997) rightly argues, among the Chukchi of Siberia there are seven genders.

But what makes Hollimon's work doubly important for archaeologists interested in questions of sex (or gender) is her application of this knowledge to the archaeological record. So often, gender theorists are criticized for not really being able to *do* gender archaeology, or to put theory into practice. She presents a series of hypotheses concerning possible means of identification of these individuals in the material record and then tests each. From an examination of the mortuary data, both bodies themselves and artefacts (Hollimon 1988, 1997), she has tentatively identified biologically 'male' individuals who may have lived as 'two-spirits'. From a sample of 210 burials, only two male individuals showed severe spinal arthritis possibly indicating repetitive activities like digging (either harvesting tubers or digging graves). These same two individuals were the only males to be buried with both digging-stick weights and baskets (the payment given to 'two-spirits' for performing the burial ceremony), lending added support to the osteoarchaeological evidence. Linking this back to the ethnographic sources, they recorded up to three 'two-spirits' per village among the Chumash, which again fits well with Hollimon's findings. On a more general level, she has shown that at no time in prehistory did gendered artefacts (digging-stick weights, baskets = female; projectile points, fish-hooks, nets = male) match the sexes of the burial in a dichotomous fashion (Hollimon 1996). The bifurcated structure of gender with which we are familiar does not fit societies even in the recent past, so we cannot always expect the material data to cohere to such a model. In identifying 'two-spirits', it may be more productive to differentiate the material culture of another (third) gender rather than simply looking for 'males in women's clothing', since in such societies they were not considered men who dressed as women and did their work. Hollimon is also careful to account for other variables, such as status, occupation and rank, rather than simply prioritizing gender. As a final comment, I'd like to stress again that, while the term 'gender' may actually describe Native American cultures quite well from our perspective, we should be continually aware that this inheres a biological sex:cultural gender construction which was likely to have been unknown to them.

But what of the ancient data and categories of sex/gender? Are such models applicable or even relevant given their cultural specificity and discursive production? In fact, there are many examples which challenge our false foundational premises of gender by stressing the contingency of the category. Consider the changing discursive categories of identity and gender constituted through the creation of eunuchs in the Byzantine empire (Tougher 1997). Eunuchs held high status positions and played key roles in Byzantine society for almost one thousand years. Until the ninth century AD, the term 'eunuch' actually referred to anyone who could not, or would not, bear children: men who were sterile, men who lacked sexual desire, men and women who chose to live a celibate life (Ringrose 1993: 86). It also included a large category of castrated men, whose reasons for castration were considerably varied. Throughout this time, however, biology and social construction became blurred categorizations: Galen posited that castrated men became more like women. This fits nicely into Thomas Laqueur's (1990) proposition of a one-sex model prior to the Enlightenment. However, Clement of Alexandria thought there were three categories: men, women and eunuchs. Thus, several intellectual traditions sat side by side, a single-sex structure and a bipolar model (Ringrose 1993: 89). And because eunuchs participated in sex with male and female partners, their sexuality did not help place them in a clearly defined gender. From the tenth century AD onwards, the term for eunuch literally meant 'cut' and referred to the surgical removal of the testicles, rather than the looser bio-social category which had preceded it. These individuals were described as ποικίλος (changeable) or ἀμφίβολος (ambiguous) or, more disparagingly, as stiff, sickly, shrill-voiced, beardless, boyish and womanlike (Ringrose 1993: 93). Eunuchs formed a nebulous category, sometimes a gender on their own, often not, their definitions and boundaries constantly changing.

Byzantine eunuchs, Indian *hijras*, Native American 'two-spirits', eighteenth-century mollies, Latin American *travestis*, Omani xaniths,

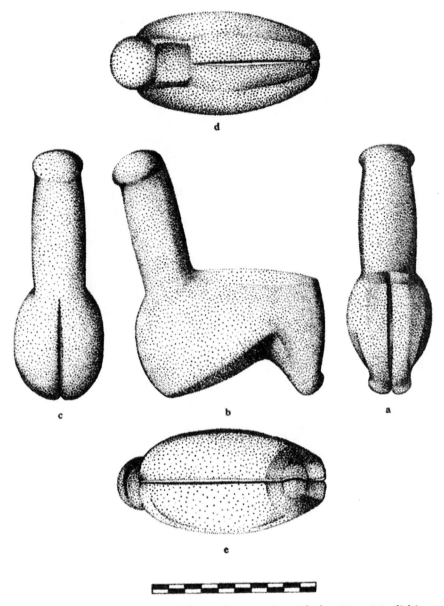

**Figure 2.1** Limestone seated figure from Sotira *Arkolies* (Late Neolithic, height 16 cm, length 11.1 cm). (a) Front view; (b) side view; (c) rear view; (d, e) top and bottom views (Cyprus Museum, no. 1981/VIII-19/1, courtesy of Stuart Swiny)

Balkan 'sworn virgins', intersexed individuals, hermaphrodites, Sambian *kwolu-aatmwol* – there are countless examples of groups and individuals, from a host of cultures and epochs, who challenge the sex/gender status quo of the West. They destabilize our own notions and present very different genders, as the 'stylized repetition of acts' (Butler 1990a: 140). But how might archaeologists approach the prehistoric record? Is there any evidence that sex (or gender) or sexuality was conceived of in radically divergent ways? Here again I'd like to return to the work Bernard Knapp and I undertook to explain the ambiguous nature of some Chalcolithic Cypriot figurines (Knapp and Meskell 1997). We examined a number of steatite and picrolite figurines which were either phallic and cruciform or clearly displayed both phallic and vulvic qualities. One example from Sotira *Arkolies* (figure 2.1) is particularly evocative since it reveals both male and female genitalia depending on the way in which it is viewed (Knapp and Meskell 1997: 193–4). Its sexual ambiguity may point to the existence of conceptual categories which diverge from our own, where harmony rather than polarity was the order of the day. The Chalcolithic cruciform figures also stress the complementarity of sexual characteristics, sometimes incorporating breasts and a phallic neck and head. The desire to delineate one sex or another, in a strictly bifurcated society, does not appear to be a priority here. Whether these figurines were meant to represent conceptual categories, beings or individuals is completely open to debate. Our point in discussing the data was to extend the critique beyond the normative tropes of our own society which places inordinate value on placing individuals (and ancient figurines) in one of two binary categories. As Moira Gatens (1996: 82) reminds us, gender as it is lived in social institutions is more concerned with imaginary bodies than with a natural or presocial body. Her question is how are men's and women's morphologies lived and experienced in the present? But whatever the answers are to that complex contextual issue, they are likely to be very different from those our ancestors might offer.

## The Trouble with Gender Archaeology

This notion of gender now seems largely irrelevant or redundant, a term unnecessary for describing the vast social arrangements, contexts, and variations in the ways in which we live, give meaning to, and enact sex.

Elizabeth Grosz, *Space, Time and Perversion*

In the late 1980s Marilyn Strathern constructed an enlightened scenario where gender referred to 'categorisations of persons, artifacts,
events, sequences, and so on which draw upon sexual imagery – upon
the ways in which the distinctiveness of male and female characteristics make concrete people's ideas about the nature of social relationships' (Strathern 1988: ix). Gender was not simply about 'men' and
'women', nor was it separated out from other categorizations of
sociality. She cautioned that gender ascriptions could not be read off
in advance and it did not automatically follow that a feminine identity meshed with 'women' only. It was action that was engendered.
And, more importantly, the problem of women was never simply
about women, according to Strathern (1988). It was more about relationships. In her work on Melanesia she concluded that gender could
be related to the capabilities of people's minds and bodies, what they
contain within themselves and their effects on others. As such, a
person's gender may be dually or multiply composed (1988: 182–3).
In all her work, gendered relations are configured around economic
and social practices, rather than the constellations of ethnicity, sexual
orientation and religious difference that characterize contemporary
experience. This prompts me to ask the question: if feminist anthropologists or anthropologists of gender were already considering such
radical concepts of sex and/or gender and its permutations, why did
archaeology go down the route it did – why did it seemingly ignore
the developments in its sister discipline? Why did the filtering process
take so long, assuming it has started to happen now? In archaeology,
studies of women did, and do, occupy centre stage, at the expense of
men, children, issues of difference and sexuality. Why the time lag,
why the lack of interdisciplinarity? After all, in the case of Strathern
and her influential work, she was entrenched literally next door to the
archaeologists at Cambridge University? Why were archaeologists
running in tandem with feminist thought from the 1970s rather than
the 1980s, largely construed as second wave feminism? This is even
more troubling for American practitioners who were conveniently
housed in anthropology departments where innovative research was
being carried out. More worryingly, why did more conservative fields
like history or classics take up feminism, psychoanalysis and social
theory, at a much faster rate than our own discipline? Classics
has been much derided as a conservative field, yet seems to have
been eager to incorporate developments in other fields on sex,
sexuality and difference (as a contrast, 1998 saw the first Society for
American Archaeology session devoted to the analysis of sexuality in
archaeology).

Significant problems, both methodological and political, surround the female-dominated field of gender archaeology. While full of promise in the mid-1980s the gender movement has shown itself to be inherently conservative and lagging behind feminist developments in other social sciences (for example, Walde and Willows 1991; Wright 1996; Nelson 1997). Archaeology continues to correlate gender specifically with the study of women (for example, Wright 1996; Nelson 1997), while masculinist theory remains a relatively unknown quantity. It has been estimated that over 90 per cent of the work produced in gender archaeology is 'womanist': concerned with the actions, status or simply the presence of women in the past. Significantly, there is little overlap between feminist and womanist literatures (Joyce and Claassen 1997: 1). More than a decade ago, Marilyn Strathern warned that what was at stake for feminists was the promotion of women's interests, i.e. the promotion of a single perspective (Strathern 1988: 24). There is another serious theme here which has been borne out in the history of gender archaeology: only men are persons and there is no gender but the feminine (Wittig, quoted in Butler 1990a: 20). To date, men have not emerged as a viable subject of analysis, nor has another crucial component of difference, sexual orientation. As mentioned before, masculinist theory seeks to analyse the construction and experience of the masculine subject, and does not in any way revolve around androcentrism or the traditional studies which render women invisible. It is an important offshoot of the feminist movement and is important for feminist politics too, as Jane Flax (1987: 629) and others have noted. If we problematize women and leave men as an untheorized group, the male position is indirectly privileged and gender studies are regarded as the domain of women. Analysing masculinity may also remedy the current objectification of women in studies devoted to gender and sexuality (Meskell 1997b). So from both viewpoints, male and female, masculinist theory should be a welcome addition to social theory. In the past we have created reductionist narratives which flattened diversity and failed to record difference, obliterating men as men, and constructing a universal, sexless, atemporal screen (Fenster 1994: ix–x) which obscured social inequalities and individual experience. Neither feminist nor masculinist theory should be studied primarily by its respective sex. If these disciplines continue to bifurcate, we are simply subscribing to another limiting Cartesian dichotomy, in theory and in practice.

The pioneering work of Meg Conkey, Joan Gero, Janet Spector, Ruth Tringham and Alison Wylie has had a marked impact on archaeology (see Conkey and Gero 1997). Without their individual efforts it is difficult to imagine the state of interpretive or social archaeology and there could be no archaeology of identity or difference. However, gender archaeology could be perceived as an additive and remedial project rather than as an epistemological revolution. Doing gender is a means of rebalancing the bias of former theorizing, but it is not tantamount to theoretical positions such as Marxism, structuralism or even postmodernism. Hill contends that 'nothing within existing theoretical frameworks – whether evolutionary, Marxist, processual, or postprocessual – prevents a re-examination of these issues' (1998: 104). Yet as Alison Wylie (1991, 1992b) and Elizabeth Brumfiel (1992) have forcefully argued, processual archaeology lacked a theory of the social, thereby impeding the study of gender, class and faction. That processualists can now engage with gender is another matter; one that seems to cause great *angst*. It is clear that 'archaeologies of gender failed to emerge within a processual framework; they are possible now because of the theoretical developments in postprocessualism' (Meskell 1998b: 182).

Another important epistemological point is that much engendered research is premised on analogical arguments, and testing is undertaken on ethnographic or ethnohistoric data rather than on the archaeological material in question (Hill 1998: 106). Much of this analysis has been undertaken in South American contexts. This has often been painted as simply an evidential constraint, typical of archaeological theorizing more generally (Wylie 1992a: 25–9), though many remain unconvinced. The centrality of analogical reasoning is clearly illustrated in prehistoric case studies where general assertions about the sexes are assumed and projected on to prehistory. A classic example is Gero's study (1991) of lithics at Huaricoto which links women with production and cooking on the basis of inference. The idea that women are associated with houses and cooking is, of course, a cultural supposition on our own part. While such a link may be valid in this specific context, more recent feminist scholarship prompts us to question all such generalizations. Too often, the roles of women have been limited to cooking, weaving and tending plants and children, whereas there are plenty of cases where women hunt (Brumbach and Jarvenpa 1997), farm and fight (Guyer 1991; Prezzano 1997), while men cook (Koehler 1997) and weave. Claassen too (1997: 85) has noted this essentialist tendency in interpretations of sex roles and the division of labour. It is well documented that the innateness of gender differences in personality and character is now factually and philosophically indefensible (Alcoff 1997: 335). There are a host of different ways in which gender distinctions are operationalized in different societies. A methodology for addressing these constituents of social difference and avoiding the pitfalls of prior gender research might be found in the writings of third wave feminists. The latter approach seeks to include all social factors, rather than to privilege the axis of sex. Lastly, the current study explicitly aims to go beyond studies of women and beyond a simple engendered analysis to explore hierarchies of difference from a third wave (or equalist) perspective. By equalist, I refer to a position which does not privilege the study of women at the expense of men or other groups.

A salient example of what I see as the current crisis in gender archaeology can be found in Sarah Nelson's (1997) recent volume. Although entitled *Gender in Archaeology*, gender does not figure here at all – it is uncompromisingly a study of women. *Ipso facto* women have gender, concomitantly, men do not. Gender and feminism are conflated (Nelson 1997: 14), resulting in a situation where only women can undertake engendered analyses. The text is characterized by a parodic rendering of the views of male scholars, even those who have *demonstrated* feminist sympathies (for example, Hodder 1991a: 13); quotes are taken out of context simply because the scholar is male. Astoundingly, she seems to support James Mellaart simply because he had a vision of matriarchy (Nelson, 1997: 146). Scholarship is clearly being sacrificed in the name of misplaced politics. One has to question why it is appropriate for female scholars to discuss power in the past, but not their male counterparts – even when addressing female inequalities. Have we created exclusionary zones in archaeology, reserved only for the inner circle? Entirely missing is the past decade of theorizing over sex and gender terminologies (Nelson, 1997: 15): Nelson argues that sex is strictly biological, while gender is social. Contrary to her claims, such thinking has indeed led to continued dichotomizing throughout. Numerous polarities are expounded within these pages founded on essentialist notions ranging from *woman as weaver* to *woman as mentor*: most of us have experiences to the contrary. The volume focuses almost entirely on the American tradition and, more limiting again, on those studies which deal with prehistory. It is replete with retrospective criticisms – the now weary excursus into marginalization of women and women's studies. Gender archaeology has been predicated upon such reproaches for at least 15 years. From a hardline perspective, it is clear that, at least in North America, an entire generation of women have made careers out of gender, thereby creating a niche market for themselves. Perhaps it is time to stop the enforced ghettoization and simply get on with the business of doing a better archaeology (see Gilchrist, forthcoming). But Nelson claims (1997: 16) that we cannot study everything at once (here she refers to issues of race, ethnicity, age); however, surely this is the only way to be rigorous in our interpretations. We have to relinquish the desire to simply *do women* just because it complicates our analyses to interpolate additional factors; this seems an outdated, sloppy and irresponsible position. It seems archaeology is wavering in the untenable position of the second wave, finding (certain) *women* at the cost of all others.

## Sexual Selves

For many fields, the study of sex and gender simultaneously redescribed the entire sphere of sexuality and this has, albeit belatedly, enabled a similar overture in archaeological discourse, although it has also led to considerable elision. But how do we approach the whole topic of sexuality? This is a question which has puzzled writers of both contemporary and ancient societies. The famous sexologist Havelock Ellis regarded sex as the 'central problem of life'. Diverse thinkers, such as Freud, Lacan, Mead, Foucault, Stoller, Sedgwick, Weeks and Butler, have struggled with the issue and have adopted radically different accounts. Feminist scholars such as MacKinnon (1997: 160) have suggested that sexuality be studied empirically, not just in the texts of history (as Foucault does), in the social psyche (as Lacan does) or in language (as Derrida does). Words and texts might be one dimension, but the real domain of sexuality is embedded within social relations and power relations. Anthropologist Clifford Geertz (1966) famously described sexuality in the image of an onion. In sexuality, as in culture, we peel off each layer (economies, politics, families) and imagine we are approaching the kernel, but it soon becomes clear that the whole is the only 'essence' there is. Sexuality cannot be abstracted from its surrounding social layers. Like Geertz, Ross and Rapp (1997: 155) refer to the social embeddedness of sexuality which should also incorporate kinship and family systems; sexual regulations and definitions of communities; national and world systems. These and other factors shape individual and group behaviour. As social contexts, they mirror and are experienced through the salient divisions in a given society: class, race, sex and heterosexual dominance. There are obviously lines of convergence: in traditional Irish villages unmarried men were perceived as 'boys', no matter what their chronological age, and in the French language, generational age and marital status are conflated – *vieille fille/vieux garçon* (Ross and Rapp 1997: 158). In fact, sexuality enters the social contract between the individual and society, neither operates in isolation. Economics, education, mass media, state policies, religious interventions and ethics all become prominent social forces along with personal choice and desire. Gayle Rubin (1975) famously talked about the social organization of sexuality: we have yet to produce such sophisticated analyses in archaeology, possibly because of the limitations of our data, and almost certainly because of our disciplinary reticence to engage with the topic seriously.

Following Foucault, Jeffrey Weeks (1997: 15) argues that sexuality is a fictional unity, a human invention that once did not exist and, in time to come, may not exist again. What we define as sexuality is but one 'historical construction which brings together a host of different biological and mental possibilities – gender identity, bodily differences, reproductive capacities, needs, desires and fantasies – which need not be linked together, and in other cultures have not been' (Weeks 1997: 15). Stress should fall on the side of variety not uniformity. To recover these historical constructions, Weeks suggests that we ask how sexuality is shaped by economic, social and political forces, what the relationship is between sex and power, and other variables such as class divisions and racism. Tangentially, we might also discover why sex has become such a predominant structuring principle and symbolic leitmotif for Western culture. Clearly, the points of contact between the state and personal life have multiplied since the previous century, whether it be medical intervention to facilitate or prevent sexual reproduction, interventions regarding sexually transmitted diseases or psychosexual counselling (Jamieson 1998: 112). Perhaps its importance lies in its position at the nexus of two major axes of current concern – our own subjectivity and society itself – which coalesce at the site of the body. Sexuality, like society, is an intricate web of institutions, beliefs, habits, ideologies and social practices whose interlinkages have to be unravelled (Weeks 1997: 57). An essential fixity cannot be assumed, either on biological or social constructionist grounds. And, like society, sexuality is not something 'out there'. Sexuality isn't simply what other people have, what certain groups possess and fetishize, it is part of our own, individual lived experience – and thus inescapable.

For many ancient contexts, it should be possible to investigate contextually their constructions of sexuality, yet they are likely to bear little relation to our own elaborate constructions and experiences. One might postulate that, while sexuality was a dominant characterizing force, it was not recognized as such in the ancient world: sexual preferences were acknowledged, but only as one would recognize someone's taste in food without characterizing that person as a member of a sub-species of humanity (Parkinson 1995: 59). Sexuality, in contexts like ancient Egypt, was a practice rather than a discourse or a label that one designated people with. Similarly, in the early Christian period same-sex relations were described as a particular type of *behaviour* rather than a particular type of *person* (Greenberg 1997: 182). One can chronicle the acceptance of such practices in medieval Christendom and early modern Europe. Yet analysing sexuality should not simply provide a forum for alterity, for non-normative practices – we should also study the social construction of heterosexuality. If left untheorized, it becomes, once again, normative, unproblematic and a given (see Zita 1998). If we have learnt anything from the queer movement, it is to *assume nothing*!

Any discussion of sexuality in archaeology should take into account the massive influence of Foucault's *oeuvre* (Meskell 1996a, 1998a; Knapp and Meskell 1997). And it is perhaps more pressing that students of history undertake this given Foucault's writings on ancient cultures, despite the numerous criticisms concerning his historical knowledge (Cohen and Saller 1994; Goldhill 1995). Additionally, his work has met with harsh disapprobation from feminist quarters (Diamond and Quinby 1988; Nicholson 1990; Sawicki 1991; McNay 1992). Feminist classicists have charged him with ignoring the female subject and the voices of children, slaves and other class groups (duBois 1998: 96; Richlin 1998), though he has enabled us to escape from reifying and essentializing the category *woman*. Both feminist and queer theory have benefited greatly from his controversial insights. Though many scholars find fault with the fine details of Foucault's thesis, most appreciate the overall contribution *The History of Sexuality* has made to fields as diverse as history, classics, feminist theory and the social sciences.

It is impossible to summarize adequately Foucault's three-volume *magnum opus*. The first volume is perhaps the most influential and, many agree, should have stood as the definitive work. Here Foucault demolishes the repressive hypothesis and posits that the construction of sexuality is a relatively recent development. In fact, he attempted to take the sex out of sexuality and focus on the operation of discourses in the construction or technologies of the self. From this perspective he was writing a *pre*history of sexuality. Some see this development as a reaction against Freud's work on sexuality, though Freud centred the emotions and personality, whereas Foucault denied these factors completely. He was trying to prove that psychoanalysis represented a failed attempt to explain sexuality (Black 1998). The second volume, *The Use of Pleasure* (1985), attempts to show a shift in the sexual interests of the self-fashioning subject in imperial Rome from boy love to reciprocal marriage (Larmour et al. 1998a: 27). The third volume, *The Care of the Self* (1986), extends this study, focusing on the control of the body and knowledge of bodily practices from pagan to Christian times, where ideology constructs and shapes sexuality. It is a history of the way in which the self has been constituted in its own self-relation as the subject of desire, rather than a history of moral codes (Larmour et al. 1998a: 32). These were studies in self-construction, care of the self and embodied ethics which eventually led to *scientia sexualis* or the modern mode of sexual/scientific knowledge (Black 1998: 54). In these later works, Foucault was more concerned with a hermeneutics of the self, rather than sex *per se* – which he famously said was actually boring. It should also be said that the last two volumes appeared within only days of Foucault's death, and the final, fourth volume, *Les Aveux de la Chair*, was never completed.

Foucault's work impacted on ancient world studies irreversibly. It opened up the possibility of theorizing sexuality in different, rather than descriptive, ways, and brought a number of traditions under scrutiny for their own sexual gaze. Such important work has been done by a generation of young scholars like Zainab Bahrani. In her stimulating work on ancient statuary and figurines, she highlights two fundamental levels of difference: the variable visibility of sexuality in the artistic traditions of ancient Mesopotamia and Hellenistic Greece, and the differences in contemporary scholarly readings of Eastern and Western art. Bahrani argues that Babylonian female figures denote a provocative and confrontational sexuality, rather than a purely fertile image of femininity. The vulva was the 'site and source of sexual pleasure rather than the producer of offspring'; indeed, 'none of the visual representations of nude women from Mesopotamia display a taboo of particular body parts' (Bahrani 1996: 11). Female sexual allure was paramount, as attested in Mesopotamian erotic literature which parallels the substantive artistic corpus. Bahrani argues that the female body was a sign and index of sexuality throughout the first and second millennia BC. The situation was very different in Hellenistic Greece, the much-touted home of the classical nude. Using insights from psychoanalysis, Bahrani suggests that Hellenistic Greek statuary, while displaying nudity, had considerable difficulties in rendering female genitalia. The accurate portrayal of the vulva was erased and rejected as non-existent: this ties into the trope of castration (1996: 5–6). Women's bodies become simultaneously the object of fear and desire. So the denial of the vulva says something very different about Greek notions of sexuality, possibly the distancing of the viewer from female sexuality or denying female sexuality altogether. The lack in the female body, demonstrated in the Aphrodites, both 'denied and represented female sexuality simultaneously, in order to provide an aesthetic ideal of femininity to Greek (male) culture' (1996: 7). Apart from this valuable contextual study, Bahrani offers a postcolonial critique of art history, critiquing the very terminologies used to produce difference: classical nudes versus naked Near Eastern figures. Nude suggests classical beauty and purity, whereas naked refers to a raw sexuality, even barbarism. The nude was closer to the natural ideal, an aesthetically purified image in the realm of high art, whereas the naked form was sexual, negative and without aesthetic mediation (Nead 1992; Bahrani 1996). As this example highlights so effectively, the gaze of both ancient and contemporary viewer is a sexualized one which draws on the specifics of cultural location. We cannot assume *a priori* the notion that the erotic has a stable, underlying referent. Nor can we assume that the gaze is always embedded in a heterosexual matrix.

## Queer Positions

In the third, and last, volume of *The History of Sexuality* Foucault suggested that Plutarch's *Dialogue on Love* bore witness to a movement that did not come to fruition until much later. An absolutely unitary conception of love was constructed, while the practice of pleasure was divided by a strict boundary: one that separates the conjoinings of one sex with the other and relations within the same sex. This is basically the order of things which exists today, bolstered by a unitary conception of sexuality, which enables one to delimit strictly the dimorphism of relations and the differential structure of desire (Foucault 1986: 198). That 'movement' was clearly homosexuality, though the term itself is problematic in a non-modern context. This was not lost on Foucault (1985: 187), who claimed that the entire 'notion of homosexuality is plainly inadequate as a means of referring to an experience, forms of valuation, and a system of categorisation so different from ours'. Homosexuality was an invention of the 1860s in his view (Weeks 1997: 33), whereas Halperin (1990) dates it to the 1890s. A new understanding of sexuality nevertheless emerged in the nineteenth century whereby sexual acts and desires became the markers of identity. Homosexuality as the condition, and thus identity, of specific bodies was inextricably linked to that particular historical moment (Somerville 1997: 37). So terms and categorizations like gay, lesbian, homosexual or queer are modern products with contextually specific designations and developments, and as such cannot simply be projected through time and space to overlay on to other cultures. In 1997 I gave a seminar to the Queer Theory Group at Cambridge University and discussed this very issue after presenting the available evidence from Graeco-Roman Egypt. It was universally agreed that 'same-sex relations' was the most appropriate term to deploy in ancient contexts, while, conversely, 'gay' or 'homosexual' labels were felt to be anachronistic. Again the emphasis should be upon a contextual examination.

This trouble over terminology ties into the much larger debate of essentialism versus constructionism, for which sexuality is a pertinent case in point. An essentialist position would advocate that homosexuality was a stable category that had always been present in human history, whereas a constructionist thesis would posit social forces as the mechanism through which identities are constructed and shaped. As I have argued elsewhere (Meskell 1996a, 1998a), neither discourse is adequate, since individual difference, volition and circumstance have not been factored into the equation. Yet constructionism, and certainly Foucauldian constructionism, can be useful in discussing differences between ancient and modern societies. As Foucault reminds us, the 'homosexual' is the creation of bourgeois nineteenth-century society, inextricably linked to the growth of capitalism, private property and the sanctity of the nuclear family. Given that the term heterosexual predated homosexual, the latter was singled out as marked, secondary and oppositional to the normative category of heterosexual (Larmour et al. 1998a: 22).

It is important to recognize, once more, the Foucauldian influence on studies of same-sex relations in ancient societies and for the general recognition of ancient sexualities as being multiply constituted (Feher et al. 1989; Halperin 1990, 1995; Halperin et al. 1990; Winkler 1990; Foxhall 1994; Parkinson 1995; Montserrat 1996; Larmour et al. 1998b). This is not to suggest that he was the originator of the idea – far from it – but that the impact of his work acted as a catalyst for an entire body of writing. But personal motivations have been called into question and fingers have been pointed at various groups in the gay, feminist and other radical social movements who have appropriated elements of Foucault's theory or historical research in order to advance their respective political struggles (Larmour et al. 1998a: 12). Why such subjectivities should be singled out against other political positions surprises me, as if we can ever be objective in our interests or arguments, and at least in this case feminists and queer theorists have been up-front in their politics.

In the following sections I attempt to critique a presumptive heterosexuality by examining a range of case studies from contemporary anthropology, ethnohistory, ancient history and archaeology. As each study pushes back through time towards prehistory, I hope to demonstrate that such studies are in fact possible and viable in archaeology. In the earlier section on 'Contingencies of Gender' I discussed the work of Sandra Hollimon on Native American 'two-spirits', outlining the difficulties in applying a normative Western model of sex and gender in a non-Western context. However, her work has further implications for the related field of sexuality, since sex, gender and sexuality are inextricably linked though contingently structured. The ethnographic accounts she presents highlight a particular fascination with gender roles, but have said less about sexual practices. 'Two-spirits', or 'aqi, could have sexual relations with both men and women, but probably not with each other because of the way in which categories of men and non-men were constructed. Again, this is constituted around the acts of penetration and reception. The Western categories of hetero-, homo- and bisexual are clearly inapplicable in these contexts, and relations between people of the same biological sex did not necessarily imply that these individuals belonged to the same gender (Hollimon 1998). As such our labels are meaningless.

As is made clear via anthropology (Kulick 1997), men who have same-sex relations in Latin American contexts, for example, do not consider themselves homosexual. Moreover, their masculinity is not questioned as a result of same-sex practices. So here again our categories are inapplicable in our own time, let alone for those cultures of the past. Yet the situation in Latin America is more complex: those who penetrate are gendered male, and those who are penetrated are gendered female. As Kulick demonstrates, the sex/gender system is inadequate, as is the heterosexual/homosexual classification. He argues that gender is grounded in sexuality (1997: 575) and that in this specific context the categories are constructed around men and non-men (which includes women and all those who are penetrated). His own work on the *travestis* of Brazil suggests that this system offers a framework for people to understand and organize their own desires, bodies, relationships and social roles. Contrary to popular belief, the *travestis* do not want to be women or to have sex changes, even though they modify their male bodies to look female through hormones and implants. The penis remains their prized possession and they consider themselves men at every level. So while men are at liberty to change their gender, females – of any sexual orientation – remain female. Many commentators might posit the existence of a third gender or intermediate sex, popular categories which have received much attention and have been layered on to the ancient world. However, Kulick correctly argues (1997: 579) that *travestis* only arise and are culturally intelligible within a strictly dichotomous gender system. Thus body, gender and sexuality are all enacting different scenarios which are at odds with a Western conception of their intrinsic relationships. This has further implications for general questions of identity inasmuch as identity is founded upon the stabilizing concepts of sex, gender and sexuality. So the very notion of the person is under interrogation through the emergence of incoherent or discontinuous gendered individuals who fail to conform to the normative explanatory picture of personhood (Butler 1990a: 17).

The evidence from anthropology and ethnohistory seems particularly rich (Feher et al. 1989; Herdt 1993; Cornwall and Lindisfarne 1994; Lingis 1994; Gutmann 1997), and far better than that which archaeology offers us. But certain contexts, particularly Mediterranean cultures, can provide information for a range of sexual practices which are grounded in evidence, rather than provocative speculation (for example, T. Taylor 1996). Drawing on the work of Richard Parkinson (1995), I'd like to explore the evidence for same-sex relations from textual sources in pharaonic Egypt. To begin with, there was no term for sexuality at this time, though the verb *nk* refers to having penetrative sex, and has no particular overtones, positive or negative. But the word *nkw* (a man on whom a sexual act is performed) has been used as a term of abuse and implies a passive role. Yet these words relate to practices, rather than to categories of individuals. Representational evidence is elusive and ambiguous, since official art rarely depicts sexual encounters of any nature. *Homosociality* is also difficult to separate from *homosexual* representations. We are on safer ground with the documentary record, as with the famous Pyramid Texts, in which the god Seth sodomizes Horus and impregnates him. In the Tale of Horus and Seth, a literary text from the 12th Dynasty, Seth says to Horus 'How lovely is your backside! Broad are [your] thighs' (Parkinson 1995: 70). Parkinson suggests that this is a play or parody on the ritual greeting 'How fair is your face.' From the account, the passive position of receiving sperm appears to be negative, whereas the act of penetration has no stigma attached. Seth's attempts to have sex with Horus appear to be an act of humiliation for Horus, but are a source of pleasure for Seth which he describes as 'sweet to his heart'. This suggests that same-sex desire was known to the Egyptians and could be articulated as such. What is interesting here is that terminology is used to delineate practices rather than individuals. In today's society, words are used to describe people; they are labels often to be used derisively such as homosexual, lesbian, dyke (Radicalesbians 1997: 154). This does not appear to have been the case in antiquity (see also Joyce 1998).

Another well-documented example comes from the Tale of King Neferkare and the Military Commander Sasenet, dated to the 19th Dynasty, though composed earlier. It describes the nocturnal activities of the king and his military commander, 'going out at night all alone, with nobody with him'. The king enters the commander's house for several hours and 'after his Person had done with him what he desired with him he returned to his palace.' This desire was certainly sexual. As Parkinson notes, their relationship is a continuing one and each man seems to be the sole object of desire for the other. He concludes (1995: 74) that sexual acts between men were expressed in official documents only in so far as they conformed to acceptable male gender roles and power structures – also akin to what Kulick discovered in Latin America. They were also constructed around the designations of activity and passivity as being positive and negative traits respectively. While there is attestation of sexual desire, this is not celebrated as we see in heterosexual love poetry, for example (see Foster 1992; Fox 1995). Such desire may have been seen as irregular and as such excluded from official discourse. Despite the reticence to portray same-sex relations in the same light as heterosexual ones, they were at least acknowledged rather than erased completely from all cultural discourse. Finally, I would like to re-centre Butler's assertion (1990a: 135–6) that any construction of gender coherence conceals the gender discontinuities that run rampant within heterosexual, bisexual, gay and lesbian contexts in which gender does not necessarily follow from sex, and desire, or sexuality generally does not seem to follow from gender.

## Re-embedding Sex in Egypt

As a final case study to illustrate the problematics of sexuality in archaeology and to offer an alternative way of seeing contextual constructions of sexual life, I will draw on Egyptian data from the village

**Figure 2.2**   The village of Deir el Medina (photograph by the author)

of Deir el Medina (figure 2.2). The site forms the basis of the next three chapters, although it is primarily the mortuary data that will be considered there. But by examining the domestic context we have an opportunity to discuss the lived experience of the villagers, specifically elite women of the household and their representations and relations with others. Sexuality in Egypt cannot be viewed through the same lens as classical Greece. Foucault's analyses of Greek and Roman cultures (1985, 1986) highlight their sexual regimes, bodily controls, medicalized practices and so on, whereas Egyptian culture had no such strictly articulated discourses. There certainly existed comparable dream books in pharaonic Egypt which set out the meanings of all manner of sexual practices for the dreamer in their waking life, but nothing approaches the scale of discursive control of the body and sexuality until we get to Graeco-Roman times. This should not be surprising given the pervasive cultural sphere that reflected the Hellenistic empire. As in all matters, sexuality is a contextual issue.

As in the Mediterranean (Cullen 1996), scholars of Egypt have cast woman as the signifier for concepts revolving around the body – most often seen in studies of iconography, dress, adornment, posture and hairstyles (Meskell 1997b). Egyptologists have failed to refigure the body in any nuanced sense, opting instead to focus on female exteriority in the most literal manner. Body and sexuality are thus read straight from the iconographic sources with little consideration of the social construction, much less embodied reality, of specific groups. Woman is reduced to a visual spectacle, and female sexuality is construed normatively through male-oriented artistic representations or literature (i.e. love poetry). To date, only a handful of writers have engaged with contextual constructions of sex, gender and the body using the rich suite of data Egypt provides (Montserrat 1993, 1996, 1998; Wilfong 1994, 1998; Parkinson 1995; Meskell 1996a, 1997b, 1998a). If sex and gender studies have proved to be less than satisfactory, then the entire subject of sexuality has been largely avoided or treated as an extension of normative Western categories. There is one book specifically on the subject (Manniche 1987) and it is not well regarded within the field. However, sexuality is being interpolated more regularly into engendered analyses (Wilfong 1997: 72–89). In general, there has been a connection between women and sexuality. This may be due to the cultural connection constructed in the West (MacKinnon 1997), and might not accurately reflect Egyptian society. However, it seems from iconographic evidence that there existed a whole aura of sexuality around female professions like musicians, dancers and entertainers, and adolescent serving girls (Robins 1993, 1996). These groups of women were sometimes represented on tomb walls or on various items of material culture, most often toiletry objects. These erotic genres are well known in the Egyptian context as are the informal sketches on ostraca (see figure 2.3) which show sexualized women or scenes of sexual intercourse. Sexuality is usually read off as heterosexual, while there is strong documentary evidence in mythology and didactic texts that same-sex relations existed, as previously discussed.

Because these images seem so familiar to us now very little new work has attempted to re-signify them or re-embed them in their non-Western context. Because of the obvious hermeneutic pitfalls, I want to suggest that we have misread Egyptian sexuality and cast it in our own experience. We have separated out sexuality as a socially constructed sphere, much as it exists in our own society: a Foucauldian category which is the outcome of specific cultural and historical processes. Sexuality is a constantly changing category in modern society, one that is undergoing continued monitoring and negotiation. Blurred boundaries seep into other social and legal categories, and sexuality itself is a slippery and fluid entity at the close of the millennium. Some 3,500 years ago, the Egyptians had no word for sexuality, which is not surprising given its specific Western construction. But

**Figure 2.3**  New Kingdom ostracon from Deir el Medina (drawing by the author)

there certainly existed a culturally contextual experience of sexual life in pharaonic Egypt. Perhaps it did not exist as a category then, but rather it assumed different roles and permutations within certain contexts. It seems unlikely that there was a coherent concept of sex; perhaps sexuality infused so many aspects of ordinary life that it was unnecessary to isolate it. I would argue that the sexual and the religious/ritual were often configured in ways which we could never satisfactorily align today. That they could exist harmoniously in Egypt suggests that we are witnessing real cultural difference.

For example, in tomb scenes sexual images of women served to revivify the male tomb occupant in the next life: the sexual self was an integral component of the living, embodied individual. Images were not sexually explicit; however, the message was clear to the informed viewer. Sex and religion formed unions which we would find unthinkable from a Judaeo-Christian perspective. Additionally, there were votive phalli which were offered in cult places dedicated to goddesses like Hathor (Pinch 1993, 1994), mistress of all things female and sexual. It has been suggested that they were offered in the hope of facilitating pregnancy. From our perspective, Egyptian sexual categories feature women only, which may not be surprising given that only men were trained as scribes and painters. Women's largely illiterate position has impeded our knowledge of complementary dis- courses on the sexual beauty of men: love poems supposedly penned by women probably had a man behind each papyrus. It is possible that erotic genres also existed for men, but that the subtleties of the Egyptian system simply elude us. Or that the young, muscular, beau- tiful bodies represented in Egyptian art were enough to be considered sensual. This certainly appears to be the case in the documentary record (see Parkinson 1995). In a series of illustrations from the Turin Papyrus, men are shown with enlarged genitalia, engaged in sexual activities (figure 2.4). Similar images have also been preserved on ostraca and in graffiti. This represents a more vernacular expression of male sexuality. It is true that in the West what is sexual is largely what is defined by men, in terms of their own sexuality. Perhaps it is also true of Egyptian culture, and that what we witness as onlookers is almost akin to that of the male gaze of pharaonic man – without the intrinsic cultural knowledge of erotics. We can approach it only at a base level, by recognizing nudity or gross sexual cues, although we miss out on much of the imagery's sexual specificity. In essence, sex/sexuality should not be viewed as a mutually exclusive category (see Derchain 1975) and in Egypt the situation was far more complex, or alternatively, far less theorized.

The specific archaeological context under investigation are the houses at Deir el Medina, the front rooms of which were notionally female-oriented, centred around elite, married, sexually potent, fertile females of the household. These spaces were loaded with what we would describe as sexual and ritual images. Similarly, this space may have been used for sleeping, eating and general domestic duties for many hours of the day (Meskell 1998f: 217). This room is designated as the room of the enclosed bed (the so-called *lit clos*). The majority of houses within the village have conclusive evidence of this bed-like structure in this room (figure 2.5). Their dimensions were roughly 1.7 m long, 80 cm wide, and 75 cm high. In house SE5 the *lit clos* was

**Figure 2.4**   Scene from the Turin Papyrus, New Kingdom (courtesy of the Egyptian Museum, Turin, Inv. Turin 2031)

plastered, with moulded and painted Bes figures; Bes is the male deity associated with women, sexuality, fertility, music and magic. Bes predominates in this room throughout the site. House C5 has a *lit clos* with an associated Bes painting, and in the house of the woman Iyneferti, SW6, there are also Bes decorations. The enclosed bed was associated with a constellation of features: white walls, paintings, mouldings, niches, Bes decorations, cultic cupboards and shrines. The French excavator, Bernard Bruyère termed them 'enclosed beds' (*lit clos*) in the 1930s and the concept of the bed, primarily the birthing bed, has been a pervasive explanation ever since. Although it meant something very specific in his native French culture, the notion of the bed has had a pervasive impact on Egyptological interpretations of the *lit clos* ever since. Given the size of these structures, the feasibility of sleeping one or two people cannot be ruled out. It may have also acted as a ritual place for sexual intercourse with or without conception. But there are inherent problems with the birthing bed theory. For instance, there is ample evidence, in the form of illustrated ostraca from the site, for the traditional birthing apparatus being a stool (or bricks) rather than a bed. Birth arbours shown in these representations might be specially constructed outdoor buildings; their temporary nature has precluded archaeological discovery. Other scholars have suggested that they may have been constructed on roof-tops.

**Figure 2.5**   The *lit clos* of house NE13, excavated by Bruyère (courtesy of the IFAO, Cairo)

These representations do not resemble the *lit clos*. These illustrated ostraca represent a genre of post-birthing representations which incorporate an erotic component, through motifs such as grooming, wigs, hip girdles or nudity itself. Such sexual overtones do not appear to be hampered by the presence of a child. The majority of these infants are shown to be male, by virtue of a pronounced penis. In fact, age seems no barrier to sexual representation for the most part, as we have seen already with the genre of the adolescent serving girl. This, too, is something scholars have not clearly set in its wider social setting. The concept of a pure and innocent childhood is a Western, and very recent, construction (Ross and Rapp 1997: 161). Irrespective of this, such data challenge the singular notion that the *lit clos* was exclusively a birthing bed; a broader cultic interpretation is more plausible.

Archaeological evidence for linking cultic practices with the *lit clos* can be found in individual houses at Deir el Medina (Robins 1996). In NE11 Bruyère excavated a *lit clos* containing several items: a limestone headrest, part of a statue and a fragment of a female statuette in limestone. In front of the *lit clos* was an offering table. A similar situation was present in C7. In NE15 the *lit clos* is built with an associated cultic cupboard, as it was in Iyneferti's house, SW6. This suggests a more generalized cultic function, and one which may not exclude men, given the number of finds which name men of the house: associated limestone offering tables or stelae often bear a male name, rather than a female. Room 1 assemblages consist of primarily ritual artefacts: stelae, shrine busts, offering tables and statues were counted. Taken together, this evidence warrants the general conclusion that a household cult, centred around mature females, focused in the front rooms of Deir el Medina houses. More practically, this space could have been utilized on a daily basis for domestic activities since troughs and mortars were also located in NE14 and SW1.

We should contextualize the associated wall paintings. The extant data suggest that the front rooms were heavily decorated, having white-washed walls with female-oriented paintings, scenes of nursing or grooming, and deities pertaining to women's lives. In SE1 there was a wall painting showing a woman breast-feeding, in C7 a scene of a female grooming with her attendant, and in NW12 a person on a papyrus skiff, probably female. These wall paintings show vernacular images, scenes which appeared on items of everyday material culture. In SE8 workman Nebamun must have commissioned a mural, either for himself or his wife, of a nude female musician with a tattoo on her upper thigh. She plays a double flute and is surrounded by convolvulus leaves, which the Egyptians considered symbolically erotic. This representation would have been immediately obvious to anyone entering the house, though how it was received by various groups has not been considered. How did the Egyptians view these ritual and sexual images? My sense is that they were not separate spheres. These messages of religiosity and sexuality exist side by side, but should not be viewed as sexual in a pornographic sense since ours is a highly articulated category, with a well-developed attendant discourse (Hunt 1993). Yet sexuality in Egypt was coloured by morality, as set out in dream books and didactic texts. I think we have to find another way of viewing Egyptian experience. One avenue is obviously via anthropology. For example, the contradictory nature of sexual perceptions and attitudes is illustrated in many cultures, especially in the Middle

East today (Atiya 1984; Attir 1985). Instead of contradiction, we might consider that sexuality existed in a broader social system, and because of this fluidity it enabled a certain cross-cutting of other domains, such as religious life, private life and cosmology, in a way that our Western tradition constrains.

This study attempts to make sexuality more 'ordinary' and more 'embedded' within the social fabric of life. Sexuality seemed inextricably linked to domesticity and ritual: to procreation, childbirth, nursing, various life stages, death and even beyond to the afterlife. Sexuality was such a necessary component that it should not and cannot be fetishized as we have in our own society. Sexuality was there in the beginning for the Egyptians. Drawing on the Memphite Theology, Atum-Ra masturbates, producing semen from which the air god Shu and moisture goddess Tefnut were created. As brother and sister, they had sex and created Nut, the sky goddess, and Geb, the earth god. Nut and Geb embraced so tightly that nothing could exist between them and their conceived children could not be born. Shu forced Geb and Nut apart, holding the sky goddess high above the earth, so that her body became the starry heavens (see figure 2.6). She then gave birth to Osiris, Isis, Seth and Nepthys (Pinch 1994: 24–5). The universe came into being and was sustained through sexuality. One can see how the power of sexuality filtered into the human sphere and was part of everyday thinking (Gay Robins, personal communication). As Foucault reflects (1978), it was only during the seventeenth century that sex became clandestine, circumscribed, policed and its discourse became coded. After that time Western societies experienced a period of taboo, non-existence and silence. Some might argue that the erotic aspects of Egyptian literature were ambiguous and encoded (Guglielmi 1996), yet this does not equate to the social and legal strictures of later European history. This was not how the ancients perceived sexuality and we should not conflate those experiences – in Egypt sex was a practice rather than a discourse. Foucault's reminds us that 'what is peculiar to modern societies, in fact, is not that they consigned sex to a shadow existence, but that they dedicated themselves to speaking of it *ad infinitum*, while exploiting it as *the secret*' (1978: 35).


## Conclusion

At the close of her book *Gender Trouble*, Judith Butler (1990a: 142) again reinforced the phantasmatic status of the 'we' in feminist dis-

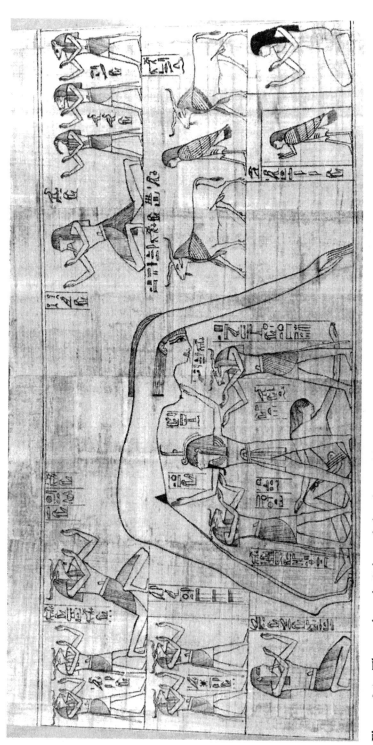

**Figure 2.6** The earth god, Geb, and the sky goddess, Nut, are separated by their father, Shu, the air god. The deity Heka is shown adoring in the bottom left corner. The owner of the papyrus, a Theban priestess, is shown in the right-hand corner, alongside her *ba* in the form of a bird, c.950 BC (courtesy of the British Museum, EA 10554/87)

course. The radical instability of the category brings into question the foundational restrictions of political theorizing and opens up new arenas for genders, bodies, selves, as well as politics. We do not necessarily need a foundational concept of the subject; rather, we should celebrate the freeing up of feminist epistemology. Moreover, as is common throughout this volume, feminist-inspired questions of identity are concerned too with issues of race, sexuality, ethnicity, class which are followed by the proverbial *et cetera* as Butler so cleverly notes. But the openness of that *et cetera* allows for all manner of possibilities and suggests that there can be no single situated subject, but rather an illimitable process of signification. In *Bodies that Matter* (1993: 168) she took this further, suggesting that all the distinct spheres of power separated by those proverbial commas (gender, sexuality, race, class) formed relationships we had not yet figured out. Yet we knew they were marked, thus opening them out to further investigation. It is for these reasons that the *et cetera* appears in the title of the current work. This proposition meshes more closely with the complex constructions of identity and embodiment that characterize social life and offers new opportunities for feminist politics. To my mind, this is a significant and lasting contribution of feminist theory and is an achievable aim in archaeological praxis. While we displace the primacy of *finding* women in the material record, we can replace it with a more nuanced account of difference, with all lines of convergence and divergence between a host of social demarcators, which offers a more representative picture of life in the past.

The work of Judith Butler has been incisive for my own questions concerning the increasing fracturing of feminist theory and gender research and how the burgeoning study of sexuality has impacted upon those fields. By adopting a third wave feminist position, we open ourselves up to a wider arena of issues and individuals: we are impelled to examine the construction of masculinity and queer sexualities, for example. Evidence for both areas of study can be gleaned from the Egyptian data as well as many other archaeological contexts. At the heart of such contemporary musings is the concept of difference which, undoubtedly articulated in other ways by the ancients, was still a powerful structuring principle in social life and daily negotiations. It is, and was, a way of seeing yourself and those around you as either conforming to, or diverging from, certain normative scenarios – most often involving class position, financial status, ethnic origin, religious persuasion, age group, sexual preference or sex category. Westerners have a particular gloss on those taxonomies: ticking boxes, adopting labels and fitting into pre-assigned categories. In ancient Egypt we know that sexuality was a practice rather than a category; being foreign might mean coming from another province in Egypt, as well as from another country; and being a child might not have a special status which precluded work or sexual activity. But in each of these cases individuals were aware of their social difference in relation to the norm, i.e. an educated, elite Egyptian male.

The view presented here is less diametrical and more complex than usually espoused in gender archaeology, still largely in the throes of first and second wave feminism. I have outlined in detail the epistemological and ontological shortcomings of those approaches. While useful in drawing attention to the political issues at stake, they have become noticeably outmoded and even offensive to those groups who feel their particular issues have been elided in the past: postcolonialists, Third World feminists, theorists of masculinity and queer theorists all have voices which deserve to be heard. Apart from the obvious political indictment, an interpolation of these specific issues makes for a more complete picture of social life and a more dynamic exchange between past and present. Sexuality is an important case in point. Throughout I propose that Egyptian sexualities were fluid and multiple, although certainly not susceptible to the forms of discourse and categorization we find in the West. As the houses at Deir el Medina demonstrate, sexuality suffused so many aspects of 'ordinary life' from religion to child-rearing that it defies Western definitions. What we would term 'same-sex' practices were just that – practices: they did not serve to demarcate Egyptian individuals as homosexual or heterosexual. The sensuality of their lived experiences should not be teleologically construed through our own narratives, something that I hope will become obvious when we examine the Egyptians' own views on the self and the body, death and sexuality, emotion and the afterlife in the following chapter.

# 3

# Body and Soul in the Archaeology of Egypt

*If you call burial to mind, it is heartbreak;*
*it is bringing the gift of tears, causing a man misery;*
*it is taking a man away from his house,*
*and throwing him on the high ground.*
*You will not come up again to see the sunlight!*[3]

We all face now, and have faced in the past, the same basic experience: existing as a uniquely important individual, looking out into a world that recedes away from the circle of daily life into a wider society of common culture and institutions, to more distant and foreign societies lying beyond, all within the context of earth and heavens and the powers of luck, fate, destiny and the will of supernatural beings....

Barry Kemp, *Ancient Egypt*

Since the body has become a central area of analysis within the social sciences, archaeology is in a unique position to draw upon, and contribute to, these timely developments. In previous chapters I have suggested that some archaeologies might lack sufficient data for such sophisticated theorizing. Conversely, fields like Egyptology, which have sophisticated data sets, are often reticent to engage with mainstream archaeological theorizing. Yet Egyptian data are particularly rich in terms of bodily preservation, representational material and, most importantly, a well-defined ideology surrounding corporeality, selfhood and death (Meskell 1996a, 1998a, forthcoming b,c). Here the fields of archaeology and Egyptology might engage in some productive dialogue in an attempt to understand the contextual experience of Egyptian embodiment and selfhood. This chapter explores such possibilities of disciplinary exchange.

## Bodies Ancient and Modern

For many cultures the locus of the self is the body, though person-hood is not necessarily bounded by corporeal zones (Strathern 1987; Moore 1994; Strathern 1996). The framework of the body is the base upon which the project of the self is constructed. The Egyptians pos-sessed a notion of unbounded selfhood which transgressed bodily borders and death itself. Therefore, the body, self and death are inex-tricably linked and should be analysed in an integrated way. The concept of death is so central to our experience of *being* human and to our concepts of embodied existence, as it was for the Egyptians, that it ultimately shapes our lived experience. Issues such as these, which have been at the forefront of sociological and anthropological research this century, have a long lineage. The Egyptians, too, were concerned with such questions: about being and non-being, about the meaning of death, the nature of humanity and the cosmos, and the basis for human society (Hornung 1992: 13). One of their most complex sets of ideas surrounded notions of the body, the self and all its multiple constituents, and the experience of death and the here-after. Questions involving these concepts still absorb scholars, though we now realize that our explanations must be grounded in a specific temporal and cultural location.

From the outset I have argued that scholars such as Giddens have sought to privilege high modernity and discount other cultural ex-periences. He proposes that modern people have become increasingly associated with their bodies and that the prospect of death poses specific existential problems at this specific juncture in history (Giddens 1991). Egyptian ideology and practice suggest that such concerns are *not* specific to our own era. Additionally, Giddens posits that the body has moved from the sphere of nature to that of culture, a suggestion that seems to reflect a structuralist desire to separate past and present experience using one of the oldest dualisms – nature: culture. Not only does such a false dichotomy infer negative:positive connotations, it could only ever account for change in the most simplistic and reductionist manner. It posits modern technological control over the body (or culture) as foremost, discounting the pos-sibility that other cultures have *technology*-specific connections to the body and death. The technology of death in Egypt was highly devel-oped, articulated and embedded within the fabric of society, as was the maintenance of life through medical techniques (there is a sub-stantial corpus of ancient writings on medical conditions and diagno-sis, see Nunn 1996; Walker 1996). The elaborate technologies of death were socially influenced by an individual's status, wealth, age, sex and ethnicity – clearly evidenced at the site of Deir el Medina. It would simply be wrong to privilege our own culture as relating to the body as a (narrowly defined) cultural product: such a judgement can only be by degree rather than invention.

Many studies have sought to draw the boundaries between modern and pre-modern concepts of death, though most refer to European evidence rather than that of ancient cultures such as Egypt. Contemporary sociologists see the body as the cultural product *par excellence*. Bourdieu, Goffman, Elias, Featherstone and Shilling all propose that the modern body represents a more elaborate, culturally manipulated project than that of the past. The pervasive images of the commodified body in our own society reflect the separation of the body (particularly its reproductive capacities) from the political and economic structures of society. These socio-cultural changes have been tied to the demise of the feudal system based on land ownership, the rise of industrial capitalism, and the emergence of postmodern society – itself based around control of communications and sign systems (Turner 1996: 2). Bryan Turner posits that the move towards a post-industrial system, premised upon a global economy, service industries, control of advertising and communications, has eroded the traditional relationship between property, the body and sexuality. Following on from this, one might link Giddens's (1992) observations that our contemporary focus on self-understanding, individualism and self-realization represents a transformation on a social level. Emotion and intimacy are part of a new pattern of expressivity concurrent with new formulations of the body and the self. More value is added to the body in high modernity through processes of commodification and enhancement, and self-identity is now linked more closely to the corporeal self. Elias would say that the modern body has been socialized, rationalized and individualized (Shilling 1993: 167). This entails a desire to overcome the biological limitations of bodily existence, to control the emotional aspect of selfhood, and to define ourselves increasingly as individual, self-contained entities. If this trend is truly a demarcator of high modernity, then its reflection in the context of death should diverge markedly from ancient perceptions and experience, so far as they can be known. It may therefore prove illuminating to compare present practices with those of the past.

Protestantism and the privatization of death supposedly mark the great watershed in the history of death, since death was then removed from the public sphere; the public nature of death and death rituals are taken as explicit markers of pre-modern societies. However, important elite individuals still elicit communal and highly ritualistic burials and tributes (i.e. military and state funerals). One could say that distinct public and private practices exist in modern society. Moreover, the Egyptian funerary industry was highly specialized and subject to commodification. It was an industry in the modern sense of the word with specific groups, such as embalmers, mourners or libation pourers, who made a living out of funerary services. The act of burial could be a highly visible, communal ritual for those of elite status, or conversely a small-scale, individual affair both for poorer people and for whole groups, such as children. There is evidence that both styles of burial existed side by side at Deir el Medina (see chapters 4 and 5). Another proposed distinction surrounds the negation of mortality in the modern context, as exemplified in the funerary industry and practices of embalming (Shilling 1993: 189). This obviously has direct parallels with practices and technologies developed in Egypt and cannot simply reflect the modern condition. Zandee's (1960) comprehensive work on Egyptian concepts of *Death as an Enemy* also stresses the underlying commonalties. Both cultures chose, where possible, to segregate settlement and cemetery spatially; in Egypt the west was generally designated as the domain of the dead. One could go as far as saying that the Christian belief parallels its Egyptian precursor. Christianity claims that death represents termination of the body, not the person (Bauman 1992: 13), that the soul continues, and that the individual is subject to resurrection. Egyptian religion also recognized bodily death. The body could be preserved, then regenerated, and resurrection itself was a cyclical phenomenon. Certain aspects of the person (for example, *ka* and *ba*) survived death and were active in the hereafter. The similarities here should not be underestimated. This does not undermine the distinctiveness or complexities of death and dying in the modern era, or the ideological constructions woven around the phenomenon, such as increasing medicalization, desacralization and socialization (Shilling 1993). Nor do I advocate an essentialist paradigm that links all contexts, past and present. Rather, I would say that we have underestimated the complexities of ancient cultures – Egypt being one of the most important. The concepts outlined above are not unique to contemporary Western discourse, although they may have become more rigorously analysed and articulated. Technology has enabled greater monitoring and intervention, in a truly cyborg sense, over the modern body. Yet Egyptian technologies of the body were complex and sophisticated, suggesting that, while knowledge changes, the desires expressed are not necessarily unique: transcending bodily death being a cogent example. Both cultures share another trait: it is more likely that the elite will have access to transformative bodily treatments, in life and death, so that an enhanced bodily status is inextricably tied to privileged social status. The Eastern Necropolis at Deir el Medina, discussed below, provides evidence for this.

## Embodying Egypt

Because Egypt provides a historical context, it is possible to interweave information derived from the texts, such as attitudes to corporeality and selfhood, with archaeological data in the form of mortuary reconstructions. The body, or physical form, could be perceived in a variety of ways. The living body was called *ḥˁ* (the phonetic symbol), and written with the sign for flesh or *ḥt*, with the sign for belly (primarily referring to the torso), while the corpse, *ḥȝt*, was sometimes written with the image of a mummy on a bed. The term *ḏt* refers to the theological concept of the body, the eternal form which transcends the living body. The word *ḥˁ* also referred to the self and person (Walker 1996: 3, 17). The human being was viewed as a complex composite of many parts, each essential to individual existence, but existing within a unified framework. The loss of one meant the loss of all. Some of these elements were thought to exist during life, while others were only activated after death. In the 18th Dynasty Theban tomb of Amenemhet (TT 82)[4] some of these constituents are mentioned: his fate or *šȝ*, his corpse or *ḥȝt*, his lifetime/character or *ˁḥˁ*, and all his manifestations or *ḥprw*. They are presented each as divinities which can receive offerings and confer blessings, yet they are still integral elements of the individual, Amenemhet. Another constituent often mentioned was the heart, *ib*, which was the seat of reason, memory, conscience, desire and emotion. It was also the centre of free will and had a personality of its own. In the Memphite Theology, the heart and tongue are said to have power over all other organs (Hornung 1992). The name, or *rn*, was vitally important and similarly had its own identity: to destroy the name meant the total destruction of the individual. Defacement of the name of the deceased was seen as a negation of a person's existence and their opportunity of attaining the afterlife. The use of the name perpetuates the personality: you do not have a name, you *are* a name, just as you *are* a body (Milde 1988). The name was not an abstract entity since it belonged to the physical world. Recently, Bolshakov (1997: 154) has interpreted *rn* as the name in its daily and ideological aspects. It was the identification of a person, his or her essence, and the bearer of his or her individuality. The name resembled the conception of the human shadow: it was able to carry and transfer power (Hornung 1992: 179). These various components of the person cover a multiplicity of aspects: an individual's vitality, capacity for movement and effectiveness, physical appearance, personality, his or her mysterious shadow, as well as his or her intellectual, emotional and moral dimensions (Lloyd 1989: 120). Despite the depth of detail, our sources are literary, artistic or metaphorical in nature and must be tempered by their inherent conventions.

There is significant evidence for the divisible nature of the person in ancient Egypt, yet as John Baines (1991: 145–6) has described so clearly:

> Most of these aspects came into their own in transition between this world and the next, or between generations, rather than being constant features of people's this-worldly existence and awareness. In this life, the social person was a unity despite this partitioning. The diversity of these aspects dramatized questions of motivation, accountability, and freedom, especially those associated with the vital transitions of birth and death.

According to the Egyptian belief system, individual selves persisted after death and were in fact multiply constituted. Five essential components of the individual may survive after death: the name or *rn*, the shadow, *šwt*, and his or her personal magic, *ḥkȝ*, along with the *ka* and *ba* discussed below (Zandee 1960: 20; Pinch 1994: 147). Not only did the corporeal body have a tangible trajectory after death, it too could be seen as divisible or multi-faceted. The self was comprised of several elements, none of which is exactly equivalent to a *soul*. There was the *ka*, which was the vital force or double self and inextricably linked with the physical body. Alternatively, the *ka* has been described as a series of relations and representations. It was the memory of the deceased, and physical representations served to activate this memory – acting as a door, reviving the image of the person in the memory (Bolshakov 1997: 145–52). The Egyptians objectified their recollections, yet the *ka* remained a fundamental property of reality. It was a copy of a whole person's individuality in both appearance and personal characteristics (Bolshakov 1997: 152). Correspondingly, the *ba* seems to have retained the character of the individual, although it depended on the physical body for existence. It had material needs as well – bread, beer and everything else a body requires (Hornung 1992: 181). This entity was usually depicted as a human-headed bird which journeyed between the underworld and this world and was also at risk of dying a second and final death. After surviving various trials, the deceased might attain the status of $3\underline{h}$, a transfigured and effective spirit (Pinch 1994).

According to the Maxims of Any, one should 'satisfy the *akh*; do what he desires, and abstain for him from abomination, that you may be safe from his harms.'[5] There were other troublesome spirits named *m(w)t* or the 'dangerous dead'. They seem to be entities which retained the lifetime sex of the individual, and female spirits seem to have been more feared. Hence, the dead were not sexed differently. So within this schema the various elements remained, although an individual could ultimately adopt specific trajectories through time, benevolent or otherwise. An individual could be multiply constituted within his or her own body. Textual evidence serves to embody Egyptian individuals in the manner specific to their own culture and imbues our interpretations with some measure of legitimacy.

If one were to examine Egyptian views on the body and death anthropologically, one would find that death itself was a transitory state and it did not prevent people from involving themselves in the world of the living. The texts reveal that the self continued after death and indeed living and dead were part of the same earthly world (see Whaley 1981: 2). The dead could intervene in daily affairs, although memories of the deceased did not appear to transcend the generations (Baines 1991). Requests, advice and magical intervention could all be sought from the deceased, as the textual evidence from the New Kingdom illustrates. Deir el Medina provides vivid testimonies to the Egyptian belief that the dead not only exist but could be a powerful force in the world of the living. Additionally, there were letters from individuals to their deceased relatives, like that of scribe Butehamun to his dead wife, Ikhtay, written in the 20th Dynasty. In the extract of the letter below Butehamun asks Ikhtay to petition the Lords of Eternity on his behalf. We see clearly Butehamun's sense of the inevitability of death together with its unknowability, while his doubts that his words will reach his wife in the afterworld contrast strikingly with the hopefulness expressed by the act of writing at all (McDowell 1999: 106). In fact, the deceased holds a privileged position being closer to the gods and acting as intercessor for human individuals in the living world. Texts like these were usually left at the tomb of the deceased, evidenced at Deir el Medina during this period. In magical terms it would appear to be the most promising point of

contact with the other world. Such a practice testifies to the continuing social interactions between living and dead individuals:

> *Said by the scribe Butehamun*
> *of the Necropolis to the songstress of Amen Ikhtay.*
> *Pre has gone,*
> *his ennead following him,*
> *and the kings of old likewise.*
> *All the people in one body*
> *follow their companions.*
> *There is not one of them who will remain,*
> *and we will all follow you.*
> *If one can hear me*
> *(in) the place where you are,*
> *tell the Lords of Eternity,*
> *'Let (me) petition for my brother,'*
> *so that I may make ... in [their] hearts,*
> *whether they are great or small.*
> *It is you who will speak with a good speech in the necropolis.*
> *Indeed, I did not commit an abomination against you*
> *while you were on earth,*
> *and I hold to my behaviour.*
> *Swear to god in every manner,*
> *saying 'What I have said will be done!'*
> *I will not oppose your will in any utterance*
> *until I reach you.*
> *[May you act] for me (in) every good manner,*
> *if one can hear.*[6]

The Egyptian belief system challenges many normative assumptions we might make about bodies and selves. The texts suggest that
persons were multiply constituted throughout life and death, and that
spiritual and corporeal selves were inextricably bound together. The
Egyptian view of embodied individuality and self was as a fluid and
unbounded entity, giving rise to experience that was conceptually
closer to non-Western cultures, than to the personal boundedness
extant in the West. Such a context serves to reaffirm further the
complex link between identity, body and death.

## The Body in Pieces

Textual evidence suggests that the Egyptians perceived their bodies
as fragmented, much as Lacanian psychoanalysis posits a notion of

the fragmented self in the construction of identity. Psychoanalysis might seem a suitable lens through which to view Egyptian culture, yet, as Ricoeur remarks, psychoanalysis provides a hermeneutics of culture which changes the world by interpreting it (see Heald et al. 1994: 3). However tempting it might be to draw parallels, the cultural context of psychoanalytic development in Europe precludes such an application. The Egyptians produced numerous amulets in the shape of separate body parts: hearts, eyes, hands, feet, heads (Andrews 1994: 69–73). There was also a class of votive offerings based on body parts, mainly model breasts, female genitalia and phalli (Pinch 1993: 235–45). Textual descriptions of Egyptian bodies tend to evoke body parts separately, often with separate characteristics and emotive attributes attached. It was common to write 'my heart was happy', instead of 'I was happy', since it was the heart which was the seat of such emotions. It would seem that the body was a networked series of parts, on the one hand separated and, on the other, presenting a whole. This fits with the general precepts of Egyptian thought with its pervasive duality, since Egyptian ideology managed to reconcile radically different concepts. Oppositions can be real, but do not need to cancel each other out: they complement each other (Hornung 1983: 240). The body in death is a clear example of this fragmentation: 'Your eyes are given back to you, in order to see, your ears, in order to hear words. Your mouth speaks words, your feet go. Your arms and shoulders serve you, your flesh is strong. Your veins are sweet. You rejoice at all your limbs. You count all your limbs, while they are healthy.'[7] There were even spells in the Coffin Texts and the Book of the Dead, which united the parts of the body after death. Consider the descriptions of the gods in anthropomorphic form: bones of bronze, limbs of gold, hair of lapis lazuli. Related to this are ideas that the flesh of the gods is gold and their bodies are made of the most precious materials (Hornung 1983: 134). According to the Book of the Dead, Ra 'created the names of the parts of his body. That is how these gods who are in his following came into being' (Lesko 1991: 113). The Litany of Re cited below demonstrates the ancient theme of member divinization. A person was made divine in stages from the top of the head down (Hornung 1992: 172–3). As a last point, in iconography the gods were also depicted as amalgams of human and animal parts, that seem to be ideographic manifestations of deities. Instead of being destabilized entities, these forms appear to have been viewed as harmonious constructions.

*... My face is a falcon*
*The top of my head is Re.*
*My eyes are the Two Women, the Two Sisters,*
*My nose is the Horus of the Netherworld,*
*My mouth is the Sovereign of the West,*
*My throat is Nun.*
*My two arms are the Embracing One,*
*My fingers are the Graspers.*
*My breast is Khepri,*
*My heart is the Horus-Sunen ...*
*My anus is the great flood.*
*My phallus is Tatenen,*
*My glans is the Protected One in Old Cairo.*
*My testicles are the Two Hidden Ones,*
*My thighs are the two Goddesses ...*
*The gods have transformed themselves into my body ...*[8]

In Egyptian iconography the human body is clearly depicted as a series of individual body parts which are unified by imaginary lines of closure (there are a handful of informal exceptions). According to Gay Robins, artists drew each part of the body in its typical aspect and put these parts together to form a composite diagram. The result was immediately recognizable, although it does not exactly correlate with reality. Thus, the eye is always depicted in its frontal position, yet the head/face is canonically in profile, leading to a disjuncture in realistic portrayal. From this perspective, an eye is an eye in any context, and an eye is best symbolized in its frontal manifestation. Similarly, the torso was presented in frontal mode, while the breast was in profile as were the hips, legs and feet. Until the 18th Dynasty, both feet were always shown from the inside because the artists simply encoded the idea of a foot and appended it to their image without distinction (Russmann 1980; Robins 1994b: 13). Right and left hands, and their portrayal, pose similar problems. Differences on the basis of the sexed body are also noted. The portrayal of female body parts (usually arms) in relation to the male is also problematic: emphasis on the superiority of the male body is traditionally paramount. Yet the Egyptians managed to incorporate this series of discrete aspects in a very convincing aesthetic system. Body pieces were thus incorporated into a single corporeality. The formally represented body is a coherent network of individual parts with their own distinctive representations. Egyptian artists depicted the human body as a series of concepts to be related rather than realistically portrayed, resulting in a unitary composition.

This notion of the networked self also carries over into concepts of relatedness or kinship. The individual was depicted as being connected to family members in an extended network of connections. The individual came from the body of the parent, and this was often expressed literally (Pinch 1993: 126). This embeddedness is reminiscent of Marilyn Strathern's work in New Guinea, where she argues that only in certain societal conditions does the *person* seem to emerge as autonomous. Only 'a minority of highlands kinship systems facilitate such a conceptual disengagement of "persons" from the nexus of kin relations' (Strathern 1987: 272). As in Egypt, one is tied to persons such as parents and children as extensions of self, especially in kin-based social interactions, although a person was still considered an individual in the legal, economic, religious and wider social frames of reference.

Drawing on evidence from Late Antique Egypt, Terry Wilfong further demonstrates this predilection for the disjoining and fragmenting of the human body, which he argues occurs along gender lines. In texts referring to women and their appearance, and especially medico-magical matters, this fragmentation seems clear. Magical spells and curses were often directed towards individual female parts of the body such as the heart, womb and mouth (Wilfong 1998). The same can be said of love spells or spells of compulsion. The male body was also reduced to significant parts, usually the penis. Curses specifically attacked the individual's penis to make it like 'a rag on a dung-heap', a 'corpse lying in a tomb', or 'like an ant frozen in winter, tiny and frozen' (Wilfong 1998: 121). Wilfong argues that normally the male body does not appear in *disjecta membra*, while the female body rarely appears otherwise. He takes his analysis through from Pharaonic, Late Antique and Christian sources, ultimately seeing the identification of the body parts of the Virgin Mary as a direct result of this lineage. But the notion of bodily fragmentation was also central to pharaonic tales of the body, the most notable examples being the Osiris myth and the Late Egyptian Tale of the Two Brothers (Lichtheim 1976: 203–11). In both narratives the penis is severed, thrown into the water and swallowed by a fish. The Osiris myth goes further since the god is dismembered and his parts scattered throughout Egypt. Osiris's body was later re-assembled in the form of a mummy by his wife Isis from which she then conceived the god Horus.

## Multivalent Hearts

Of all the body parts mentioned in the texts, the heart (*ib* or *ḥ3ty*) appears most frequently and was accorded the highest status since it was the seat of intelligence, memory, emotion, rationality, truth and religiosity. The word *ib* commonly connoted the human will, mind and emotions, whereas *ḥ3ty* was the physical organ of the heart (Walker 1996: 151). The latter was viewed as the powerhouse of the body, its source of energy, but was not deified like the *ib*. In life, as well as death, the heart was indispensable and could not be corrupted. It was perhaps the only thing that the deceased took with him or her along the way to judgement before entering into the afterlife. The heart played a crucial role on the day of judgement, where it was weighed against the feather of truth, symbolizing Maat, to determine whether the individual was just or evil during his or her lifetime. The heavy heart indicated corruption and was subsequently thrown to a monster which devoured it, consigning the individual to damnation and a 'second death'. If the heart was balanced perfectly with the feather or figure of Maat, then the deceased was ushered off to join Osiris, lord of the Underworld. The ibis-headed god Thoth kept records of the judgement ceremony, as shown in the representation of the psychostasia, a good example being in the Ptolemaic temple at Deir el Medina. So the heart represented the entire person in this situation, and quite often the human figure replaced the image of the organ (Hornung 1992: 177). One might say that the heart formed a synecdoche for the individual. Yet the heart was also the seat of free will and could turn against its owner (for example, Book of the Dead, chs 30 A and B), the gods or the order of the created world. Spells were necessary for ensuring that one's heart stayed loyal during death (see Brunner 1977). In earlier burial procedures the heart was removed from the body and an artificial heart put in its place. Texts on heart scarabs bear this out, and those in the Book of the Dead chapters 27 and 28 also prevent one's heart being taken away (Zandee 1960: 155, 174–5). In later times the heart was left in place, though the heart scarab was still employed (this is attested at Deir el Medina). In view of the heart's centrality, there was much concern for demons tearing the heart from the breast or destroying it after death.

From various textual sources one can build up a complex picture of the polyvalency attributed to the heart. For example, in Coffin Text Spell 1130 the heart is the receptacle of good deeds for the just and, conversely, the site of evil for those of poor character. In the Tale of Sinuhe, the heart is both a place of longing and where homesickness is most deeply felt and also the source of insincerity and panic. But it was often tied to sincerity and to true emotions. A neglected friend writes to his companion at Deir el Medina 'What is with you? Write and send me the thoughts of your heart, so that I can enter into them.'[9] On a more official monument, a stela of Senwosret III (c.1846 BC), the heart is related to strength and courage: 'he is making the enemy's heart strong. Aggression is bravery'.[10] In didactic texts the heart appears as the bearer of wisdom, truth and honesty: it could also be represented as a twin self or mirror image of the self, as in the Teaching of Amenemhat I. The heart could be the site of decision-making and action as well. Although it was very much part of the individual and his or her character, it also had a life of its own and an independent will (much as we might say colloquially today 'follow your heart'). This is evident from Maxim 11 from the Teachings of Ptahhotep:

> Follow your heart as long as you live!
> Do no more than you are told!
> Do not shorten the time of following the heart;
> to destroy such a moment is a horror to the spirit!
> Turn away no chance in the course of a day,
> beyond the needs of establishing your household!
> Property will exist regardless, so follow your heart!
> Property is of no avail, when the heart is disregarded.[11]

To summarize, the heart had a rather malleable set of attributes associated with it, both spiritual and earthly. It was the seat of highly charged emotions, of character (good or evil), pleasure and desire. It formed the ethical core of the individual, and was a significant aspect of the self – running in parallel, or opposite to, the embodied self. The *ib* should be viewed as one of a person's transformations along with the *ba*, *ka*, shadow, rather than among the physical organs of the body. The *ib* could be the psyche, mind or spirit, but no single Western term easily coheres with the Egyptian concept (Walker 1996: 185). The heart should not be viewed as a singular entity, but instead as a poly-valent series of spiritual and physical associations.

## The Body in Death

Moving now into more specific discussions concerning the psychology of death in the Egyptian social system, Alan Lloyd (1989: 124–31) summarizes Egyptian rituals of death in the following steps:

a mourning period, preparation of the corpse, interment and regular cultic practices for the deceased intended to be maintained indefinitely. These immediate practices were often preceded by the much earlier construction of the tomb. Such an emotional and material investment presumably affected the experience of death, if only in terms of preparation and determinacy. John Baines (1991) states that the Egyptians, like many groups, tended to dramatize their loss on a communal scale, thus making loss bearable through its public display. Further, loss creates loose ends in terms of orphans, widows and the aged, who have no tangible source of support. The death of an individual manifests in disorder and grief at many personal and embodied levels. One could see the phenomenon of death as linked to a psychological infrastructure. Lloyd sees a project of three stages (similar to Hertz and Van Gennep): separation and bereavement; recovery and readjustment; maintenance, where the dead are incorporated into the world of the living via continuing rituals. At the first stage, public grief was displayed and preparations of the body were undertaken, supposedly lasting up to 70 days. This number was probably an ideal or possibly even magical (Baines and Lacovara 1996). For the deceased, the body and personality were preserved, while the deceased was transferred to the next level of being. Through ritual activity the *ḥkȝ*, or personal magic, was activated. For the living, this extended time period enabled family and friends to adjust and reintegrate the deceased into the group in a new social form. The recovery stage was marked by the funeral, operative on a community level, after the process of mummification was completed. When hired, the embalmer used the materiality of the body to make a lifelike, lasting image that could be revived and given a new soul at any time (Hornung 1992: 168), though we know that many bodies at Deir el Medina were not fully embalmed. A form of revival occurred at the funeral, which encompassed rituals of transfiguration such as the Opening of the Mouth ceremony which sought to re-animate the bodily functions and lead to rebirth. The internal organs of the body became independent entities in the New Kingdom and were often treated like the body itself, being wrapped and placed in small mummy cases of their own (Hornung 1992). In essence, the deceased took on the identity of the resurrected god Osiris. To maintain the deceased in the afterworld, social support was required, in the form of continued spells and rituals, by family and community members after death.

For a full afterlife the corporeal body itself had to be physically intact, and there is a plethora of textual references to fear about bodily destruction (Zandee 1960: 14–19). Terror and disgust were evoked through confrontation with the dead body, and spells like those from the Coffin Texts or Book of the Dead could be invoked to maintain the transitional state of the corpse. There was an explicit concern over bodily fluids, such as sweat, and with the dead body's loss of integrity through the presence of maggots. Sensual descriptions of death are common, and the Egyptians were not reticent to write about the smell of the decaying body, the disintegration by parasites, the rotting of flesh, mutilation, the eyes perishing and so on. This horror was reconciled, even remedied, with the culturally specific practices of embalming and evisceration. Surprisingly, at a particularly literate village like Deir el Medina, we still do not know exactly who performed these bodily preparations or where they took place. Contradictory to the catalogue of known effects of bodily death, texts also stress the beauty and god-like quality of the deceased, particularly the imperishable 'bones of bronze' and 'limbs of gold' (Zandee 1960: 58). Fear and acknowledgement of decomposition were juxtaposed with claims of god-like preservation and perfection. As Parkinson (1997: 151) reminds us, 'death was respected by the Egyptians, but also feared . . . its horror and its blessing, and the uncertainty about what comes after death.'

The corporeal self should have integrity in death and the coffin itself acted as a regenerative casing that would facilitate the emergence of the transfigured body free from earthly imperfections (Willems 1988; Hornung 1992: 169). At Deir el Medina, from Ramesside times onwards, we can see how the coffin became the primary focus of funerary wealth and elaboration (Meskell 1997a, 1999). This process of resurrection did not occur on one auspicious occasion, but took place every night in the depths of the underworld, where dead individuals took command over their bodies. In a sense, existence formed a continuum that was only interrupted in a minor way by the experience of death. The needs of the body also extended into the afterlife, including sexual and material pleasures. The physical body could only really attain divinity through confronting the ultimate challenge to its integrity – death itself. Again, the notion of human divinity is mirrored materially in Ramesside bodily practices, specifically evisceration and embalming, which only became characteristic at Deir el Medina in this period. Religious systems and social ideology allowed for the possibility of a 'good burial' in ancient Egypt. Bloch and Parry (1982a: 15–16) refer cross-culturally to notions of the good death as being pious and dutiful in life, which is subsequently followed by the proper burial ritual – a scenario parallel with ancient Egyptian conceptions. A good death promises a rebirth for the individual, while a bad death represents the loss of regenerative powers. In the course of life, one could internalize these meanings and thus transcend the contingencies of life (Shilling 1993: 179).

John Baines and Peter Lacovara have referred to the mortuary practices of pharaonic Egypt as forming a 'mausoleum culture'; given the powerful associations of the tomb, this would seem a particularly apt description. Tombs were constructed largely during the tomb-owner's lifetime and as such were very much part of life, the superstructure being a visible and tangible reminder of one's death and the hereafter. In principle, the tomb formed a concrete, yet liminal, installation for maintaining the deceased in life, where the world of the living and dead overlapped. The preservation of the deceased's mummified body, the grave goods and the integrity of the tomb itself was fundamental (Baines and Lacovara 1996). The associated mortuary chapel facilitated the mortuary cult, which was integral to the maintenance of the deceased. So the Egyptian cult of the dead incorporated various human reactions to loss and bereavement and culturally specific constructions of the self, the individual's relationship with society, the cosmos, and afterlife beliefs. Despite a well-developed ideology concerning death and the hereafter, the texts reveal a profound scepticism about mortuary provision, the survival of monuments and bodily destruction. Harpists' songs proclaim that people should live for the day because 'no one who has gone has come back', suggesting that all these elaborate earthly preparations were futile. The visible decay of the tomb itself was a potent reminder (Baines and Lacovara 1996). Baines comments (1991: 129) that, in general, humanity had far more contact with the dead than they did with the gods. Moreover, in Egyptian thought, the life of the deceased resembles that of the living, and it is integrated within daily life and practices, such as rituals, oracles, magic and intervention. In this way, the material constructions (tombs, chapels, shrines, tomb goods), preparations (mummification), practices (domestic, mortuary and commemorative rituals) and beliefs (about the individual, death, afterlife, cosmology) combined to produce the Egyptian experience of death with a particular focus upon the individual.

So far I have concentrated on the body of the deceased and its transmutations during death, burial and beyond. However, the bodies of relatives and mourners were also transformed through the experience of death. As Dominic Montserrat (1997) points out, mourning was expressed via certain forms of body modification; for Roman Egypt this is often documented as shaving or cutting hair. Both men and women partook of these ritual observances. He also suggests that more transient practices occurred, such as scratching the face, heaping dust or earth on the head, and the rending of hair and garments – all practices that were common in pharaonic times (D'Auria et al. 1988). The mourner was said to be 'head-upon-knee'. Documentary evidence (P. Oxy. III 528) suggests that prohibitions on washing and dietary and dress regulations were also operative. In some New Kingdom wall paintings mourning women wear strips of blue cloth tied around their heads to mark the immediate household of the deceased, a custom with analogues in modern times (D'Auria et al. 1988: 56). The classical historian Diodorus Siculus (I 91.1–2) reported that 'whenever anyone dies among them, all the family and friends cover their heads with mud and go about town making lamentation, until it is the time for the body to be treated. Furthermore, during this time they allow themselves neither baths, wine, or any expensive foods, nor do they wear brightly-coloured clothing' (Montserrat 1997: 36). This strongly parallels the New Kingdom iconographic data and evidence from the Book of the Dead spells, suggesting a significant lineage to these discursive practices. That the living, grieving body is modified might suggest a parallel with the dead body, in its transitional phase. There is an extensive corpus of writing on the symbolism of hair (Eilberg-Schwartz and Doniger 1995), especially in its ritual associations. Hair was loaded with meanings revolving around sex and death. The dishevelling of the hair, face and body may relate to concepts of disorder, denial of bodily existence and the inevitability of the death of the physical body in this world. Such an open display of what would normally be perceived as anti-social, primitive behaviour may have enhanced the experiential, emotive or even eroticized state of the mourners: it made grief embodied and palpable. Parallelism may have further been at work in abstinence from food, wine and bathing, since all of these functions are necessary to life, but not necessary in death.

## Sex and Death

Death, with its accompanying rituals and experiences, has been a central focus of anthropology and has generated an attendant body of theory. One set of long-standing ideas surrounds concepts of rebirth in funerary rituals and the linkage between life and death. This has immediate relevance to Egyptian afterlife beliefs, the changing focus of tomb goods, and the preparation of bodies themselves. Indeed, fertility, rebirth, sexual potency, revivification and appetite are all aspects of the association between sex and death (see Behrens 1982). In the Book of the Earth, illustrated in the tomb of Ramesses VI, a procreative god is depicted with his phallus bound to the goddesses of the hours (Hornung 1990: 85), linking sexuality and rejuvenation. For vivid illustration, Coffin Text spell 576 states 'my phallus is *baba* (?)...there is sperm in my mouth...NN has the disposal of his desire'.[12] This reinforces the idea that the body transcends death and maintains its fundamental character beyond the boundaries of death. It could also represent a reluctance to accept the consequences of death, and that is also manifest in the elaborate treatments of bodies in an attempt to sustain life, the inclusion of artefacts from the world of the living, and visual representations from life and people in their alive state. These factors are evident in 18th Dynasty tombs, although we witness a shift in emphasis from the Ramesside Period and later (Meskell 1999). Even coffins such as Heqata's, from the Middle Kingdom, bore texts which stressed sexuality. Here the *ba* of the deceased is described as being free to have sex with both goddesses and earthly women alike. The *ba's* sexual abilities had the purpose of guaranteeing a full life for Heqata after death (Willems 1994: 311). The connections between life, death and sexuality are fundamentally important and ritual practice is the medium through which they were most often united.

Studies that sought to identify this cultural phenomenon began with Bachofen in 1859, then Frazer in 1890, Harrison in 1911, followed by anthropologists such as Evans-Pritchard, Hertz, Goody and Geertz. Bloch and Parry (1982b) followed with their collection *Death and the Regeneration of Life*. Central to many of these interpretations was the double aspect of funerals, first proposed by Hertz. In some societies this may entail burying the individual twice, secondary burial after excarnation or similar treatments or, as in the case of Egypt, a lengthy processing of the body after death and then a ritual interment. One phase focuses on pollution and sorrow (embalming and preparation), the other on continuity and negation of death. The linkage between sex and death also involves the interplay of liminality or liminal states. Van Gennep (1960) developed the notion of liminality, elaborated upon by Victor Turner (1967), positing that one could expect rites of separation, transition and incorporation respectively. He found that rites of transition were those with the greatest duration and complexity and as such should be seen as autonomous. Where Egyptian perceptions might differ is in relation to the state of the individual in this transitional phase. Many of the anthropological studies cited for the double aspect of the funeral also document communal fear surrounding the state of the deceased, as a spirit, throughout this liminal phase. The transference of the soul from one domain to the other involves a dangerous period when spirits are malevolent and socially uncontrollable. Thus, the funeral acts for the living in perpetuating the status quo, rather than being merely for the deceased (Bloch and Parry 1982a). While the Egyptian texts do not explicitly state this view, it may be a point worth considering. Related to this were Egyptian notions of the *dangerous dead*, previously mentioned, who figure strongly in the texts and in personal letters (Pinch 1994: 45, 148). The deceased individual could threaten or bless the living long after the period of death, preparation and burial. So in the liminal phase following death the whole society of the dead was more dangerous than the living community. For the Egyptians, the deceased was incorporated into the realm of the living and continued to be a potent force, unlike groups for whom the deceased is put to rest after the second burial. As a last point, Whaley (1981) has posited a connection between biological fascination and knowledge of the body and its sexual association, although his study focuses upon the Enlightenment. He suggests that the symbolic link between sex and death emerges from a scientific preoccupation with the corpse. If this is the case, then we could argue for a similar interest in the body during pharaonic times, especially given the elaborate bodily practices undertaken after death.

It is well documented that rites of passage often employ metaphors of life and death, since it is perceived that change entails the death of the former self, and the birth of a new one. Death rites are often filled with the symbolism of birth, and this is true of the Egyptian context. In the Egyptian poem, The Tale of Sinuhe (Parkinson 1997: 34), Sinuhe says: 'What matters more than being buried in the land where I was born?' Maurice Bloch (1982) explains the linkage between birth and death by stating that both negate the notion of eternal unchangingness. The closest association of these two states in Egypt occurs in the ritual Opening of the Mouth, immediately preceding burial. Ann Roth (1993) suggests that this ritual mimicked the birth and maturation of a child and its purpose was to take the newly reborn deceased through the transitions of birth and childhood, so that he or she could be nourished by the (adult) food amply provided in the Egyptian mortuary cult. She goes as far as saying that the ritual implements used created links with the placenta, the severing of the umbilical cord, nursing, weaning and teething (Roth 1993: 60). Drawing on a spell in the Old Kingdom Pyramid Text from the pyramid of Unas, Roth presents evidence for this parallelism. The *nṯrwy* blades were used to split open the mouth, while the *psš-kf* knife was used to make the king's jaw strong (i.e. ready to breastfeed), meaning that the umbilical cord had been severed (Pyr. 30a). Roth also suggests the birth scenario to explain the splitting of the king's mouth in death. At birth the baby's mouth is obstructed by mucus and must be cleared to facilitate breathing. Although syringes are now used, the doctor still uses a little finger to test for any abnormalities in the palate. She argues that its size, softness and sensitivity make it appropriate for this task and similarly suitable for clearing out the mouth. The blades are shaped like two little fingers (right and left) and slightly curved. In other spells, two jars were presented (Pyr. 31), one empty and the other full of milk, and were explicitly called the breasts of Horus and Isis. Later in the ritual, weaning and teething are suggested by offering various soft and hard foods. The latter cut the teeth, and wine was offered to dull the pain (Pyr. 36). Though these associations derive from Old Kingdom texts, they continue into the New Kingdom ritual repertoire as well, evidenced in the tombs of Amenemhet (TT 53) and Tutankhamun.

So the moment of death is not simply related to the process of the afterlife, but indelibly linked to life experience, and to concepts of ageing and to reproduction. Death relates inextricably to life, specifically the recent life of the deceased and the lives of his or her offspring (Metcalf and Huntingdon 1991: 108). Sexuality is also tied to these constructions, whether it be at Malagasy or Nyakyusa funerals or in ancient Egyptian ones. Consider the New Kingdom tomb scenes of naked servants and dancing girls painted with erotic motifs (Derchain 1975: 66–9), the depictions of the goddess of sexuality Hathor, and the fishing and fowling scenes replete with sexual puns (both visual and literary) which were a material reflection of continuing sexuality. These images were concrete (i.e. painted on tomb walls), not passing enactments, displaying their continued importance for the deceased. As previously noted, it was thought that the deceased remained a sexual being with sexual needs and desires. Implicit in this construction was that the deceased was sexed male and there are no comparable tomb scenes which cater specifically for female sexuality: heterosexual narratives were also tacitly assumed. The tomb itself was a normative construction deemed to eradicate difference and to present regulated aspirations for a perfect hereafter.

Tied to the idea of sex and death was the notion that women were explicitly linked to the sphere of death and funerals. Though women are associated with fertility and sexuality, in many cultures they are given to dealing with aspects of pollution and mourning – the emotive dimension. Grieving was subject to a sexed difference: compared to the quiet attitudes of men in tomb iconography, women's mourning gestures are vehement (Milde 1988: 18). In many cultures weeping at funerals is not only tolerated but required by custom (Metcalf and Huntingdon 1991: 44). Weeping also occurs on cue. In New Kingdom Egypt, this performance was largely delegated to women as a form of profession, like the wailing women in the tomb of Neferhotep (Zandee 1960: 45) or Minnakht (figure 3.1), and it could be a hereditary one (stela Turin 50053 in Tosi and Roccati 1972: 88). As such, these displays were probably mediated by class or status prerogatives: many at Deir el Medina could not have afforded such displays. This is not to say that people – men, women and children – were not individually moved to tears by the passing of a loved one at the point of burial. But textual evidence suggests that emotionality was not prized in general by the scribal elite, rather cool-headedness and reservation seem to have been rewarded. Indeed, 'silence was golden'. Testimony to this is found in autobiographies such as the Middle Kingdom stela of Intef: 'I was silent with the wrathful . . . I was cool, free from haste

**Figure 3.1**   Wailing women in the Theban tomb of Minnakht, Overseer of Granaries, dated to the reign of Tuthmosis III (courtesy of Dominic Montserrat)

... I was collected, kind, merciful, who quietened the weeper with a kind word' (Parkinson 1991: 61–3). Cross-culturally, the display of emotion is often designated a female domain, as in the ritual lamentation in Greece (ancient and modern), the Bara of Madagascar, the Nyakyusa or Kuranko of Africa (Jackson 1989: 69; Metcalf and Huntingdon 1991: 47) or modern Egyptians (Abu-Lughod 1993). In Roman Egypt, as well, personal letters express the linkage between women and emotionality. A second-century letter to a man called Horion states 'because of what has happened to them, the mother of the deceased and his sister have been unable to write anything to you, but they have asked me to write to you about his death' (P. Haun. II 17 in Montserrat 1997). There were obviously exceptions, and I am not suggesting an essentialist position in terms of emotive responses. Various groups do not display strong emotional responses at funerals, as Geertz (1973: 153–62) documented for the Javanese. Attitudes to death across time are characterized by diverse emotions – fear, sorrow, anger, despair, resentment, resignation, defiance, pity, avarice, triumph, helplessness – and can manifest in a complex mixture for any individual (Whaley 1981: 9). Taken together, this reaffirms theories of cultural specificity in terms of emotion, display and mortuary ritual, which in turn reminds us that we are faced with both the strange and the familiar in our own world. Such an amalgam must also be considered for antiquity.

## Intention, Emotion and the Experience of Dying Young

the artifactual accoutrements were in place to re-create a historical drama but the sensual and the emotion were not – there was no 'smell of death' and for me Ramses is neither god, hero or father.
            Susan Kus, 'Toward an archaeology of body and soul'

In the many mortuary studies carried out in the Egyptian context, and within archaeology as a discipline more generally, a significant component appears to be missing. This fundamental aspect is comprised of intentionality, emotion and embodied experience (Meskell 1996a). Recent archaeology has focused upon power strategies and the negotiation of social status and prestige display (Tarlow 1992, 1999), reducing individuals to passive social actors fulfilling prescribed roles (Melhuus 1993; Meskell 1996a, 1998a). According to Tarlow (1999), cemetery analyses have focused on the expression and negotiation of social relationships, particularly under the influence of archaeologists such as Parker Pearson (1982) and Shanks and Tilley (1982). From this perspective, the deceased are manipulated for the purposes of status aggrandizement (Parker Pearson 1982: 112) and people are simply motivated by self-interest to accumulate power. Out of the recognition that the burial context was manipulable, and did not necessarily reflect social reality, came the realization that the manipulation of symbolic meanings in the creation of social relationships (mostly power relations) was in itself an exciting area of study (Tarlow 1999). The centrality of *power* has overshadowed the realization that death is a deeply moving, personal experience and that grief has embodied, yet individual, responses. The possibility that preparations surrounding death and burial were not necessarily driven by social aspirations is seldom acknowledged (Nordström 1996). We should not give primacy to the routine aspects of ritual life at the expense of a powerful emotional life (Rosaldo 1989: 13). We have conducted an archaeology of burial, rather than an archaeology of death (for example, Barrett 1988). Similarly, there is a distinction between the bereaved members of the deceased's domestic group and the more public ritual group. Our analyses, therefore, must be multi-dimensional. Cultural descriptions should seek out force as well as thickness, and they should extend from well-defined rituals to a myriad less-circumscribed practices (Rosaldo 1989: 16). Our clinical, sanitized treatment of Egyptian death has been highlighted by Susan Kus in her critique of the Ramesses II exhibition in America (1992: 170–1). The *experience* of death is entirely lacking; the fact that we are dealing with human beings rather than body counts and ceramic assemblages seems paramount. As Kus (1992: 172) reveals:

> we talk about desire for power, about awe before the gods and before kings, about magic as the audacious confrontation of human and natural forces, and about ideological notions of purity and danger being tied to physiological processes. The physical and the emotional are part of our social theoretical discussions just as much as are cold, calculated motives and logics.

The problem of ascribing emotional values or indices to other cultures has become a major focus in anthropological theorizing. The social construction of emotions and the cross-cultural variance of those emotions have been widely documented, thus challenging the biological determination of emotional life. On the basis of semantic differential studies, the phenomenology of what we have come to regard as the basic, fundamental human emotions can vary in shades of experience, in accordance with particular patterns of socialization, such as sex and class (Heelas 1986: 239). This recognition is one aspect of a general theory of the socio-cultural constitution of individual experience, developing out of the critical positivist tradition of post-Enlightenment social philosophy (Armon-Jones 1986: 32). Emotions are defined as culturally constructed concepts which point to clusters of situations calling for some kind of action (Lutz 1981: 89). Emotional elements might be universal but emotional experiences are not, although some might say that fear is an exception. Cultural difference is highlighted by the fact that a number of groups do not make the Western distinctions of mental:physical, mind:body and emotion: cognition. Egyptian experience may belong to one of these non-Cartesian groups. Accessing culture-specific emotions is an integral part of the project to identify bodies and selves, particularly in the context of death.

If anything is to make us reconsider our over-arching theories of power and aggrandizement in mortuary studies and take into account the emotive dimension of death, it may be the bodies of children and the care which seems to have been assigned to them as they embarked on their journey to the afterlife. This group of individuals was particularly important for my analysis, since my first recognition of the missing emotive dimension in mortuary analyses came at the time when I was interpreting the Eastern Necropolis at Deir el Medina (Meskell 1994a, 1997a). Here most of the village children were buried throughout the 18th Dynasty. The death of children and their subsequent burials seems to me a clear example where power-based explanations of aggrandizement fall short. Far from presenting a 'soap opera' approach, we must acknowledge that in our own culture the deaths of children elicit a specific response of sadness and deep regret. I am not suggesting that ancient Egyptian sentiments were commensurate with our own, but the evidence suggests that they shared some element of this feeling evidenced by their careful interments of children. Egyptologists still remain locked in the language of objectivity, so that the subjective experience is excluded. This serves to negate past subjective experience as well.

We have no conclusive textual evidence as to how children were perceived by various groups, if they existed within a liminal zone or were considered incomplete individuals until a certain age. There exist only two books devoted to the subject (Janssen and Janssen 1990; Feucht 1995); both focus on textual and iconographic material. Here archaeology might prove invaluable. I also suggest that we have left the significance of this important social group untheorized or have relied too heavily on gleanings from other pre-industrial communities. Phillipe Ariès' (1962) work on the history of childhood has been influential in claiming that people could not allow themselves to become too attached to something that was regarded as a probable loss. He also posited that children were not perceived as having a fully developed adult personality because too many of them died. The sociologist Robert Hertz (1960: 76) maintained that, in general, the death of a stranger, slave or child will go almost unnoticed, arousing no emotion nor ritual since these individuals were not fully incorporated into the social order. Moreover, since society has not given anything of itself to the newborn, it remains indifferent and unaffected by the child's disappearance. The demographer David Heer (1968: 454) also suggested that there is a connection between mortality rate and the amount of emotional energy that parents invest in each of their children. Thus, where infant mortality is high parents may develop strategies of lower emotional involvement in children as individuals. Lloyd De Mause's (1974) evolutionary stance led him so far as to state that the further one went back in history, the lower the level of child care and the greater the likelihood of murder, abandonment, beating, terrorizing and sexual abuse (see McFarlane 1981), as if there were some inverse relationship between neglect and civilization. This presumably reflects the author's cultural and temporal chauvinism, which is not necessarily borne out by the ancient data. One need only point out that, locationally speaking, society in the twentieth century cannot claim impunity from murder, violence or the sexual abuse of children.

Data from Deir el Medina, particularly that from the Eastern Necropolis (Meskell 1994a), cast doubt on the theories put forward by Ariès, Hertz, Heer and De Mause. Their views, while outdated, are still influential and are reproduced in modern accounts of death and bereavement across cultures. According to two clinical specialists, '[i]n countries where child mortality is currently high, the death of a child is often perceived as inevitable, with mourning lasting no more than a few days' (Young and Papadatou 1997: 197). Burials of children at Deir el Medina demonstrate the care and concern given to children through a spectrum of ages from neonates onwards. Significant energy was expended upon tomb construction and provisioning, even though it was sometimes proportionally less than that expended on adults at this time. Concern that children should attain an afterlife is demonstrated, for example, by the inclusion of pottery vessels and foodstuffs. The concept of burial was central to Egyptian society. It was a personal aspiration that appears to have transcended social aggrandizement and display for many middle- and lower-class people.

Marginal situations, the major experience being death, push at the borders of our bodily existence, they force us into the recognition that the world is unstable and open-ended and that the meanings we attribute to our bodies and our world are based on nothing more solid than human activity. Death undermines and calls into question the cognitive and normative operating procedures of ordinary life. It threatens the basic assumptions upon which society is organized, as well as the dread of personal meaninglessness, especially when it touches the very young. It thus challenges the individual's sense of what is real and meaningful about their embodied selves and the world around them (Shilling 1993: 178–9).

I am not arguing for an essentialist position that binds 'people' across spatio-temporal boundaries, as if the total experience of death was somehow commensurate anywhere. However, some measure of empathy, which lies beyond the rigid framework of social constructionism, must be considered. We cannot dismiss the corporeal nature of the bodily experience since aspects of individual bodily existence lie outside the range of power-based narratives, whether it be living, dying, sleeping, eating or experiencing pleasure, pain or violence. The discourse of constructionism, whether it be power, prestige or social aggrandizement, cannot be entirely adequate here. Not only does such a position eliminate agency and the individual, it undermines human intentionality as well as the emotive and experiential dimension. The vigorous return to embodiment we witness in a host of disciplines constitutes a balancing act between a 'muted universalism at the back of an emphasis on local knowledge and local constructions of the person' (Strathern 1996: 198). As Andrew Strathern goes on to say, embodiment could be viewed as a new humanism, not exactly soteriological but none the less intended to bring us back to ourselves.

This movement in interpretation is similarly a return to incorporating the sensuous quality of lived experience and bodily perception, predicated largely on phenomenology, which is further linked to revised concepts of the person (Strathern 1996: 198–202). The concept of embodiment links the physical, social and psychic aspects of the individual. We are now in a position to explore cultural and individual experience and difference, reconciling subject and object positions. Moving further, we could create sensory biographies, including even the dense communication between persons and things. In Egypt, the body in death assumed different positions in specific contexts: it was subject during living experience and it was object in the sphere of death. In the mortuary context, the elaborated body, subject to social practices and technologies transformed the living body into dead, yet deified individual, who became closer to the divine pharaonic body, and closer to the gods themselves. Such a process is historically contingent and at Deir el Medina becomes evident only after the Amarna Period, in Ramesside times. The body has a long and fluid history at the site from the 18th Dynasty to Christian times, with a host of concomitant social ideologies woven around it. Concepts of the body changed radically during that time and notions about individual bodies were similarly linked to social axes of difference – age, sex, class, ethnicity, marital status and wealth, as I hope to demonstrate in the following chapters.

## Conclusion

I have argued that modern sociological accounts of death fail to accord ancient societies the emotive dimension of death: the individual was mourned and buried in ways that were meaningful within Egyptian culture. The technologies of death were well-developed and have ultimately influenced some of our own Western cyborg techniques for the body in death. Although a well-developed ideology accounted for bodily death and the hereafter, the Egyptians still feared death and sometimes expressed nihilistic sentiments about the next world. From cultural and textual data it is possible to reconstruct Egyptian views on the self as multiply constituted. There were many facets of the self in death; individuals were partible, divisible and each somatic identity was considered to be active. In transcending death they operated as intentional and powerful agents, creating links between living and dead members of the community, as is well attested at Deir el Medina. Using data from the site, I suggest that the incidents of death involved significant numbers of villagers. Individual members grieved and mourned and buried their dead. Additionally, female mourners participated in the more elaborate funerary displays. But before this stage was reached, builders had constructed the tomb, artists and scribes has decorated it, artisans had created shrines, statues and the material culture of death itself, and others had embalmed the dead. An entire array of individuals was indelibly involved, some emotionally linked, others by social and economic forces. Women played significant roles in the social drama of death, not only in funerary preparations and grieving, but conceptually in the revivification process itself. A successful burial and afterlife was ensured through the invocation of sexualized practices – at least for men. Whether it be mythological, iconographic or ideological, the connection between sex and death was an integral one. Here again we see the pervasive presence of sexuality as a practice that infused cycles of life and death, rather than operating as a series of stylized events or taxonomies. Finally, at Deir el Medina individual tombs encircled the village in constant view of the living community, encroaching on the very edge of their existence, suggesting that the ancestors were ever present in living experiences and negotiations (Meskell forthcoming c). Egyptian mortuary practices also extended beyond interment. Commemoration and memorialization were fundamental both to a successful afterlife (for the dead) and to a prosperous earthly existence (for the living). Cycles of life and death were inextricably linked and as complex and deserving of study as in any modern context.

> *A night vigil will be assigned to you, with holy oils*
> *and wrappings from the hands of Tayet.*
> *A funeral procession will be made for you on the day of joining*
> *the earth,*
> *with a mummy case of gold,*
> *a mask of lapis lazuli,*
> *a heaven over you, and you placed in a hearse,*
> *with oxen dragging you,*
> *and singers before you.*
> *The dance of the Oblivious ones will be done at the mouth of your*
> *tomb-chamber*
> *and the offering-invocation recited for you;*
> *sacrifices will be made at the mouth of your offering-chapel,*
> *and your pillars will be built of white stone.*[13]

The evidence presented here impacts upon areas other than the archaeology of death and burial. It also serves as an example of the potential of an embodied archaeology that draws on contextually specific knowledges of the complexities of Egyptian physicality and personhood. The primarily textual and iconographic data combine to present the cultural complexities of Egyptian perceptions of the body in a non-Western vision, more akin to anthropological accounts than to Foucauldian or Giddensian ones. Similarly, the evidence forces us to re-think the body project, which has been too readily cast in reductionist terms that focus upon clothing, jewellery and hairstyles. These exterior factors are not tantamount to the body, or to embodiment. Egyptian personhood, in all its multiple manifestations, also defies Western logocentrism. The self in death was perhaps the most elaborate construction and was potentially different from how one experienced oneself throughout life, which I discussed as a 'networked self'. Parts of the self survived after death and could take on either benevolent or malevolent characteristics, yet importantly it retained the essential identity of the individual. Textual accounts and archaeological evidence show that personhood also extended to children from the point at which they achieved form in the womb onwards. Their deaths were accorded particular types of burial and there was a demonstrable concern for their well-being and prosperity in the afterlife. Modern Westerners are not the only privileged group to possess manifold concepts of the body, embodiment, emotionality and sensuality. If anything, our notions of the person and the self seem infinitely more simplistic than the sophisticated set of ideas the Egyptians developed to comprehend their own being-in-the-world.

# 4

# Mapping Age, Sex and Class at Deir el Medina

The relationship of behaviour to the material world is far from passive; artifacts are tangible incarnations of social relationships embodying the attitudes and behaviours of the past.

Mary Beaudry et al., 'Artifacts and active voices'

In the construction of the cultural world, all dimensions (the height or colour of pottery for example) already have meaning associations. An individual in the past is situated within this historical frame, and interprets the cultural order from within its perspective. The archaeologist seeks to get 'inside' the historical context . . . .

Ian Hodder, 'The contextual analysis of symbolic meanings'

Deir el Medina is the most documented settlement site of New Kingdom Egypt. Additionally, archaeological evidence from the village houses has yielded significant patterns of social inequality among individuals in the Ramesside Period (see Meskell 1998f). Ironically, the most substantive evidence for social difference emanates from the mortuary sphere which offers more secure archaeological contexts and a greater time-span from which to analyse changing social trends. Since the mortuary sphere was intended to be a continuation of the living world in Egyptian ideology, the information gleaned from burials may be more socially informative than one can generally assume in archaeology. While visual representations may reflect an 'ideal life', many of the actual goods were owned and used by specific individuals and, as such, are telling in terms of inequality. Social factors can be apprehended on various levels: by general statistical patterning and by reconstructed narratives focusing on individual tombs and their occupants. Such an approach may remedy the tensions between prioritizing *society* or *individual*, outlined in chapter 1, currently polemical in archaeological theorizing. Similarly, the material illustrates how archaeologists might tap into complex social negotiations in relation to age, sex, class, ethnicity *et cetera* and how specific individuals experienced those interactions. Evidence correlating to each of these vectors of difference is available from documentary or archaeological sources or from both. Throughout I employ a third wave feminist approach advocated in earlier chapters which, I argue, fits the ancient data best. Thus in terms of sex, my results suggest that this was not simply the primary structuring principle operative at Deir el Medina and that other potent factors became more critical at specific times, which can be clearly demonstrated. I argue that difference and inequality were structured around complex issues that were subject to change, according to status, life-cycle and temporal context.

## Methodological Considerations

The cemeteries of Deir el Medina (figure 4.1) contain approximately 400 tombs, published by Bruyère in numerous volumes of site reports (Bruyère 1924, 1925, 1926, 1927, 1928, 1929, 1930, 1933, 1937a,b, 1939, 1948, 1952, 1953). The tombs were found in a variety of states: intact, partially disturbed, looted, re-used, mixed period burial and so on. Flaws in the data due to looting or re-use might be balanced out within the large corpus of tombs under investigation. Without this type of statistically based research many of the assertions made about New Kingdom mortuary practices for the middle and lower classes will remain unsubstantiated or incorrect. In a similar, smaller-scale project, Stuart Tyson Smith argues (1992: 196) that a rigorous methodology applied to the data will allow us insight into the logic of the burial system. He prefers to smooth over variability in an attempt to isolate broad systemic tomb requirements, whereas I posit that such variation is the most illuminating area of study for us to pursue in the attempt to identify individuals. In sum, both general and particularistic data are necessary for representativeness and individuality to be fully illustrated.

Statistical analysis of the tomb data was undertaken using SPSS 6.1.3. First, bar charts were produced for discrete 18th Dynasty tombs, Eastern Necropolis tombs, 19th and 20th Dynasty tombs and complete tomb assemblages covering all periods. Frequency charts quantified goods; together with the coefficient of variation rating, these illustrate the reliability and variation within the types of goods. Total counts were produced for individual tombs, and tomb profiles were devised to show the total assemblage for each tomb. Cluster

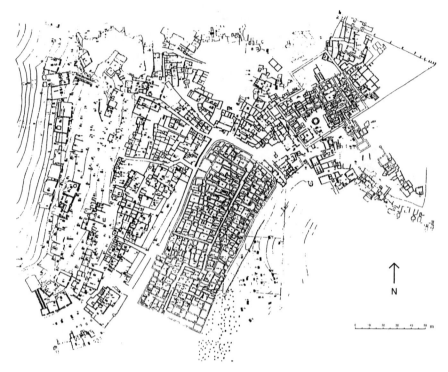

**Figure 4.1**  Map of Deir el Medina (after G. Castel, *Deir el-Médineh 1970, fasc. 1, Gournet Mar 'eï Nord*, FIFAO 12.1, Cairo, 1980)

analyses, using factor and correspondence analysis (ANACOR), were also used to demonstrate grouping on the basis of total number of artefact types for each period as well as grouping of tombs themselves on this same basis. Factor analysis enabled examination of the relationship between two nominal variables (tomb number and object type) graphically in a multi-dimensional scatter plot. Tombs with contents of mixed periods were excluded from these analyses (see Meskell 1997a).

The statistical procedures provide a quantitative framework from which to discuss general social trends in New Kingdom society, predominantly on the basis of age, sex, class and socio-economic group. Sex-linked variation is more obviously demonstrable from intact tombs and should ideally focus on the burials of individuals, couples and small family groups. For this purpose I have profiled the tombs of discrete individuals (Kha and Merit; Sennefer and Nefertiry; Setau; Eastern Necropolis individuals), examining the factors of age, sex, class, wealth as they intersect with each other. Burial goods were assigned to individuals primarily on the basis of names inscribed on objects, rather than extrapolating from our own preconceptions. The large-scale statistical analyses enable general quantitative statements to be made about the period, the class, the socio-economic group *et cetera* in question. Statistical analyses are better suited to quantitative generalizing theories, whereas a form of qualitative interpretation or narrative reconstruction is more appropriate to position individuals within that schema. In this way one can move reflexively from the case studies of individual people back to the larger society in which they were embedded – and they may correspond to, or contradict, that social picture. The mismatch of society and selves offers the most interesting avenues of research, allowing insight into the construction of new identities and shifting boundaries in an ever-changing system. I am not proposing here that society and self are separate entities, but rather that each constitutes the other. By accessing individuals, I am referring to individual identities as they are represented in specific tombs; textual records of these people are usually absent. This analysis by-passes many of the gross generalizations about women or men, for example, in New Kingdom Egypt, which I would argue have been largely unsubstantiated in quantitative and qualitative terms.

## Status and Class: Ranking Deir el Medina

From the playground bully to Ramesses the Great, it is striking how freely, and with what zeal, we indulge the spirit of inequality.
           Paul Wason, *The Archaeology of Rank*

Concepts of class and status cannot be objectively located in a given society, whether ancient or modern, since they are theory-dependent. As Crompton (1995: 44) reminds us, they are not simply 'out there'. Even census data, while seemingly objective, are gathered with regard to specific theoretical assumptions that may not always be explicit. The emphasis on social structures or systems has been criticized for its 'over-socialized' conception of human nature, and the resultant shift has focused on the significance of human/individual action. As Garfinkel argued, human beings are neither structural nor cultural dopes, but act reflexively in their social setting (Crompton 1995; Meskell 1996a). From the 1960s onwards, there has been an active critique of the closed system where the social world is perceived as a cohesive totality, resilient to change and with a tightly arranged hierarchy of power (Bauman 1995: 77). Comparative studies of civilizations have demonstrated that no human population is confined within a single system, but rather in a multiplicity of only partly coalescing organizations, collectives and systems. We all know of instances where an individual has defied his or her social position or risen above it. At Deir el Medina men such as Paneb and Qenherkhopishef were adopted as boys (L. Lesko 1994a) and rose from meagre beginnings to prominent status and wealth.

Althusser, Foucault and Bourdieu have diffused the image of society as an implacable machine that serves to maintain inequality, power and privilege (Touraine 1995: 85), and this vision persists in archaeological theorizing, particularly in mortuary studies. The growing interest in rank within archaeology emerged out of a broader trend towards a social archaeology, largely stimulated by the work of Childe, Clarke, Renfrew and the Cambridge school (for example, Hodder, Miller, Tilley, Shanks). Following the work of Service and Fried, archaeologists in the US, such as Yoffee and Earle, pursued models derived from anthropology (particularly the big man, chiefdom, stratified society and state typologies) to describe the evolution of complex society. Most of these archaeologists were aiming to identify institutionalized status inequality, i.e. any hierarchy of statuses that form part of social structure and extend beyond age, sex, individual characteristics and intrafamilial roles (Wason 1994: 19). While this is one important layer in the social stratum, so too is the very sub-stratum that Wason wants to avoid, that is, the individual dimension. Both are interdependent categories that must be addressed in order to offer a representative and accurate picture of social life, as experienced by individuals and not categories. Lewis Binford once talked about the social persona as a composite of the social identities maintained in life (Chapman and Randsborg 1981: 7; O'Shea 1984: 4), although he was more interested in generalizing strategies than in contextual ones. Again, he was interested in accessing the larger social system at the expense of individuals in all their variability. The present study aims to conduct a more nuanced analysis of status and wealth between individuals at Deir el Medina, taking into account both synchronic and diachronic change.

Rank at Deir el Medina may be examined through social and material data in a number of ways. To date, the villagers have been analysed by economic status (Janssen 1975) or on the basis of individual professions (Bierbrier 1982; Keller 1984; L. Lesko 1994b). It should also be possible to discuss rank by using the spatial distribution of tombs, tomb construction and expenditure, i.e. tomb wealth. More broadly, one should properly talk about rank and status rather than class, since the workman's community represented a spectrum within the 'middle class', with lower-class individuals relegated to the village environs. There are real problems with this terminology in an Egyptian context, since 'class' usually refers back to Marx and the notion of a mobilized and politicized group (Bourdieu 1998: 11). Although the villagers rallied together and went on strike against the administration, they were not necessarily unified with other groups outside the village. Understandably, many scholars wish to avoid the term 'class' altogether, but all such terms are culturally loaded and there is no obvious alternative.

## Socio-economic Interactions

There has been much debate over the financial standing of the villagers of Deir el Medina. For such purposes the villagers are often treated as a single unit, rather than as a group of individuals of varying status and financial position. The major work on this aspect of the village was undertaken by Janssen (1975) who has argued for the superior wealth and status of the inhabitants of Deir el Medina. His study revealed considerable wealth, or rather debt, for many villagers. For instance, in the text O. Gard. 204, a woman named Shedemdei owed a man called Penne some 76 *dbn* (hereafter 'deben', a weight in copper, about 91 grams; see figure 4.2).[14] The same sum, 76 deben, was owed by Nebsmen to Khnemmose. Penne and Khnemmose were ordinary workmen, while Nebsmen was a policeman and Shedemdei a chantress of Amun (Janssen 1975: 533–4; 1994: 130). Janssen claims that people with outstanding debts such as these cannot be called poor, yet many similar situations exist in modern life among less-than-wealthy individuals. Relative wealth and inflation are difficult to determine from the documents alone. Janssen uses the example of 'expensive' cattle, which seem to have been bought by chief workmen and lowly doorkeepers alike. To me this infers that cattle were within the purchasing power of a range of individuals, from high to low status, rendering the notion of 'expensive' somewhat problematic.

Janssen's thesis (1975: 536) is that there was a three-tiered social stratification in the village: an upper class of chiefs and scribes, a middle class of ordinary workmen, and a proletariat of *smdt*, water carriers, wood cutters, fishermen and gardeners. He claims that the latter two groups resided outside the valley itself. With 68 houses inside the walled village and numerous others outside, it is difficult to

**Figure 4.2**   Egyptian weights in a variety of shapes and sizes with measuring equipment, now held at the Louvre (photograph by the author)

imagine that some ordinary workmen were not inhabitants of the valley. For example, Khawy in NE15 was only a guardian, while several other house owners were neither scribes nor chiefs. It is entirely likely that the lowest class Janssen outlines may have lived outside the village, though making frequent visits and spending protracted periods of time there. Slaves or servile people are another category of lower-class individuals he does not mention, and these people may have lived within the village or have been transported in on a daily basis. Moreover, from Janssen's own records it appears that ordinary workmen were heavily involved with the economic transactions of Deir el Medina, so that they must be included as a necessary part of the village. Did they not also have tombs in the necropoleis? In sum, Janssen has derived his information from purely documentary data, with only passing reference to the variable wealth indicated in tomb construction.

Archaeological analysis also provides evidence for ranking, and for how this ranked system changed over time. Two types of data prove informative: the spatial distribution of tombs; and the hierarchic scaling of tomb construction and expenditure. In the context of New Kingdom Egypt, tomb location and construction can be used as indices of rank (see Brown 1981; O'Shea 1984). However, I am not advocating that such indices can be used in all cross-cultural contexts (Tainter 1978; Bard 1994). In the 18th Dynasty the spatial distribution of cemeteries was based around two hills: Gournet Murai (Eastern Necropolis) and the western rise overlooking the valley (Western Necropolis). At this time there was an additional spread of tombs to the north and south of the original 18th Dynasty enclosed village. The northern group remained as tombs, whereas the handful of southern tombs were incorporated into the Ramesside village when it expanded, being transformed subsequently into domestic cellars. From Bruyère's plans of the extended village there appear to be fewer than 20 of these earlier tombs. Another observation from this original plan is that the tombs of the Eastern Necropolis on Gournet Murai (see figure 4.3) appear to be oriented north–south on their major axis, whereas the 18th Dynasty tombs in the Western Necropolis are generally oriented east–west, as one would expect given the funerary beliefs of the Egyptians. At present this anomalous situation cannot be explained adequately.

There must have been some prominence bestowed upon those buried in the Western Necropolis by virtue of its location and outlook towards the Nile valley. Their entrances faced the rising sun, associated with the concept of daily resurrection. The sun passed directly overhead and set behind these tombs on the West Bank. The Egyptians held the west to be the sacred domain of the dead, so that one might imagine the Western Necropolis of Deir el Medina, which was itself on the West Bank, as being the most ritually potent place to be buried. Being most desirable, it appears that there were constraints on exactly who was buried in this location, as in so many cultures where certain locales take on meaning for elite groups and are thus at a premium. To date, archaeology has paid little attention to the generational use of cemeteries: what is the changing relationship between the availability of space and the decisions made by living

**Figure 4.3** View towards the Eastern Necropolis (Gournet Murai) at the time of excavation (courtesy of the IFAO, Cairo)

members of the community concerning the interment of different age, sex and status groups (Chapman and Randsborg 1981: 15)? Tombs of the 18th Dynasty Western cemetery were reserved primarily for substantial single-vaulted and multiple-vaulted tombs, and some that had tomb chapels associated with them. In this spatial zone there is a significant lack of simple pit tombs or simple single-vaulted tombs, almost entirely designated to the opposite hill, in the Eastern Necropolis. Similarly, no prestigious tomb constructions are sited in the Eastern Necropolis, although the burials themselves are not always exceedingly poor. Tomb type and tomb location are closely related, suggesting a distinctly ranked community at Deir el Medina in the 18th Dynasty. Figure 4.4 indicates a range of tomb types in this period, with the most elaborate constructions being in the minority. The most common tomb type, the substantial single-vaulted tomb, occurs in both cemeteries but is rare in the Eastern Necropolis.

(a)

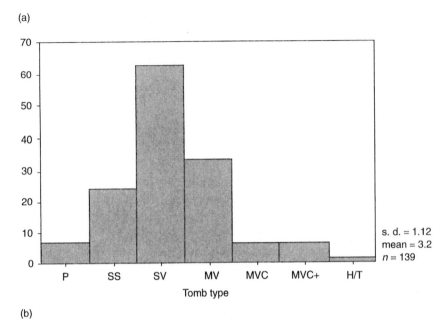

(b)

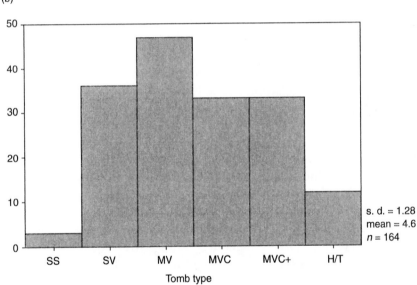

**Figure 4.4** Types of tomb construction for (a) 18th Dynasty and (b) 19th/20th Dynasties (P = pit tomb; SS = simple shaft tomb; SV = shaft and vault; MV = multiple vault tomb; MVC = multiple vault with chapel; MVC+ = multiple vault, chapel, courtyard and pyramid complex; H/T = house/tomb complex)

A case could be made for the two distinct spatial zones reflecting varying degrees of differential wealth and differential status, although these two vectors of difference intersect in divergent ways. In the Eastern Necropolis the burials of children, adolescents and single people tend to predominate. Some of the young children are buried with equal or more care than those discovered in the Western Necropolis at this time. In that zone children were not given separate burial, rather they were interred with other family members, usually a husband and wife. For the most part, the two cemeteries evidence very different burial patterns. The Eastern Necropolis also possesses very poor pit burials for children and possibly older individuals. The statistical analyses include only those pits which Bruyère described and numbered. The number would realistically be much higher, since he maintained that the lower portion of Gournet Murai was riddled with these shallow burials (Bruyère 1937a: 11). In sum, the Eastern Necropolis demonstrates a number of practices and burial types that are often affected by age, sex and financial status. It is likely that wealthy, high-status individuals (and couples) buried in the Western Necropolis buried their children, sisters, and perhaps even divorced wives, in the Eastern Necropolis. This suggests a very fluid expression of rank at Deir el Medina in the 18th Dynasty, and that decisions were made on a rather individualistic level. For example, individual parents might decide to bury their child in a roughly constructed pit in the Eastern Necropolis, or with them in a lavish, expensive tomb in the Western Necropolis. Both options were possible.

When we move into the 19th Dynasty the spatial zone designated for burial was reduced to the Western Necropolis alone. Tombs were compressed within the confines of the slope, extending to the gebel, and towards the northern edge of the site. The burial of individuals in the Eastern Necropolis ceased, possibly with the exception of foetuses and newborns, who are sometimes accompanied by undatable material. The burial areas become homogeneous, with little if any clear demarcation of segmented or ranked zones. It is possible that the larger, more elaborate tombs that were newly constructed (as opposed to re-used vaults) were built up against the escarpment at the highest elevation of the Western Necropolis. This may be a result of limited space, a desire to construct new tombs, or a function of chapel building, which was possibly facilitated by cutting directly into the gebel – or a combination of these factors. From the Ramesside Period onwards, the Western Necropolis was the prime location for burial (figure 4.5).

**Figure 4.5** Tombs 218 (Amennakht, father), 219 (Nebenmaat, son), 220 (Khaemteri, son) in the Western Necropolis at Deir el Medina (photograph by the author)

Tomb construction evidenced in the Western Necropolis for the 19th and 20th Dynasties shows a movement towards standardization and appears to be less ranked than its 18th Dynasty counterpart. Analysis demonstrates that there were very few poor or simple tombs at this time. Most were multiple-vaulted tombs with chapels and/or pyramids. The financial outlay on these various tomb types was almost commensurate, in contrast to the vast disparity between a simple pit burial and an expensive tomb-complex witnessed in the 18th Dynasty. It would seem that the later tombs show a levelling process, and that is in keeping with social developments I will discuss later. Basically, we see fewer tombs at this time, though they are more homogeneous and show a greater overall expenditure in energy and cost. This is a logical outcome since the tombs were now generational structures, often containing scores of bodies from successive generations as well as extended families. Fewer tombs were built because fewer were needed and older 18th Dynasty vaults could be modified or simply re-used; tombs no longer housed individuals, rather they became the repository of kin groups. Furthermore, overall tomb expenditure could be increased if resources were pooled for communal structures.

When factor analysis was applied to the tomb data for each period, in order to examine clustering on the basis of total burial assemblages in each tomb, it was clear that the 18th Dynasty represented a more ranked community than that of the 19th and 20th Dynasties. While factor analysis cannot by itself establish this notion of graduated rank, the evidence gleaned from cemetery location, tomb construction and mortuary practice lends weight to the argument. This evidence goes some way towards supporting Kemp's thesis that New Kingdom Egypt did not manifest a tripartite socio-economic system, but rather that status formed a continuous and graduated continuum with complex socio-economic relationships (1989: 294–317; Smith 1992: 196). Smith's work on intact tombs in the Theban region employs Deir el Medina data coupled with elite tombs. He concludes that there are no abrupt socio-cultural breaks that would indicate a sharp class division, supported by the gradual increase in the number and variety of tomb goods as one goes up the social scale (1992: 197). It should be noted that the poorer tombs of the Eastern Necropolis contained a large variety of tomb goods, which date to the 18th Dynasty, so that the equation of number of goods with status must be too simplistic. Take, for example, tombs 1370 and 1379 which have almost as many classes of artefact as elite Western Necropolis tombs like that of Kha (tomb 8), and certainly more than Sennefer (tomb 1159A) (see figures 4.6 and 4.7). A better way to access individual wealth and status is by examination of idiosyncratic goods or non-standard burial items. In the case of Kha, these elements included the 'gold of valour' necklace given to him by pharaoh, his gold cubit and electrum cup. Variability itself may be a clue to an individual's status and wealth and as such cannot be smoothed over in any statistical analyses.

## Village People: the Question of Ethnicity and Origins

There has been a resurgence of interest in the issue of ethnicity in archaeology (Graves-Brown et al. 1996; Jones 1996). Ethnicity has now come to represent a mode of action and representation, according to Cohen (1994: 119), which entails decisions people make about themselves and others symbolically as the bearers of certain cultural identity. Whether such terms of reference are useful in antiquity is debatable, and an Egyptian notion of ethnicity would perhaps be significantly different from our own. Yet we know that the Egyptians were keen to set themselves apart from other groups in the Mediterranean and Africa. Eriksen claims (1993: 12) that ethnicity is an aspect

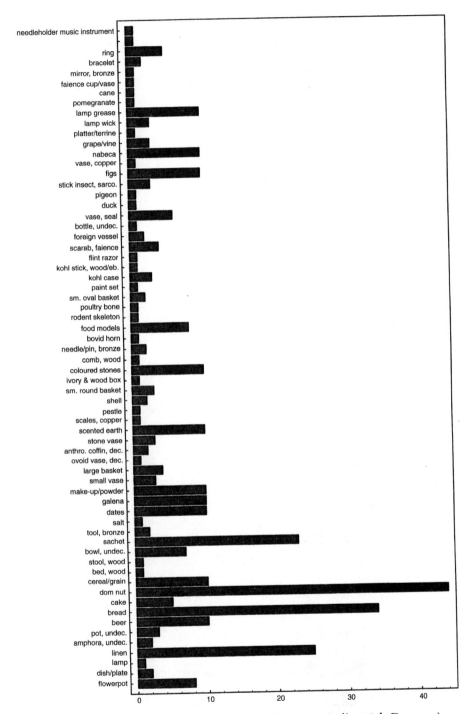

**Figure 4.6**  Profile of tomb goods for tomb 1370 (Madja, 18th Dynasty), Eastern Necropolis

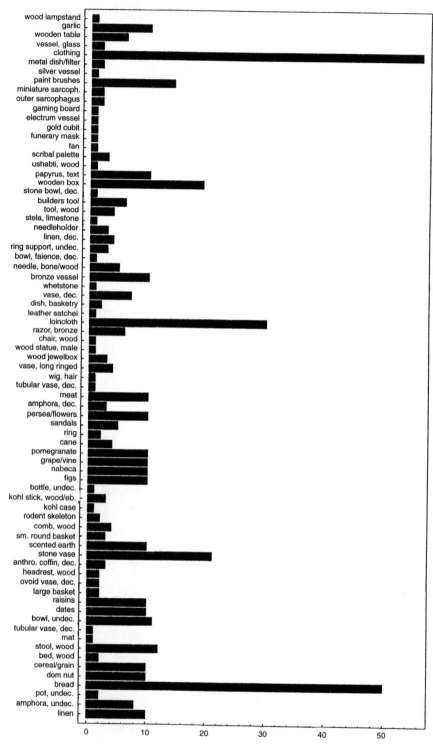

**Figure 4.7** Profile of tomb goods for tomb 8 (Kha and Merit, 18th Dynasty), Western Necropolis

of social relations between individuals who consider themselves as culturally distinctive from members of other groups with whom they have a minimum of regular interaction. On the one hand, the state presented an image of ideological unity, and, on the other, Egypt was open to the immigration of foreigners in all periods and its neighbours were of great significance (Baines 1996: 362). In terms of Deir el Medina, it has long been generally thought that the villagers were a highly heterogeneous, culturally mixed community, though this may be more a modern fiction of an 'artists' colony' than a demonstrable situation in reality.

In the current state of research the data present an interesting, yet frustrating, paradox concerning the composition of the Deir el Medina community. In the first place, we know little of the organization of the 18th Dynasty workers, and even less about their daily life from the domestic record. We know more about their burials due to the significant number of intact, or nearly intact, tombs. By contrast, our domestic data and the plethora of textual material all derive from the Ramesside Period, whereas the burials from these dynasties are the most disturbed. Our picture of the village is very much constructed from the Ramesside textual data (Meskell 1994b), though the character of the 18th Dynasty village must have been very different. The small village of the 18th Dynasty and the relatively unimpressive burials of the majority of workmen in the Eastern Necropolis contrast directly with the inextricably inter-related community of the 20th Dynasty and its impressive and expensive personal tombs and monuments. It would be wrong to view the nature of the community as commensurate throughout these dynasties. The villagers who abandoned Deir el Medina during the Amarna Period were not necessarily the same as those who re-established the community in year 7 of the pharaoh Horemheb. Many individuals were assembled there for the first time. Deir el Medina in the Ramesside Period took on a new character that is seen not only in the texts but also in the archaeological record: tombs, monuments, artefacts, even bodies themselves. The Ramesside Period has a certain multi-cultural flair in everything from foreign individuals to the use of foreign names. The influx of new people diminishes in the 20th Dynasty, towards the end of village occupation, when all the families are basically inter-related; there is a dearth of newcomers and a more general feeling of homogeneity.

William Ward (1994: 61) claimed that in the New Kingdom foreigners were a prominent part of the population, including individuals from Mycenae to Persia. Whether this picture of exotica is correct or somewhat overstated, evidence for an international community at

Deir el Medina requires a significant amount of teasing out. Ward's primary data set was his collection of proposed foreign names from Deir el Medina, among which he identified names of Libyan, Nubian and West Asiatic origin, the latter including Canaanite, Ugaritic, Hurrian, Cypriot, Akkadian and Hittite. He concluded that the majority of these individuals lived in the village, that their recent ancestors were foreign, and that many of the women were 'housewives' to ordinary workmen. These people did not reach the position of scribe or chief workman, suggesting a possible link between ancestry/ethnicity and status. He suggested that local custom or prejudice may have restricted their social mobility. Problems arise when a name has meaning in two languages, as Ward himself pointed out. Here one should also consider local onomastics, since it is possible that names were associated with the specific locality of Deir el Medina. Although it is tempting to subscribe to Ward's theory of ethnicity, his ascriptions should be seen as tentative and may be modified in future – many Egyptologists remain sceptical. It is not that the presence of diverse ethnic populations at this time should be questioned, but rather the degree to which Ward sees the phenomenon as ubiquitous.

One avenue to access the ethnicity of individuals not mentioned in the Ramesside texts, i.e. the 18th Dynasty population, is via the mortuary archaeology and individual bodies. From the 28 interments of the 18th Dynasty in the Eastern cemetery two females were thought to be of foreign extraction. In tomb 1379, the woman Iabtina (or Ibentitina) was considered foreign, perhaps Nubian (Bruyère 1937a: 170–2). Also considered Nubian was the woman Nubiyiti, in tomb 1382. Whether these assignments were made solely on the name or on the body itself is not specified in Bruyère's text. Because of the paucity of recorded documentation it is impossible to ascertain whether individuals were drawn from different Egyptian localities at the foundation of the village, but the possibility should not be ruled out. At this time tombs contain significant numbers of foreign vessels (Bell 1982). However, these are predominantly of Mediterranean origin and reflect trade and internationalism, rather than the presence of foreign individuals.

The Ramesside Period offers both material and textual data. In tomb 339, Bruyère (1926: 51–61) recorded finding a woman's body with prominent cheekbones, her eyes replaced by obsidian and ivory: this special type of preparation of the body indicated to him that she was Syrian, her name being Takharu, literally translated as *the Syrian*. Such practices tend to be rare and it is likely that assimilation into community life might mask an individual's ethnic origins. The adoration of several foreign gods, such as Reshep or Anat, might be taken as evidence for an influx of foreigners to the site, but these deities were widely worshipped in the New Kingdom and cannot be taken as proof of ethnicity (figure 4.8).

Although the term 'ethnicity' has taken on an international connotation in our own society, to the Egyptians similar associations of difference may have been attached to people coming from the Delta,

**Figure 4.8**   Stela belonging to Huy, workman at Deir el Medina, showing deities from Syria and Canaan. Huy and his son Seba kneel below the deities Kadesh, Min-Amun and Reshep (Louvre C. 86 [N.237]; photograph by the author)

Abydos or Aswan. In a country defined by the vertical projection of the Nile, the distances between various localities may have seemed enormous. Regions must have taken on quite clear local identities, although this localization has yet to be fully studied. There has remained a tendency to generalize from Thebes or Memphis outward, as if Egypt itself was a monolithic entity. This study can only attempt to answer questions concerning Deir el Medina in its specific cultural, spatial and temporal context, rather than employing the site as a template for settlements elsewhere.

At this local level, there is evidence that the population at the site came from various areas of Egypt, attested from both textual and archaeological sources. Deities were associated with specific locales, so it is interesting that we have evidence for the cults of Seth of Ombos, Montu of Armant (McDowell 1994) and the triad from Elephantine, Khnum, Satis and Anukis. Evidence for the latter is represented on the naos shrine of the workman Kasa, now in the Turin Museum (Valbelle 1972). The prominence of this triad on such an important funerary monument indicates that the family of Kasa probably originated in Elephantine and brought their local deities with them to Deir el Medina. This triad was found elsewhere at Deir el Medina (Valbelle 1981) and its occurrence may reflect nothing more than a passing trend. Yet we know that skilled workmen were transferred from various institutions to the site when the team needed to be increased in order to complete a royal tomb as a pharaoh neared death. McDowell cites three such individuals and their families taken from Karnak: Pashed, Qen and Ramose in the time of Ramesses II. She also states that the scribe Amenopet seems to have links with Kush (McDowell 1994: 42–3). These individuals brought not only their families, but their expertise, customs and personal wealth – all adding to the character of the community. We cannot rule out the possibility that there were intra-national and international members of the village, and though much of the diversity may be masked by the homogeneous nature of the material culture, such variations must have been felt more noticeably in the living social relations of the village.

## Patterns of Sex and Age in the Western Necropolis

In this section I examine the representation of individuals in the mortuary sphere on the basis of age, sex, status and wealth and how social inequalities are mediated through material culture, as well as through bodies themselves. Due to the excellent conditions of preservation, many of the bodies recovered by Bruyère had their flesh and hair intact and so sexing individuals and ascribing approximate age was relatively unproblematic. It was also possible to ascertain the inequalities in bodily treatment and practices between individuals. Material inequalities had serious repercussions for community members in terms of attaining an appropriate afterlife, as well as reflecting social dynamics on a lived and experiential level. I begin by discussing the Western Necropolis data, from the earliest occupation of the village in the 18th Dynasty through to the 19th and 20th Dynasties. I then compare this necropolis with the Eastern Necropolis, where there is a significant degree of temporal overlap, discussing the burials from the Eastern Necropolis in detail and focusing specifically on those of individual children. Few studies have sought to discuss this cemetery in terms of social dynamics, and few, if any, have considered the specific character of the children's burials in detail (Meskell 1994a, 1997a). By quantifying goods ascribed to men, women and children, within the temporal parameters, gross patterning can be highlighted according to age and sex. Many assertions have been made about the status of women in Egypt, specifically their favourable and egalitarian circumstances (B. Lesko 1994, 1994–5). Fewer, if any, analyses have sought to identify the position and visibility of children in tomb assemblages (Nordström 1996). Examination of sexed tomb goods in securely dated tomb contexts does not support the notion of egalitarian treatment in terms of possessions. Deir el Medina offers a unique opportunity to determine changing social relationships involving a range of groups over some 400 years, shedding a broad light on New Kingdom social dynamics.

A clear pattern emerges from the 38 Western Necropolis tombs of the 18th Dynasty with clearly sexed goods. The majority of tombs have some male goods, whereas this is not the case for female or children's objects. In one tomb there are over 196 items solely ascribed to men. The highest number of ascribed female goods for the 18th Dynasty is 39, and these belong to the wealthy burial of Kha's wife, Merit. Her case illustrates the point well: although her personal items were of value in themselves, their relative wealth was particularly low when compared to those of her husband, Kha (Meskell 1998c: 371–5). In terms of percentages, 87 per cent of the tombs contain male goods, 24 per cent contain female, 11 per cent shared items and 5 per cent contain children's items. As wealth and status increased, the relative wealth of female family members declined significantly. It is only at the lower socio-economic end of the spectrum that we see any measure of equality in the value of tomb goods between males and females, illustrated by the Eastern Necropolis burials. The notion that New Kingdom women of the middle class were well provisioned in death is a fiction derived from looking at their personal effects in isolation, rather than measured against their male counterparts. The tomb goods of Merit may look expensive and are indicative of the status of the family, yet they are a pale reflection of the extensive tomb assemblage of her husband, Kha. The numbers of shared goods, where both male and female are mentioned, are extremely small. Objects such as stelae, statuary, lintels, architectural features and pyramidia were often inscribed for husband and wife, since they referred more generally to the provision of the structure of the tomb itself (figure 4.9). This obvious wealth has masked the character of New Kingdom social dynamics – a system which saw wealth and status

**Figure 4.9** Inscribed lintel of Qenia and Tuya, 18th Dynasty (now held in the British Museum 918, 1243; photograph courtesy of the IFAO, Cairo)

concentrated around elite males and other male family members.

Sexual partnerships in Egypt should perhaps be viewed in a more fluid way than for much of European history. Unions appear to have been based upon real feelings of love, rather than simply upon social or economic prerogatives. Parents might have orchestrated some marriages; however, most documentary evidence points to consensual arrangements between men and women. Here I am reminded of the descriptions of intimate relations in the medieval village of Montaillou (Le Roy Ladurie 1980: 144), where 'relations between couples were naturally complex, including every possible variety of marriage and concubinage. There were grand passions, ordinary marriages with or without love, and liaisons both temporary and habitual, venal and affectionate.' Interestingly, there was no formal marriage ceremony in Egypt, which suggests that 'marriage' was a private rather than a public event. Egyptian phrases have been interpreted as analogous to this arrangement: 'bringing a bundle', 'to live with', 'to found a house'. In terms of 'bringing a bundle', this might refer to the provision of bridewealth (Toivari 1998: 1158). These acts of reciprocity also had significant import when things went wrong. A marriage could be dissolved in a manner similar to its instigation. And there are numerous instances of marital problems, adultery and divorce. Both men and women could instigate a divorce, but the ratio demonstrates a salient disparity – 12 : 3 in favour of men divorcing or threatening to divorce women (Toivari 1998: 1162). Take the case of Hesysunebef, who began his life as a slave and was later adopted by his master to became a member of the team of workmen. He rose to the important rank of deputy. Devoted to his adoptive parents, he named his children after them and dedicated a stela to his father (McDowell 1999: 50), a considerable financial outlay. His wife Hel formerly lived with the workman Pendua, but was unfaithful to both these men with the same man, the notorious Paneb. As Andrea McDowell (1999) suggests, this infidelity may have prompted the divorce, especially since Paneb had threatened to kill Hesysunebef's father. Intense social relationships and ruptures seemed to have been enacted rather publicly in the village and were subsequently recorded for posterity.

*Really, it was not in order that you might become blind to your wife that I took you aside and said, 'You should see the things that you've done [on behalf of (?)] your wife.' You rebuffed me only to become deaf to this crime ... I will make you aware of those adulterous acts that your [wife] has committed at your expense.*

*(Response to the preceding): But she isn't my wife! Were she my wife, she would cease uttering her words (charges?) and get out leaving the door open.*[15]

There are numerous texts recording the absolute breakdown of marital relations, which similarly reflect that these ruptures were always to the detriment of women. Economically and socially, the exclusion of women from their familial home meant a life of insecurity and poverty. Divorce sealed their fate, and unless their own children provided for them or they re-married the rest of their lives were guaranteed to be difficult. This was especially true of their burial, which was primarily a male concern. For the most part, women were included in the tombs of their husbands, examples being Kha and Merit or Sennefer and Nefertiry (Meskell 1998c). But in the Eastern Necropolis some were buried on their own or with other women; these women might have been single or divorced, and are discussed more fully in chapter 5. If fortunate, they may have been able to prepare their own funerary arrangements or, alternatively, relied on their children, mainly sons, for such preparations. Such individual women, buried alone and perhaps living outside the parameters of family life, probably represent a larger sector of the community than previously realized. Such circumstances were part of many women's experience at various stages of their lives. The fluidity of the marriage union meant that its dissolution was equally unconstrained, resulting in a number of individuals who found themselves outside the gendered arrangements of the family.

Since 18th Dynasty burials could include a male, female and in some cases a child, the under-representation of the latter two groups in real numbers is significant. Not only do women appear to be relatively invisible in the material record, but the number of children present is almost negligible. Their objects are confined usually to a coffin, small pieces of jewellery and sandals. Only the two wealthiest tombs in this data set, those of Sennefer (tomb 1159A) and Kha (tomb 8), have children's objects. Sennefer's tomb has the box-burial of an infant. Kha's tomb does not even contain the burial of a child. We can postulate that in the 18th Dynasty children were mostly buried in the Eastern Necropolis in simple tombs or pits, though the numbers discovered are small in relation to the probable level of infant mortality. The provision of burial for children in the Western Necropolis at Deir el Medina seems to have been a low priority in the 18th Dynasty, or it was spatially demarcated in another region such as the Eastern cemetery or perhaps under house floors. Box burials were found under house floors within the settlement enclosure, under the house walls of SE VI and in the northern sector of the site. Excavations of the settlement at Qasr Ibrim also produced several intra-site infant burials, most recently under the floors of a fourth-century AD building. One of these children was wrapped in a cloth and a sandal was placed with the body (Scott 1992: 88). Geraldine Pinch (1994: 132) has explained this practice as representing the desire for the soul of the child to return to the mother in the form of another child. It has been claimed that this tradition survived into recent times among Egyptian women in an effort to facilitate future births. When Flinders Petrie found similar examples at the Middle Kingdom settlement of Kahun he saw this practice as unorthodox and undesirable, believing that it did 'not reflect much credit on the manners and customs' of the inhabitants. On the basis of current interpretations, one would posit the presence of house burials at Deir el Medina as yet another burial practice in the rich repertoire of New Kingdom society.

For the assemblages of the 19th and 20th Dynasties, it should be possible to trace any social changes at the intersection of sex and age. A total of 27 tombs from this period have clearly sexed tomb goods. Again, male goods predominate, but we see noteworthy increases in female and shared items. In percentage terms, 89 per cent of the tombs contained inscribed male items, 29 per cent female, 37 per cent were shared and 15 per cent had children's goods. This fits the pattern of increased tomb size and complexity, coupled with the provisioning of extended families within those structures. The higher number of bodies interred would presumably have incorporated increased numbers of women and children. The increase in categories of shared named goods, such as inscribed architectural features, stelae and combined statuary, fits with this shift. Yet the actual numbers of inscribed female goods, or of goods directly attributable to women, remain relatively low. Women might be more visible across the spectrum of tombs of the 19th and 20th Dynasties, yet their comparative wealth and ownership of goods are still markedly inferior. Whether this relates to social status in life is another matter, but a significant concern is their representation in death and their possibilities for an afterlife. Lack of statuary, shabtis (figure 4.10), canopic vessels, libation vessels and amulets would all have diminished that possibility. Their only chance would be if their own destiny in the afterlife was, by default, tied to that of their spouse.

**Figure 4.10** A collection of post-New Kingdom shabti figures which were intended to work for the deceased in the afterlife (now held at the Louvre; photograph by the author)

Evidence from Ramesside tombs (in all conditions) shows an increase in the number of shared goods, and of goods depicting multiple individuals. I have examined all tombs with Ramesside data, eliminating Third Intermediate Period shabtis and later material, and concentrating on inscribed data for the most part. For some 61 cases there was a total of 334 male objects, 79 female, nine shared and nine children's objects. From the 19th Dynasty onwards, it seems more common to have representations of husband and wife on a shared basis, or to incorporate several family members on stelae and statuary. This fits with the picture of familial interments, since many of the individuals represented would have ended up in a single tomb in the Western Necropolis. This does not necessarily mean that women had more goods of their own, but rather that they tended more often to be shown as associated with their husbands. The same could be said for children. This pattern diverges markedly from that of finds evidenced in the 18th Dynasty tombs of Kha (tomb 8) and Sennefer (tomb 1159A). It is further at variance with less wealthy tomb assemblages from the Eastern Necropolis, which show a more one-for-one distribution of finds between men and women.

## East v. West

The previous section focused on social patterning in the Western Necropolis in terms of large-scale temporal change, coupled with intra-period trends according to sex and age. The situation in the Eastern Necropolis appears to have been very different (figure 4.11).

The construction of elaborate rock-cut New Kingdom tombs, as in the Western Necropolis, not only reflected world building and cosmological belief structures, it was a huge endeavour in the construction of self – for eternity. While the self had individuated characteristics, individuals were also influenced by a particular and formulaic vision sanctioned by over-arching religious and social forces. Wason (1994: 85) has proposed that if rank is not based on hereditary lines, then status rivalry will be at a premium and this is likely to be manifest in competitive funerary display. Personal aggrandizement could be seen as a locational device which ensured that construction of self was firmly rooted within a corporate group identity, often through the deployment of exaggeration and propaganda. Similarly, the material manifestation of death was a social phenomenon, on all levels, with organized, regulated communal responses and practices – even down to hired female mourners. These practices do not undermine the fact that death was an emotive, personal experience for the participants, family and friends, but they do illustrate the discursive canonical practices of an adult male elite. It is this prevailing vision of death, replete with pyramid chapels, decorated walls, gilt sarcophagus, furniture and grave goods, mourners in white, flowers and smells, which dominates the Egyptian way of death.

Prestige, propaganda and social display were not foremost in the minds of poorer families burying their dead children at Deir el Medina. Whether they were stillborn or verging on adolescence, buried alone or in family vaults, there was an immediate concern for their chances of attaining an afterlife, rather than with social aggrandizement that could enhance the status of their parents. Concepts such as aggrandizement seem almost alien with regard to the group of children buried in the Eastern Necropolis. The excavator suggested (Bruyère 1937a: 7) that the Eastern Necropolis simply represents a lower socio-economic group. However, I would suggest that at Deir el Medina the level of variance in the way in which children were buried across the spectrum of class is marginal, as opposed to the significant change in adult burials.

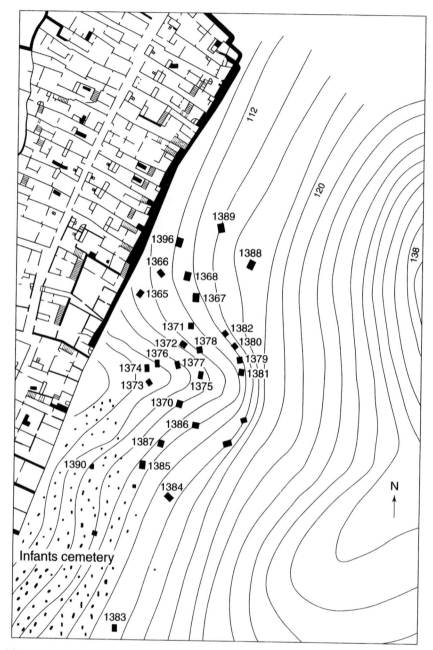

**Figure 4.11** Map of the Eastern Necropolis (after B. Bruyère, *Rapport sur les fouilles de Deir el Médineh (1934–1935)*, Cairo, 1937)

The Eastern Necropolis appears to be segmented in zones along age-determined lines. The lowest part of the slope was reserved for very young children. Bruyère found not only infants, but neonates, foetuses, placentas and organic residues that defied identification in among bloody cloths, the remains of viscera and the mummification process itself. This represents a meaningful deposition, since the Egyptians tried not to let any part of the bodily existence escape: this extended to materials that had come into contact with the corpse (Hornung 1992: 169). Bruyère claimed (1937a: 11) that this southern extremity of the village was riddled with small pits, circular, square or rectangular, cut 40–90 cm deep into the rock without any internal or external masonry. They were filled with sand, pebbles and a few large stones to cover these holes and prevent hyenas and jackals from disturbing the burials. Adolescents of both sexes were assigned to the middle section of the hill and adults to the upper portion, with women being more numerous than men. This last point is not surprising given the limited burial options for women. Generally, the construction of a tomb was a male enterprise and men presumably financed the overall project. Thus, women would have largely been reliant on the support of a male, whether father, husband or son, for the provision of burial. And those individuals who undertook the responsibility of burial were presumably entitled to priority in matters of inheritance.

Of additional note are the excavations carried out by Georg Möller between 1911 and 1913 (Anthes 1943) which few scholars have incorporated into their discussions of the site or of the Eastern Necropolis. It is worth summarizing briefly the evidence uncovered by these earlier excavations. Möller chose to excavate the lowest sector of Gournet Murai, the region with neonates and infants. Four tombs were uncovered. Each of these were shallow pit burials with no trace of a superstructure. Tomb DX1 was a basket burial containing a child's body wrapped in linen, above which was placed a decorated pot containing vegetable matter. To the north of the basket was another ceramic vessel with resin inside and superimposed upon that was a cup with a black rim. Burial DX2 contained another basket with the body of the child wrapped in linen but without grave goods. Burial DX3 was a particularly unusual interment: it contained two wooden boxes, with two statues and grave goods, yet no bodies were found. The tomb was intact and covered with undisturbed stones. One might speculate that a twin birth may have occurred with an unhappy outcome; perhaps the bodies themselves did not survive for burial. We know that twins represented a particularly problematic category for the Egyptians, and were considered very differently from single births (Baines 1985). The twin statues in DX3 may have stood in as simulacra for the physical bodies of individuals, possibly as a means of ensuring a successful and complete afterlife. Although the evidence is not conclusive, the unique nature of the find indicates an anomalous situation which presumably called for a highly individualistic and personal response. The boxes both contained a wooden statue wrapped in linen, suggestive of some magical practice. The burial assemblage consisted of some 18 ceramic vessels, two baskets and a wide variety of foodstuffs: emmer, bread, grapes, dates, figs, pomegranates and nuts (Anthes 1943: 55). Lastly, burial DX4 contained a body in a basket, next to which were plant remains. In the fill was a well-preserved pot with a roughly executed white painted pattern (1943: 55). The nature of the finds, the particular ceramics, statuary and foodstuffs, indicate an 18th Dynasty date for these burials.

## Patterns of Sex and Age in the Eastern Necropolis

Several tombs in the necropolis were dated securely to the 18th Dynasty by the excavator, whereas others have been dated here on the basis of pottery, classified by Pamela Rose, and coffin types. If we consider that poorer village inhabitants had to make do with white-washed chest coffins, crudely cut and decorated, and that these tended to go out of use in the mid-18th Dynasty (Smith 1992: 97–8; Taylor 1996), then many more of these tombs can be securely dated to this period. Table 4.1 draws on data from Bruyère's excavation reports, as well as on this new information. On the basis of similarities in the funerary assemblages, I suggest that most of the burials listed below as *unknown* were also likely to be 18th Dynasty interments. Here, as in the Western Necropolis at this time, the burials of individuals and couples predominated. It is the predominance of women and children buried alone or as couples which is strikingly different. Here women cannot be dismissed simply as a subordinate group: individual agency and choice were open to them, even at this socio-economic level. Furthermore, this complex cross-cutting of identity categories contrasts with the arrangement of the Western Necropolis, illustrating that the interplay of social factors was fluid and contextual.

The early date of many of these tombs suggests that this area was used most extensively in the first stage of occupation of the site. It is more difficult to date tombs in the Western Necropolis to this early period because there was the substantial mixing of objects from

**Table 4.1** Eastern Necropolis burials

| Tomb no. | Date[1] | Details |
| --- | --- | --- |
| 1365 | Possibly 18th | Individual coffin burial, looted |
| 1366/1367 | Unknown | Individual burial, looted |
| 1368 | Possibly 18th | Individual burial |
| 1369 | Unknown | Individual burial, looted |
| 1370 | Early/mid-18th | One male, old, and one female, old |
| 1371 | mid-18th | One female |
| 1372 | Early/mid-18th | One young female, two infants not sexed |
| 1373 | Unknown | Male infant, basket burial |
| 1374 | Early/mid-18th | Infant, basket burial |
| 1375 | Early/mid-18th | Female infant |
| 1376 | Early/mid-18th | Individual, basket burial |
| 1377 | Early/mid-18th | Individual, not sexed |
| 1378 | Unknown | Infant, basket burial |
| 1379 | Early/mid-18th | One male, old, and one female, old |
| 1380 | Early/mid-18th | One young female |
| 1381 | Early/mid-18th | One young female |
| 1382 | Early/mid-18th | Two females, one young, and one male, old |
| 1383 | Unknown | Infant, basket burial |
| 1384 | Unknown | Infant, box burial |
| 1385 | Unknown | Infant, basket burial |
| 1386 | 18th Dynasty | Two middle-aged males, one male infant |
| 1388 | Early/mid-18th | Two females |
| 1389 | Early/mid-18th | One male |
| 1390 | Unknown | Male infant, box burial |

*Burials excavated by Möller in the 1911–13 season*

| | | |
| --- | --- | --- |
| DX1 | Early/mid-18th | Infant, basket burial |
| DX2 | Unknown | Infant, basket burial |
| DX3 | Early/mid-18th | Twin box burials, no bodies |
| DX4 | Early/mid-18th | Infant, basket burial |

[1] Dated on the basis of coffin type, ceramics or burial goods.

various burials that is not evident in the Eastern Necropolis. Contemporary Western Necropolis tombs that have been identified include 1069, 1157, 1165A, 1166, 1169, 340 and 354. Among these, only a minority would be of people in the upper echelon because the community was ranked with two chief workmen, a handful of scribes and a majority of ordinary workmen. However, the paucity of burials, particularly of men, demonstrates that the Eastern Necropolis cannot have been the only cemetery for the early period of occupation. None the less, the small number of burials for the early 18th Dynasty in both cemeteries parallels the size of the village and the number of workers at this time, probably a total of less than 40: the later walled enclosure of Tuthmosis I encompassed only 40 houses.

The data from the Eastern Necropolis burials include 12 females, six males, one female infant, three male infants and ten unsexed children. The prominence of women in this spatial context might be explained in various ways. First, given the 18th Dynasty trend toward burials of individuals, specifically individual men, it is not surprising that there would be a surfeit of women left needing provision. They may not have had the resources to construct a tomb, and women do not appear to be buried individually in the Western Necropolis. Bruyère recorded finding a female body in several disturbed tombs (for example, tombs 1420, 1266), although the violated condition of such tombs suggests that we have only a partial picture of the original inhabitants. No intact tomb in the Western Necropolis conclusively illustrates the single burial of a female, whereas we have such examples for men, such as tomb 1408. Some of the women in the Eastern Necropolis may have been divorcees, single, widowed women or even concubines if such a role existed. Bruyère suggested (1937a: 178), on the basis of the inscription on the coffin of a single female in tomb 1380, that she may have had such a status in life. A similar inscription was found on a statue base in tomb 1379. Most of the women in this cemetery are buried in anthropomorphic, inscribed coffins whereas the males tend to be buried in casket coffins which are often uninscribed (Claudia Näser, personal communication). Whatever the reasons for the greater number of women present in this cemetery, they are still far fewer than their male counterparts if one considers all cemeteries. This situation also extends to children.

On a first examination, the burials in the Eastern Necropolis (Bruyère 1937a), especially those of adults, might seem to be significantly poorer than in the Western cemetery. They none the less contain items of considerable wealth: bronze mirrors (tombs 1370,

1371, 1380, 1382), wooden statuary (1379), bronze razors (tombs 1379, 1380, 1381, 1388, 1389), gold (tombs 1379, 1380, 1381, 1382, 1388), ebony (tombs 1380, 1388) and ivory (tombs 1370, 1375, 1377, 1380, 1381). The assemblages closely correlate with the richer 18th Dynasty tombs, as opposed to the Ramesside ones. Tomb 1352 (Bruyère 1937b: 95–107) in the Western Necropolis seems to be an example of an intermediary tomb, its assemblage falling neatly between the Eastern Necropolis burials and those of the upper echelons, such as Sennefer and Kha.

The Eastern Necropolis also provides a clear example of the pitfalls one may encounter in assigning goods on the basis of sex from a contemporary Western perspective. For example, sexed bodies and associated finds support the claim that both men and women could be buried with jewellery, make-up, toiletries, perfume jars, razors, combs, tools and canes. Many of these items have strong sex-linked associations in many cultures and might be specifically designated to one sex or the other. These goods were presumably used in life by both sexes, as well as forming part of a repertoire of tomb possessions which were to be included in 18th Dynasty burials – thus challenging normative assumptions about the sexes and their essential characteristics. In tomb 1370 both the aged woman Madja and the unknown man have in their coffins kohl jars with make-up, jewellery and folded linens (Bruyère 1937a: 150–7). Both were wrapped in approximately ten layers of wrappings. As for differences, Madja had a bronze mirror over her heart while the man had a lyre placed within his coffin. Three mirrors are directly associated with a female (placed on the body) in the Eastern Necropolis, while the fourth (tomb 1382) was in a vault containing a male and two females (Bruyère 1937a: 183–8). Another mirror known from the site had its handle engraved with the name of the man, Harmose. However, since mirrors were closely associated with the goddess Hathor, one might expect women to be more strongly associated with these objects. In tomb 1380 a young female had two bronze tools within her coffin. Bronze razors have been found in female burials, for example tombs 1380, 1381 and 1388. Assumptions about sex-linked artefacts cannot be based on modern categories and predilections and we must factor in a considerable amount of ambiguity in terms of sexual differentiation of such items. Some goods may reflect a trend for sex-linkage, such as work tools, yet even these may cross sexed boundaries and one must remember that such boundaries are culturally constructed in the first place. In general, the Eastern Necropolis assemblages are not as clearly demarcated on the basis of sex, in comparison with the wealthier Western Necropolis; this difference is perhaps telling in terms of sexual equality at the lower socio-economic level.

The Eastern Necropolis not only had a higher representation of women, admittedly in a smaller sample than the Western Necropolis, but burials seem to have been more egalitarian on all levels than in the Western Necropolis. The vast disparities on the basis of sex present in the tombs of Kha (tomb 8) and Sennefer (tomb 1159A) are not reproduced in these less expensive tombs. The pattern here would be best described as equally distributed wealth, with little variance in the tomb assemblages and bodily treatments of men, women, and even adolescents to some degree. Age becomes a substantive factor in the style of burial regimen with small children, babies and foetuses. Figure 4.12 illustrates the distribution of goods on the basis of sex and age in the Eastern Necropolis. Sexed goods are designated on the basis of inscription, or if there is a single occupant then all tomb goods are assigned to that person.

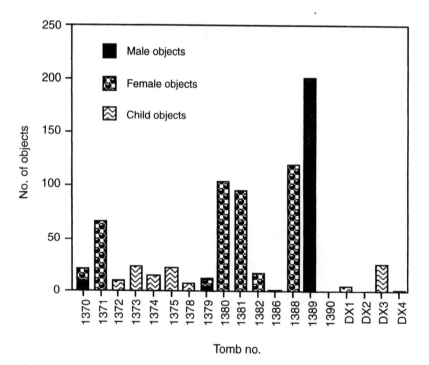

**Figure 4.12**  Goods ascribed to men, women and children in the Eastern Necropolis

## Embodiment in the Eastern Necropolis

*Do not say: 'I am too young to be taken'*
*For you do not know your death.*
*When death comes he steals the infant*
*Who is in his mother's arms,*
*Just like him who reached old age.*
                    The Instruction of Any[16]

I now want to consider concepts of the body, embodiment and individuals in the specific spatial context of the Eastern Necropolis. This cemetery clearly illustrates the constellation of attributes (age, class, sex) at work in the burial of individuals, couples and family groups, and in the presentation of selfhood. The necropolis has many children's tombs and the intact nature of specific burials, with full assemblages, allows for narrative reconstructions through which the individual can be accessed. Here one could apprehend highly personalized constructions of identity and move fluidly between commentaries on society and self. Together with ethnicity, sex and class, age is one of the four dimensions of individual and social experience, but it has yet to receive its due attention (Laslett 1995: 4). The data suggest that children were, to some degree, socialized into Egyptian society at birth, yet those processes intensified as they reached adolescence. Age is the major factor structuring difference in the Eastern Necropolis, marital status being the next most incisive determinant. The data also illustrate how difference and variability were played out in burial practices during the New Kingdom, but more specifically in the 18th Dynasty.

Most Egyptian families, elite and non-elite, probably had numerous children. As Baines comments (1991: 133), this would have been a requirement if they were to increase or reproduce themselves because only a minority of children survived to become adults. He cites evidence from Roman Egypt which suggests a life expectancy at the age of 14 of 29.1 years. At birth, average life expectancy must have been much lower than 20 years. The magisterial work on Roman Egypt, conducted by Bagnall and Frier (1994) and based on census data, suggests that only 20 per cent of women survived from their teens into their sixties. At birth, female life expectancy was some 22.5 years, whereas the male equivalent was at least 25 years (1994: 100). However, the Deir el Medina data demonstrate a higher general life expectancy. Boyaval (1977: 350–1) believes its numbers of elderly people to be quite unusual with the village's average age at death being 25+ years. However, the methodology involved is never stated explicitly and determining exact ages at the site would be almost impossible given Bruyère's reports. A more recent general study (Nunn 1996: 22), based on work with Turin collections, suggests that the arithmetic mean age at death for dynastic individuals was 36. Again such a general study can only impact very superficially upon the Deir el Medina data.

In the Eastern Necropolis, Bruyère identified five types of inhumations for infants. The first was burial within pottery jars or amphorae, made in coarse fabrics, both decorated and undecorated. These were common domestic vessels, not originally created for a funerary purpose. Some bear engraved marks which may have indicated the name of the child's family. The majority of vessels contained a foetus, neonate or even a placenta wrapped in stained linen. Associated grave goods, such as beer and ceramics, did not belong to the world of the child, but to an adult world and, as such, were symbolic of adult conceptions of a desirable afterlife. The fact that the placenta, known to represent the twin self and a powerful spiritual force (Pinch 1994: 130), was buried lends weight to the argument that these children were already perceived as embodied individuals – perhaps the physical body itself was all that was necessary to constitute a person whether it survived birth or not. In most cases, a sharp flint, probably used in delivery, accompanied the burial (Bruyère 1937a: 12). We know that items such as these that had close contact with the body of the individual were ritually important, and for that reason were integral to the burial.

The second mode of burial was in re-used baskets or fish baskets made of rushes, simply tied at the two ends. Usually, a torn, darned or imperfect piece of cloth enveloped a small body, most often a stillborn baby. Bruyère (1937a: 12–3) considered this type of interment to be the poorest and least common. There is no evidence of amulets or jewellery, although occasionally these children were buried with several small vases containing bread, raisins, dom palm nuts and grains. These goods were part of the standard adult burial assemblage, rather than a specific constellation constituted around children. The third category, also of wicker work, comprised round or oval baskets, at the bottom of which the child was placed and covered with a shroud or rag. The body was placed in a number of positions, the most common being stretched out upon the back with the hands falling on the lower stomach. Often the child was too tall for the basket, which had to be cut open leaving the shrouded feet exposed at one end. Here again, jewellery was absent, although vases of food for the afterlife were sometimes included.

The fourth form of inhumation was in boxes and chests, primarily re-used household containers. Small children were also placed in roughly hewn wooden boxes that were designed specifically for the funerary context. The burial of a young boy named Iryky merits particular attention (Meskell 1998a: 155). The family that lost this child suffered throughout his life and death – Iryky was so badly deformed that surviving beyond birth must have been somewhat of a miracle. His torso and head were abnormally large and his limbs stunted. He was not the only deformed child in the cemetery who had survived beyond birth; in tomb 1373 there was another, unnamed boy, some 80 cm tall, who suffered from scoliosis. He was buried with jewellery, vases and plates full of bread, grain and dom nuts in an oval basket. Iryky's family also took considerable effort to bury him in a decorated chest, painted yellow with black borders, with hieratic script in black ink, including his name (Bruyère 1937a: 14). That he was supported through life and cared for in death suggests that the welfare of children was a concern in Egyptian society. It is important to add here that box burials were also located under house floors within the settlement enclosure, namely under the house walls of SE VI. Another was found in the 1970s' excavation in the south-western corner of the village (Bonnet and Valbelle 1976: 325). Two other box burials, previously described, were located by Möller in his 1911–13 excavations in the north-eastern sector of the settlement (Anthes 1943).

Coffins are the last relevant category here. These were used for small children and adolescents alike, some coarsely hewn from a tree trunk, others in anthropoid form. While all construction techniques evidenced here were rough, some coffins have a coat of lime wash, and others have yellow painted and varnished figures and inscriptions. In the case of the three children found in tomb 1372 (Bruyère 1937a: 161–4), one is prompted to ask why they were not interred with a family group, which would have been a common alternative. Perhaps, for this socio-economic group a family vault for communal burial could not be afforded, or the parents (or sets of parents) had not begun to construct one at the time of their death. However, this is not in itself a poor burial *per se*. Apart from two anthropoid coffins and one casket, there were six pieces of jewellery, twenty-four objects including ceramics (one a Cretan import), as well as food offerings and unguents. Moreover, there is a simple box burial in the tomb of Sennefer (tomb 1159A) in the Western Necropolis, and considering his own opulent burial plus the rich decoration of this tomb, he could have easily afforded a more elaborate burial for the child. This suggests that age, rather than class or possibly sex, was the determining factor in methods of burial. From this perspective, purely materialistic explanations cannot account for the myriad symbolic factors which may have affected the style of burial chosen for these individuals. The fact that children were often buried on their own lends weight to claims that they were considered individuals and as such warranted their own tombs.

The segmentation of the Eastern Necropolis along age-determined lines also has implications for status and enculturation. It could mirror the status of children in their respective stages of socialization. We know little of these stages, since so little was written about children; some Egyptologists claim that there is evidence for puberty rituals, such as male circumcision, in the textual and iconographic record (see Janssen and Janssen 1990: 90–8). Integral to this socialization was body modification such as changes in hairstyle. For example, there was a tradition of shaving children's heads which we see in both the iconographic and mortuary record, so that Egyptian culture was inscribed upon the body. Perhaps those broad stages of life were represented in the layered organization of the cemetery: neonates in the lowest sector, infants further up, adolescents toward the top with the adults. This would suggest that neonates were considered as embodied or that flesh itself was an integral part of personhood, and may reflect their integration within the family and community (contra Carr 1995: 184). Without textual data on such personal issues we can only surmise at the underlying ideology.

For children, the Deir el Medina burial assemblages were not generally derived specifically from the sphere of childhood as we might expect, with toys or things from the world of children in any modern sense. The objects fall within the standard range of adult grave goods, if a microcosm of it. What might we infer from this? Were these assemblages the result of expediency and lack of thought for the specific context of childhood on the part of the family – in this case almost every family at Deir el Medina? There are exceptions, such as the baby burial under the walls of house SE VI where Bruyère (1937a) recorded finding hieratic ostraca and clay toys – a horse, a 'doll' and a wooden spoon. However, these could have been toys or have simply been interpreted as such due to the context and our own preconceptions of childhood (Robins 1994c: 234–5). It is well known that such 'dolls' form an enigmatic class of objects and have been variously interpreted as dolls, concubine figures and fertility figures, as well as magical, ritual and even sexual aids (Pinch 1993, 1994).

An examination of 18 relatively intact tombs containing children from the Eastern Necropolis reveals that only two burials contained objects that could be interpreted as being specifically made for children during life. In tomb 1378 (Bruyère 1937a: 170) there was a cake in the shape of a male, which the excavator termed a 'doll', and in tomb 1375 (1937a: 167), accompanying a small girl, was a broken figurine. The range of possible interpretations for the latter have been previously discussed. Both objects could be explained in terms of magic and ritual practice which operated at a highly individualistic, rather than state, level (Kemp 1995: 26). Both tombs 1375 and 1378 and the remaining assemblages are remarkably congruous with the large number of adult burials from various sectors of the site. Since it has been suggested that children were named at birth (Feucht 1995: 107), it could be inferred that they were regarded as individuals with tangible trajectories in life and death. According to Hornung (1992: 178), children were named immediately, since without a name the individual did not exist. In addition, if the placenta was treated as a twin self, could it not be argued that form itself was the constituting factor in the formation of an individual, even if he or she did not attain personhood? Obviously the bodies of neonates and children were perceived as different, yet they still possessed a full persona. Feucht (1995: 94) argues from the Hymn to the Aten that the foetus was considered a living being and protection for the unborn was an important requirement in society at large. The mortuary evidence suggests that children as social beings were multiply constituted in the same way as adults. They too must have had all the strands of the person, the *ka*, *ba*, *rn* and so on. However, while the emotional investment in them may have been analogous, the financial outlay in their burial may have been less. Undoubtedly, some children were given much poorer burials which leave no archaeological trace – as also applies to poorer adults. We cannot assume, however, that child burials excavated at Deir el Medina represent quick and meaningless 'disposals' of bodies.

What might we infer archaeologically from the burial of these individuals, apart from the emotive component? First, the Deir el Medina data suggest that burial assemblages were not generally designed specifically for the sphere of children. I suggest that very young children were already considered embodied persons, and their untimely deaths warranted personal responses and care, even at a microcosmic scale, in the same manner as adults. Children were recognized as significant social beings at a very early age, and archaeologists should not simply view their burials as merely reflecting upon the status of their parents (Moore and Scott 1997). Secondly, examination of the Eastern Necropolis tombs suggests that age and class are substantive determining factors, even before sex. Further, sexed difference between small children is not immediately apparent and childhood might have been the pervasive conceptual category. Thus, a contextual analysis at an intra-site level is required if the hierarchical ordering of constituents is to be determined. Evidence from hundreds of tombs in various cemeteries at Deir el Medina suggests that sex should not be privileged or ranked first as the pivotal determinant from which all other forms of difference stem. The tomb data also indicate that analysis at the level of the individual may be more conducive to the multi-levelled historical data available for such a site.

## Conclusion

The Deir el Medina data have much to offer the social archaeologist in terms of hierarchies of difference: rank, wealth, ethnicity, age and sex. I have provided an interpretation of the statistical analysis for ranking at Deir el Medina using tomb data. Socio-economic data, derived from documentary sources, have also been employed to discuss ranking and differential wealth. Other determinants of difference, such as ethnicity, were gleaned from textual as well as funerary data. This chapter has provided the evidence for the major axes of social inequality, namely wealth, sex and age, as identified in the mortuary archaeology, as well as a social framework from which to discuss social inequalities. These variables intersect in fluid ways. In the 18th Dynasty burials of the Western Necropolis difference is constituted around sex and to a lesser degree age. For the less affluent individuals in the Eastern Necropolis the major issue was age and perhaps marital status. So the primary social divide was really based upon wealth, which then splintered off into inequalities based on age or sex, depending on cemetery context. This is in keeping with other cross-cultural findings (Carr 1995: 175), substantiating that vertical social position and age take precedence over sex as structuring principles.

Intact 18th Dynasty tombs from the richer Western Necropolis suggest that as wealth and status increased the relative wealth of wives or female partners declined significantly in the mortuary realm. As described, there is a host of social reasons for women's position throughout life becoming more tenuous, and social ruptures might leave them without support and provision in this life and the next. In contrast, the situation for children appeared to be basically consistent across the social strata. The situation in the later Ramesside period, for which we only have data from the elite Western cemetery, was markedly different. There was a move to generational tombs encompassing many individuals, and while the visibility of women and children increases, together with the decline in Eastern Necropolis tombs, there is still a material discrepancy in favour of elite men and their male relatives. The increase in numbers of individuals present and the more favourable general treatment of women and children continues at Deir el Medina until it reaches an apex in the Graeco-Roman period (Meskell 1997a; Montserrat and Meskell 1997). Without a general and quantifiable background, the highly specific discussions of individual burials appears too idiosyncratic. Both levels of analysis are necessary.

This analysis seeks to provide Egyptology with several demonstrable social and material patterns that fluctuate over space and time, while offering archaeology a critical case study in the fluidities of social relations and cycles of life and the importance of re-centring embodiment. The study illustrates that isolating gender as the primary vector of difference is misplaced, and that our way out of this impasse is to conduct an archaeology of individuals. This corresponds with the findings of third wave feminism, described in chapter 2, according to which a range of social signifiers must be introduced into the debate. Difference is experienced in fluid ways, often through the lenses of class or ethnic inequalities, rather than simply as a result of being male or female. Here we might approach the multiple subjectivities which constitute individual identity. The funerary record at Deir el Medina substantiates that position. According to Cannon (1989: 455), an understanding of social dynamics and the changing meaning of particular symbolic expressions must first involve a study of the historical context of change in mortuary expression. However, understanding social categories or structures is only one part of the process: placing individuals within (or outside) social schemas is the other fundamental dimension in the analysis of social relations and realities. Finally, by reflecting on the complexity and messiness of the social setting of Deir el Medina we may conclude that ours is not the only society to face the dissolution of marriage, the mixed constitution of families and the fluid nature of intimate relations, often grounded on nothing more than ephemeral desire and temporal cycles. We might share similar sentiments and uncertainties, yet the cultural resolutions and historical trajectories are deeply embedded in contextual specificity.

# 5

# Accessing Individuals at
# Deir el Medina

[P]ost-processual archaeology, for the first time in archaeology, seeks
to open up an adequate discussion of the processual relationship
between individual and social norm. More distinctly, however, it does
for the first time introduce something other than process.

Ian Hodder, *Reading the Past*

This chapter returns to the issue of the individual and identity which
I presented at the outset, and demonstrates what can be done to
uncover fragments of life histories. Since concepts of body, person and
self were treated in chapter 3, here I draw out more specific information about individuals and their biographies. Much of the archaeological data comes from discrete tombs that are not supported by
accompanying texts: we are fortunate to find a coffin bearing an
inscribed name. Much of this analysis resembles the silences of prehistory, although I would posit that a sensitive and sensual interpretation is still possible. My approach to these issues is explicitly third
wave feminist. Sexed difference is not simply the key determinant:
other more fluid axes of difference were most often at play. I consider
how factors such as ethnicity, age, class or sexuality were expressed
in terms of material inequalities and bodily treatments. Because we
have substantive economic data from Deir el Medina, such material
differences can be quantified using the 'deben' system. This reflects
more upon the Egyptian experience of inequality, rather than simply
projecting our own cultural notions of quality, expense or difference
between individual burials. Finally, I consider the disjunctures
between the social relationships of living individuals, emotional relationships of love and affection, and the material consequences of
social inequalities which inhered in New Kingdom Egyptian culture.
We should not expect these variable pictures of the past to cohere
neatly, since contradiction and rupture are characteristic of all aspects
of social life.

## An Archaeology of Individuals

How is it possible to locate individual constructions or representations of self from the mortuary record at Deir el Medina? In quantitative analyses individual variation is usually smoothed over for reasons of coherence or in order to establish a clear pattern without background noise and outliers. Such variation, and the construction of interpretations surrounding it, is seen as anecdotal and inconsequential in relation to broader issues. Such a view from the top down does not facilitate an archaeology of the individual or of difference and tends to gloss over the abundant variability present. The very aim of identifying representativeness in effect negates individual variation. When a K-means cluster analysis was applied to the tombs it was immediately apparent that only two or three tombs could be grouped together out of the several hundred that had been entered into the SPSS database. This suggested that the variability was such that clustering on a straightforward basis would be impossible – the range of goods present was too variable and mixed. In many ways, there is no such thing as a typical 18th Dynasty tomb or a typical Ramesside one, though I suspect that 18th Dynasty tombs may demonstrate more individual variability by virtue of their focus on goods from the living world.

At Deir el Medina we can overcome the tension between social structure and individual agency by paying closer attention to the tomb data, especially the material from more secure contexts. It is in these contexts that individual resolutions or negotiations of the factors of age, sex, class, marital status *et cetera* can be examined in reality, rather than simply as a heuristic enterprise. While burial data are of a specific form and may not directly correlate with life experiences (for a general survey, see Wason 1994), the particular nature of Egyptian mortuary practice means that some measure of overlap with the living sphere can be assumed. Mortuary practices are meaningfully constituted: they are chosen to varying degrees in relation to personal intentions, social strategies, attitudes, beliefs and world-view themes (Carr 1995: 117).

The mortuary practices we witness are not passive reflections of social organization; they are the product of active social and personal choices and strategies that might even compromise the dynamics of social relations. It is now axiomatic that mortuary practices can be seen to either idealize the practical, daily social relations that comprise social organization or to invert or mask social relations (Carr 1995: 111). Perhaps we have to view such social relations/realities as operative on several levels, acknowledging that there are tensions and disjunctures between those social levels. In the first instance, there were emotive relationships as experienced between living individuals: between lovers, partners, parents and children; significant textual data and material practices substantiate this. Interconnected with this were cultural practices and beliefs about the social positions of husbands, wives, children and family members. I suggest that the social negotiations we witness, materially, in the 18th Dynasty tombs at Deir el Medina were influenced greatly by these interactions. Personal relationships are a key form of social cohesion. They also structure social and sexual identities and are crucial in sustaining societal patterns and maintaining social divisions (Jamieson 1998: 3). This provides our material basis for the quantification of social inequality discussed in chapter 4. Contrasting with these social experiences are the material expressions of partnerships and familial bonds. Tomb assemblages, like those of Sennefer and Nefertiry, may not replicate any real equality of feeling between husband and wife; rather, they reflect the social inequality of the sexes at this elite level. Moreover, in an Egyptian context the domestic, mortuary, textual and iconographic data might each present different and conflicting profiles of life. Each of these dimensions existed in antiquity, creating their own specific social stresses and contradictions. We have to move reflexively between an analysis of how social structures impact upon people's lives and an analysis of how individuals shape those structures through choice and action (Collier and Yanagisako 1987). Indeed, moving from the general analyses (nomothetic) to the identification of individuals (idiographic) always gives rise to some disjuncture. We should not expect these dimensions to cohere easily and should perhaps suppress any inclination to produce smooth, seamless narratives.

## Material Culture and Life Histories

From the rich and varied suite of artefacts present in Deir el Medina tombs, it is possible to make social inferences based upon material inequalities. There are straightforward indices of variation, neatly summarized by Wason (1994: 93–4): differences based on type, quality, raw material source material and purpose. Each of these taxonomic differences is present in the tomb data from Deir el Medina and potentially offers insight into individual experience and life histories. As Ian Hodder rightly asserts, 'to look at objects by themselves is not really archaeology' (1991b: 4); rather the extrapolation from material culture to social meanings should be our primary concern.

The people of Deir el Medina made very specific, individual choices concerning funerary arrangements at the point of burial, and presumably for a significant period of time during life, since so many resources went into these preparations. Death and burial were pivotal experiences in the lives of the Egyptians, and were considered transitory events in the larger scheme of things. Yet this did not deter people from expressing fears and grief over its acknowledgement. Inbuilt within Egyptian culture was the facility of preparing for one's own death, as well as for those of the immediate family. The villagers must have prepared for their own burials, especially by contracting for tombs to be built and coffins and statuary to be made. The text O. Berlin 12630, from the time of Ramesses III–IV, documents the scribe Amennakht's purchase of a coffin, in exchange for a calf, from the workman Mose (Wente 1990: 162). Tomb assemblages were highly variable at this time, reflecting individual life experiences and personal choices rather than standard responses to death and the afterlife. The deceased, however, could not orchestrate the moment of burial, and we know from texts such as the Will of Naunakhte (Černý 1945) that family members, particularly sons, were responsible for the funeral and interment. Sons (and/or daughters) must have been prepared during life for the deaths of their parents and instructed as to their wishes: individual choices were made concerning bodily treatments, possessions to be included, favourite items and foodstuffs, the funeral arrangements. Much of this must have been discussed during life, and negotiations made between kin as to what should be interred or, alternatively, inherited. This range of individual, personalized behaviours can be hypothesized from the tomb assemblages we see in the cemeteries at Deir el Medina.

More generally, the data suggest that certain groups of artefacts or artefact types give insight into daily practices and individual beliefs: items of magic, work-related objects, leisure items, toiletry articles and so on (see figure 5.1). These artefacts reflect the unique personal world of the individual to a greater degree than perhaps do mundane ceramics, linen or furniture. While these can be informative on an individual level, our reading of specific forms of material culture is often hampered by a lack of cultural knowledge. At present, for example, archaeologists can say more in social terms about magical items than they can say about linen. Among magical or ritual items within the tomb assemblages are some highly idiosyncratic items that may defy explanation, as well as some that may be more informative

**Figure 5.1**   Figurines and statuary from Deir el Medina (courtesy of the IFAO, Cairo)

on a social level. For example, in the 18th Dynasty Eastern Necropolis tomb of the woman Madja (figure 5.2) and her unnamed male companion (tomb 1370) there was an array of unusual finds: gazelle dung in a basket, a small wood and ivory casket containing small pink and green stones, scented earth kept in a linen sachet made into a bag and tied twice, shells kept in a basket (Bruyère 1937a: 150–7). These may all have been magical ingredients. The knotting of string for such a bag was very important because it literally bound the magical forces together or acted as a blocking point (Borghouts 1994: 124). In the same tomb there were three ceramic miniature coffins, made especially for winged insects, that were surrounded by a double necklace of blue and white beads. Presumably, this couple engaged in a variety of obscure magical practices, for protection or to bring about change, or perhaps Madja was one of the 'seers' or wise women of the village (Borghouts 1982, 1994: 128; Baines 1991: 171). Dung was often used in magical spells (Pinch 1994: 128, 134), while shells had potent magico-sexual connotations since they often resembled female genitalia and could be amuletic as well (1994: 107). As noted earlier, in tomb 8 Merit wore a girdle of gold cowrie shells around her hips, presumably acting as both jewellery and amuletic protection for the after-

**Figure 5.2** Decorated coffin of the elderly woman Madja from tomb 1370, Eastern Necropolis, now in the Louvre (photograph by the author)

life. Pebbles, which were found in several Deir el Medina tombs, could also have similar amuletic functions, especially if they were suggestive in shape. The winged insects are more difficult to interpret. Many animals were part of magical practice and the fact that the insect coffins were in sachets like amulet bags may support this notion. Thus, specific items of material culture can reflect personal histories, items of magic or ritual being particularly telling examples. These artefacts have what Gell (1998: 18) would describe as 'agency' in that they have powerful roles in social life. Objects merge with people 'by virtue of the existence of social relations between persons and things, and persons and persons *via* things' (1998: 12). This allows for an archaeology of agency, intention, causation, result and transformation, regarding individuals and material culture.

Magical practices seem to have increased or become more visible in the Ramesside period. In tombs 1444, 1450, 1451 and 1453 (Bruyère 1930: 92–115), for example, magical papyri or ostraca were placed with the deceased. This development is further supported by the presence of a large number of medical and magical texts (L. Lesko 1994a: 133). Texts such as these could be placed in the tombs for two reasons:

for the benefit of the deceased or to protect the living against the dead individual (Pinch 1994: 150). Presumably these items were placed there by family members, for whom they may have been advantageous in either way. In tomb 1444 of the 20th Dynasty, magical papyri were attached to a collar on a string 55 cm long which was accompanied by a figure of Taweret and a human shape: the associated name may be female. In tomb 1453 a burnt female statuette was recovered. The burning may attest to a magical practice or simply result from post-depositional burning within the tomb. Effigies were central to many sinister spells (see Pinch 1994). Another example could be the wax statuette found in the vicinity of tomb 290 (Bruyère 1924: 10–15; Bruyère and Kuentz 1926). The wax was modelled around a stone, with the hands flat against the body. This might have been a magical figure involved in funerary rites or one that was commonly used in execration magic. While I do not attempt to document all ritual or magical practices at the site, the presence of such specific and personal items of material culture can offer insight into social relations among the villagers in the spheres of life and of death.

Other glimpses of individual identities can be gleaned from the inclusion of more mundane items. For instance, various tombs contain needles and needle holders, usually made from bronze and papyrus respectively (for example, tombs 1370, 1381, 1382, 1389, 1450 and 8). Most of these tombs contained the bodies of women and some may posit that these women were actively engaged in sewing, either privately for family members or as a means of domestic production that could be traded to supplement their income. Textual data from the site substantiate the presence of such an industry (Janssen 1975: 536), as in the case of the notorious chief workman Paneb who made various wives of the village weave cloth for him. Apparently his colleague, Hay, did much the same thing but managed to escape the community's scorn. An interesting tomb is 1389, which contained a bronze needle and papyrus holder though it had a single male burial. Bruyère (1937a: 202) decided that there must have been another occupant, the presence of the needle being used to support this hypothesis. However, it should not be discounted that men could possess these items and use them in everyday life. For one thing, in the New Kingdom weavers were commonly male; activities such as weaving should not be rigidly sex-linked.

More common are tools related specifically to tomb construction that were found in 18th Dynasty tombs (8, 1159A, 1089, 1057) and in ones from the 19th and 20th Dynasties (1, 217, 357, 1445, 337, 1060). Many of these appear to be sculptor's tools which were generally found in more affluent tombs of important individuals, such as Sennedjem (tomb 1), Ipy (tomb 217), Qen (tomb 337) and Kha (tomb 8): they therefore correlate with professional status. Kha's work tools are exceptional in both craftsmanship and expense, being worked with gold foil and ebony. They are also inscribed, and one appears to have been given by pharaoh himself. This object is obviously revealing in relation to his unique status as chief workman. Sennedjem (tomb 1) and Sennefer (tomb 1159A) also had tools relating to tomb construction, some of which were inscribed, though they seem not to have been of the same standard as Kha's. Other unusual tools were found in poorer tombs of the Eastern Necropolis, some of them bronze objects. There was also a copper balance in a wooden box (tomb 1370). This might suggest that its owner, the woman Madja, or her male partner, may have been involved in jewellery production or metal-working. They may have also been traders using the proto-currency deben. From Janssen's study (1975), we know that such transactions were frequent in village life, as were ones conducted at the riverbank, or *mryt*. One representation in the Theban tomb of Qenamun depicts a woman trading alongside other men at what appears to be a riverbank. Such activities cannot be ruled out for the villagers at Deir el Medina (McDowell 1992, 1994: 46; Meskell 1994b). Other items may reflect the presentation of the individual in the sphere of death, while also relating to experiences during life. Clothing, jewellery, musical instruments, games, figurines and statuary may also provide clues to life experiences, interests and professions. Goods of these types are more frequent in 18th Dynasty assemblages than in those of the later Ramesside or Third Intermediate Periods. The artefact classes discussed above suggest that histories and personal experiences might be teased out from the archaeological record. They offer insight into individual difference and variation which, although represented in the mortuary sphere, may also be telling in terms of life experiences.

## Individual Variability and Costings

To access individuals I have suggested profiling discrete tombs in terms of the range of tomb goods and the ultimate cost using Egyptian measures. Stuart Tyson Smith (1992: 196) has proposed that wealth and status are reflected in the variety and number of tomb goods. This can only represent the wealth index in the most general way, since many of the poorer Eastern Necropolis tombs contain a surprising amount of material, coupled with considerable internal variation. My database of Deir el Medina tombs illustrates some 341 items for the tomb of Madja (tomb 1370), while tomb 1388 had 248 items, and tomb 1389 contained 225 objects (these totals include food counts). These are all 18th Dynasty tombs, and can be compared with a wealthy contemporary tomb in the Western Necropolis, that of Sennefer (tomb 1159A), which contained only 121 artefacts. However, Kha's tomb (tomb 8) contained some 506 goods which is somewhat higher than the Eastern Necropolis examples. In terms of variation of artefacts present, Madja's tomb had some 65 separate types of goods, whereas Sennefer's had only 29 distinct types. Both were basically intact tombs. Given that looting has greatly diminished the number of finds in most tombs, no firm conclusion can be reached at this stage. But the intact examples demonstrate that one cannot make simple reductive correlations between the number of goods or the degree of variation and tomb wealth. Each case should be examined in context to determine factors such as quality, expense and outlay distribution. For instance, the construction of Sennefer's tomb and its subsequent decoration is more telling than its burial assemblage, which is quite limited.

Accessing this level of individual variation presents the researcher with a complex and time-consuming exercise, and one which is open to interpretation. One approach worth pursuing is individual costings in order to add precision to the ranking of burials on the basis of age, sex, status, marital status and possibly even ethnicity. Potentially this is the most telling means of accessing both differential status (on the basis of social factors) and constructions of self. It is possible to deduce rough estimates for New Kingdom tomb goods at Deir el Medina because we have both the material data and textual documentation from the general period recording relative prices. Ostraca from the village, recording numerous economic transactions, have been gathered and analysed by Janssen (1975). Though the barter system was operative, the villagers recorded their purchases in units of deben. However, much of the usable burial data derives from the early to mid-18th Dynasty whereas the price data are concentrated in the later Ramesside Period. Any results need to be qualified by the following assertions: (a) prices given are approximate and relative (rather than absolute), since price fluctuation and inflation probably occurred; (2) Ramesside prices are not always standard and qualitative differences must be allowed for. There may be a considerable price range for some goods such as beds, coffins, livestock and so on. I have derived individual costings from Janssen's work (1975) and

Smith's (1992) subsequent analysis. Furthermore, I have tried to take into account the quality of goods present where possible, which diverges from Smith's project. Costings in themselves are likely to rely on highly subjective decisions. Smith tended to focus on the burial as constituting a unit that normatively reflected the status/wealth of the male, rather than on the burials of discrete individuals. His aim is to demonstrate the sliding scale of wealth from the very poor tombs of the West Bank, through the middle ranking Deir el Medina burials, to the more elaborate tombs of the high officials (Valley of the Nobles) and the royal family themselves (Valleys of the Kings and Queens). This is an interesting and productive exercise that differs from my aim of addressing individuals.

In the following section I employ thick description to profile the circumstances of individuals in their burial context. Following Geertz (1973: 28), '[t]he aim is to draw large conclusions from small, but very densely textured facts.' It is an attempt to reinstate the narrative element in terms of biography and embodiment. My project has been indelibly influenced by Susan Kus (1998) and her call for an 'open-ended and continuing exploration of all the entailments, enticements and entanglements of "sensuous human practice" in practice and in theory'. I have previously explored the possibilities of biography and reconstruction by focusing on the burial of husband and wife, Kha and Merit (Meskell 1998c) excavated by Ernesto Schiaparelli (1927). This was an exceptionally wealthy tomb in which the social inequalities of a husband and wife were mirrored in the material disparities between their individual interments. The wealth present there was equivalent to a lifetime's salary, which is in keeping with the Egyptian practice of preparing for burial throughout life. From my analysis, the chief workman Kha had some 196 goods assigned to him by name, costing a total of 3,919 deben. His wife Merit appeared directly to own 39 objects, totalling 787 deben. Goods that could be described as shared, in that they name both individuals, total only 129 deben. Several of Kha's more expensive items have a supra-economic prestige value, such as his gold necklace of valour and gold-covered cubit measure, which were gifts from pharaoh, whereas Merit's do not. It is not simply a matter of *quantitative* difference, there was also a marked *qualitative* difference between the goods of husband and wife. For example, the decorated boxes of Kha are carefully painted and engraved, whereas Merit's tend to look poorly constructed and inscribed, with the exception of her wig-box. It seems likely that Merit died before Kha since she was buried in a coffin originally designed for her husband. Kha then commissioned a series of coffins with gold ornament and fine workmanship for himself. The treatment of their bodies also illustrated a substantial difference: his bodily treatment was more elaborate than hers, so that his body was better preserved for eternity. Neither body was embalmed. At present we do not know the cost or organization of such mortuary preparations. X-ray analysis showed Kha's body was adorned with substantially more gold jewellery and amulets (Curto and Mancini 1968: 78–9) than the pieces placed on Merit's body. This tomb provides a striking example of the disjunctures between relationship and reality that are common in the elite tombs of the Western Necropolis. Further salient examples are described in the sections that follow.

## Sennefer and Nefertiry (Tomb 1159A)

The rather impressive burial of the man, Sennefer, is in striking contrast to that of the woman who accompanied him into the afterlife (Bruyère 1929: 40–73) (figure 5.3). She is named only once on her rather cheap ready-made coffin, as Nefertiry. Unlike Sennefer, her body had no death mask, objects, wreaths or flowers, and was simply wrapped in bandages. The small child buried with them bore no name or association, had no objects, amulets or jewellery, and its body was poorly prepared. Considering the wealth evident in this tomb, there is a marked discrepancy in distribution on the basis of sex and age (see box 5.1). Over 25 items are either inscribed with the name of

**Box 5.1**   Contents of tomb 1159A

| Goods belonging to Sennefer | Price in deben |
| --- | --- |
| Funerary bed, painted white | 20 |
| Decorated shroud | 75 |
| Plain linen shroud | 50 |
| Stool in wood and leather, naming Sennefer | 8 |
| Elaborate anthropoid coffin | 95 |
| Funerary mask | 35 |
| Garlands of flowers | 2 |
| Large scarab necklace in black stone | 36 |
| Wood/gold pectoral | 40 |
| Wooden headrest | 5 |

| | |
|---|---|
| Bronze situla | 24 |
| Bronze jug | 24 |
| Bronze basin | 24 |
| Bronze plate | 24 |
| Bronze bowl | 24 |
| A cubit in wood and ebony | 10 |
| Sandals | 2 |
| 2 wooden shabtis, painted | 2 |
| Fan, ebony and ivory, naming Sennefer | 8 |
| Wooden measuring stick | 6 |
| *Total* | *514 deben* |

| *Goods belonging to Nefertiry* | *Price in deben* |
|---|---|
| Elaborate coffin | 95 |
| Collar | 10 |
| Bracelet | 10 |
| 2 rings | 8 |
| *Total* | *123 deben* |

| *Goods possibly shared or unknown* | *Price in deben* |
|---|---|
| 17 large bouquets of flowers | 17 |
| Wooden box | 10 |
| 2 large canes | 4 |
| Female figurine | 2 |
| 1 vase | 1 |
| 3 plates with fruit, grain and dom nuts | 6 |
| 4 bead collars | 40 |
| *Total* | *80 deben* |

| *Goods belonging to the infant* | *Price in deben* |
|---|---|
| Simple wooden box | 10 |
| *Total* | *10 deben* |

**Figure 5.3**   Coffins of Sennefer and Nefertiry, tomb 1159A in the Western Necropolis at Deir el Medina, dating to the 18th Dynasty (courtesy of the IFAO, Cairo)

Sennefer or were placed on his body, whereas Nefertiry had no amulets, but only a collar, an elbow bracelet, wrist bracelet and ring. Together with her coffin, these total five objects. As evident with Merit, Nefertiry's body is very badly decomposed and basically skeletal, in contrast with the superior treatment and elaboration of Sennefer's body.

Again, there is a clear emphasis on male wealth, with a ratio in excess of 4:1 in favour of Sennefer's goods. The adult male Sennefer's burial cost 514 deben, plus the cost of bodily preparation which we know to be more elaborate than that of Nefertiry or the infant. Nefertiry's burial, minus wrapping, cost 123 deben, while that of the child was a meagre 10 deben. Items that cannot be directly attributed to an individual or could be seen as communal totalled 80 deben. Since the tombs of Kha and Merit (tomb 8) and of Sennefer and Nefertiry (tomb 1159A) were intact burials, these results are not due to looting or post-depositional factors. The situation present in the Western Necropolis is markedly different from the early to mid-18th Dynasty burial patterns in the Eastern Necropolis. One case in the Western Necropolis which bridges the gap between Western and Eastern Necropoleis burial patterns is the late 18th Dynasty tomb 1352 of the man Setau, probably dating to the reign of Akhenaten. Some of the goods seem to be in an Amarna or post-Amarna style.

## Setau, Taat, Bakiset and the Others (Tomb 1352)

Five individuals were buried in this Western Necropolis vault, four in coffins (Setau, Taat, unnamed young female, Bakiset) and one in a box (male infant). The representation of females and younger individuals is significant. Bruyère (1937b: 95–107) surmised that Setau was approximately 60 years old and the woman Taat was in her 40s, while the unnamed female was quite young and about 1.5m tall, and Bakiset was an even younger girl, only about 1.25m tall. Bruyère gave no approximate ages for the younger girls. The representation of sexed individuals here is more akin to that evidenced in the Eastern Necropolis than appears to have been the norm in the Western Necropolis. The level of wealth and its general distribution are also in keeping with the earlier Eastern Necropolis burials (see box 5.2). The costings that can be estimated for females and adolescents in this tomb are similar to those in the less affluent Eastern Necropolis in that they are often equal to, and are sometimes even superior to, males, which is not the case in the Western Necropolis. In the latter cemetery there are no clear examples of female wealth outstripping male in either the 18th or 19th Dynasty burials.

Although Bruyère (1937b) clearly attributed the tomb to Setau, Servant in the Place of Truth, his burial was significantly cheaper than that of the unnamed female. Setau's interment cost 62 deben (plus wrapping), whereas the anonymous young female's cost 116 deben (plus the cost of wrapping). It is primarily her jewellery that accounted for the increased cost: it was made from stones such as carnelian, lapis and turquoise, together totalling 63 deben. The burial of the woman Taat cost 52 deben, which is not dissimilar to that of the young girl, Bakiset, at 40 deben, and the infant boy at 31 deben. His burial is interesting since his box-coffin was rather cheap (20 deben), but he was buried with 11 deben worth of jewellery. The older female Bakiset had no jewellery whatsoever, while the mother Taat only wore one ring, costing about 4 deben. These finds illustrate once more that jewellery cannot be ascribed as a female artefact class, and is not always correlated with older individuals who would have had time to accrue such items.

**Box 5.2**   Contents of tomb 1352

| Goods belonging to Setau | Price in deben |
| --- | --- |
| Wooden shabti | 10 |
| Wooden headrest, naming Setau | 5 |
| Sandals | 2 |
| Anthropoid coffin | 40 |
| Bronze ring | 4 |
| Long wooden cane | 1 |
| *Total* | *62 deben* |

| Goods belonging to unnamed female | Price in deben |
| --- | --- |
| Anthropoid coffin | 40 |
| Small wooden box | 3 |
| 8 faience rings | 32 |
| Bead necklace | 5 |
| Ivory earring | 2 |
| Bracelet in ivory, carnelian, lapis | 10 |
| Funerary amulet, *wḏ3t* eye | 10 |
| Faience ring | 4 |
| Bead bracelet | 10 |
| *Total* | *116 deben* |

| Goods belonging to Taat | Price in deben |
| --- | --- |
| Anthropoid coffin | 40 |
| 2 canes | 2 |
| Scribal palette of May | 1 |
| Wooden headrest of May | 5 |
| Signet ring | 4 |
| *Total* | *52 deben* |

| Goods belonging to Bakiset | Price in deben |
| --- | --- |
| Anthropoid coffin | 40 |

| Total | 40 deben |
|---|---|

| Goods belonging to the male infant | Price in deben |
|---|---|
| Wooden chest | 20 |
| Earring in ivory | 2 |
| Cane stool | 1 |
| Basket | 3 |
| Blue faience necklace | 5 |

| Total | 31 deben |
|---|---|

| Goods possibly shared | Price in deben |
|---|---|
| 2 large ceramic plates, red | 2 |
| 6 small ceramic plates | 6 |
| 1 small ceramic amphora | 1 |
| 3 small ceramic beds | 3 |
| Female figurine, ceramic | 1 |
| Reclining female figurine, ceramic | 1 |
| Wooden statuette | 15 |
| Wooden box | 10 |
| Mummy of a quadruped in fish basket | 5 |
| Bouquets of persea | 1 |
| Food models | 1 |
| Ceremonial cane | 1 |
| 2 wooden low seats | 16 |
| Oval basket | 3 |
| Unguent vase | 10 |
| Small ceramic vase | 1 |
| Decorated amphora with beer | 2 |

| Total | 80 deben |
|---|---|

This tomb exhibits other anomalies in terms of sex-linked goods. Within Taat's coffin were two canes, a scribal palette inscribed with the name of the man May, and an inscribed wooden headrest belonging to the same man. Bruyère explained their presence as being the result of robbery, yet purposefully placing goods belonging to someone else into a coffin seems beyond the bounds of stealing. There is some evidence that the contents of the tomb were disturbed in a minor way, notably because items of jewellery belonging to the unnamed young female appear to be damaged. The pilfering appears to be fairly insignificant given the amount of easily obtainable, portable material which remained on her body and in the tomb generally. It may represent petty looting accompanying a later interment. However, one should not assume differential robbery of male goods, since it is unlikely that robbery as an activity was sexed. None of this explains the seemingly male goods which were discovered in the coffin of the woman Taat. There is no reason why women cannot have owned canes and there are several examples where this is the case at Deir el Medina; so that this type of good cannot be sex-linked. As for the inscribed goods of May, it is possible that he offered these to the deceased, or that they were acquired by the family and deposited in a meaningful way. Canes and headrests were frequently found within coffins, while scribal palettes are often associated finds in the tomb. We know from the coffin that Taat was mother to about nine children and perhaps May was one of her offspring. The placement of goods belonging to offspring in their parents' tombs is also quite common; for example, with canes and boxes in the tomb of Kha and Merit. Another possibility is that Taat used those goods herself in life, although this is purely speculative. Thus, Bruyère may have been too hasty in explaining away this variation from what he considered normative and using the incident of robbery to account for individual difference. The salient point here is that one must be cautious when ascribing goods on the basis of *a priori* notions of sex and sex-linked attributes. The evidence from Deir el Medina repeatedly demonstrates that artefact categories are not easily or normatively assigned to any specific group: cosmetics, items of grooming, jewellery, perfume, razors, mirrors, tools, canes, figurines can belong to individuals regardless of age, sex or even, in some cases, status.

As a postscript to this tomb, the tally of goods which cannot be directly associated, or could conceivably be shared items, totals 80 deben. Among the array of common goods, such as ceramics, foodstuffs, baskets and beer, are three bed models and two female figurines in clay. These specific items presumably relate to female fertility (especially in the afterlife), sexuality, rebirth and potency. They are often associated with women, and have been found in both domestic and mortuary contexts (Pinch 1993). They might attest to concerns felt in the living world, or might simply have acted as a safeguard for the next. Their inclusion in the tomb might further strengthen the case for this tomb having a stronger female emphasis than usually seen in the Western Necropolis at this date. Only through a full and contextual analysis of the presentation of individuals in a given tomb can meaningful social dynamics be inferred.

## Madja and her Husband? (Tomb 1370)

The next set of tombs to be examined are those from the 18th Dynasty in the Eastern Necropolis. Here the situation prevailing between the sexes appears to be more balanced and egalitarian. Box 5.3 lists the goods belonging to the aged woman Madja and her unnamed male companion (figure 5.4). Bruyère (1937a: 150) estimated that the male died first and was buried against the east wall. He also believed the tomb had been slightly looted during the interment of Madja,

**Figure 5.4** The 18th Dynasty tomb contents of tomb 1370 from the Eastern Necropolis. The anthropomorphic coffin of Madja is behind (see figure 5.2), while the unnamed man's coffin is at the front covered with tomb goods (courtesy of the IFAO, Cairo)

**Box 5.3** Contents of tomb 1370

| Goods belonging to the old man | Price in deben |
|---|---|
| Decorated coffin | 40 |
| Alabaster kohl jar | 2 |
| Bronze tool | 6 |
| 3 scarabs | 6 |
| Folded linens | 10 |
| Musical instrument | 20 |
| Bracelet | 10 |
| Sandals | 2 |
| *Total* | *96 deben* |

| Goods belonging to Madja | Price in deben |
|---|---|
| Decorated coffin | 40 |
| Faience cup | 1.5 |
| Stone kohl jar | 2 |
| Folded linens | 10 |
| Bronze mirror | 12 |
| Bracelet | 10 |
| 5 scarab rings | 20 |
| *Total* | *95.5 deben* |

| Goods possibly shared or unknown | Price in deben |
|---|---|
| 2 wooden beds | 40 |
| 2 wooden stools | 16 |
| 2 decorated amphorae | 4 |
| Headrest | 5 |
| 3 ceramic vases, empty | 3 |
| 8 baskets | 24 |
| 2 stone vases | 30 |
| Copper scales | 5 |
| Bronze tool | 6 |
| Stick/pestle | 2 |
| Wood/ivory small box | 3 |
| Wooden comb | 1 |

| | |
|---|---|
| Bronze needles | 2 |
| Liquid fat in horn | 10 |
| Food models | 1 |
| 11 small pots of grease/fat | 110 |
| Paints | 2 |
| 2 kohl jars | 4 |
| Flint razor | 1 |
| Scarab | 2 |
| 2 cane stools | 2 |
| 3 beer amphorae | 6 |
| 1 large pot of grease | 30 |
| 8 flower pots with food | 16 |
| 3 small model sarcophagi with insects | 15 |
| 2 pots with food | 4 |
| Copper vase | 24 |
| 6 plates with food | 12 |
| 1 plate | 1 |
| 1 cane | 2 |
| A parcel of rags | 5 |
| *Total* | *388 deben* |

although it does not appear to have been greatly disturbed (1937a: 145). As the list shows, the items directly associated with the bodies of the male and female are almost exactly the same in terms of cost: 96 deben for the male and 95.5 deben for the female. Their type of burial and general expenditure is also generally comparable. There are, of course, items reflecting personal pursuits: he had a musical instrument and Madja had her mirror. Among the shared goods, which total 388 deben, the duplication of certain personal possessions suggests a substantial degree of equality. For example, there are two wooden beds and two wooden stools, which may have been the belongings of both husband and wife. Goods contained in numerous baskets may also have been equally distributed or shared possessions.

## Nubiyiti and the Others (Tomb 1382)

In this tomb Bruyère (1937a: 183–8) discovered three coffins placed side by side against the south wall (figure 5.5). Apparently, the tomb

**Figure 5.5** The 18th Dynasty tomb contents of tomb 1382 from the Eastern Necropolis. The coffin of the unnamed female is at the front and that of Nubiyiti is behind (courtesy of the IFAO, Cairo)

was intended for a single coffin, and was then enlarged to accommodate the additional two coffins. An elderly man, poorly preserved, was found in a plain white chest coffin. A young female was found in one of the decorated coffins, while the second woman was found in another decorated coffin. The latter woman seems to have been named Nubiyiti, and Bruyère thought she was a foreigner, presumably on the basis of her name. If ethnicity was a major factor in this context, it was not borne out materially. Finds can be classified as those which are directly associated with the individual, though the majority were not ascribed and were simply lined up along the eastern wall of the vault in front of all three coffins. Most of them belong to categories already seen as typical shared goods or unattributable items (see box 5.4).

Tomb 1382 shows the marked sex-based difference in tomb wealth typical of the Eastern Necropolis. Here we almost have a situation

**Box 5.4** Contents of tomb 1382

| Goods belonging to the old man | Price in deben |
| --- | --- |
| Undecorated casket coffin | 20 |
| *Total* | *20 deben* |

| Goods belonging to Nubiyiti | Price in deben |
| --- | --- |
| Decorated coffin | 40 |
| 1 pair of earrings | 10 |
| 2 small collars of gold and carnelian | 40 |
| Bracelet of 6 carnelian scarabs | 10 |
| 2 rings, enamel and carnelian | 8 |
| *Total* | *108 deben* |

| Goods belonging to unnamed female | Price in deben |
| --- | --- |
| Decorated coffin | 40 |
| Horn filled with unguent | 10 |
| Collar of enamel amulets | 5 |
| Sachet of raisins, grain | 1 |
| Collar of gold and carnelian beads | 40 |
| Bracelet of enamel scarabs | 10 |
| 2 scarab rings, carnelian and faience | 8 |
| *Total* | *114 deben* |

| Goods possibly shared or unknown | Price in deben |
| --- | --- |
| Papyrus box full of biscuits | 2 |
| 11 baskets | 33 |
| Bronze mirror | 12 |
| Small box made from bone | 3 |
| Faience decorated bowl | 1.5 |
| Faience ring support | 1 |
| 4 alabaster kohl vases | 8 |
| 2 alabaster unguent vases | 20 |

| | |
|---|---|
| Ebony stibium | 1 |
| 2 breccia/jasper kohl vases with galena | 30 |
| 2 wooden combs | 2 |
| Alabaster vase | 2 |
| Ceramic saucer | 1 |
| Beads | 1 |
| 5 small vases with nuts, figs, nabeca, grain | 5 |
| Small ceramic plate | 1 |
| 2 wooden needles | 1 |
| 2 vases with black decoration | 4 |
| 2 undecorated vases | 2 |
| 1 flower pot with nuts, bread, figs, raisins | 2 |
| 6 ceramic cups used as lamps | 6 |
| *Total* | *138.5 deben* |

where the sex-linked patterns of the Western Necropolis are inverted. This is perhaps an extreme example, but it throws into sharp relief the need to examine individual tombs and individual burials in context. Here was a very poor burial of an elderly male, totalling only 20 deben (plus wrapping). Next to him were two females with fairly similar burials which total 108 deben (Nubiyiti) and 114 (unnamed female), respectively. Each female had approximately the same amount, and kind, of jewellery, often made from the same materials – carnelian, gold and enamel. There is a greater degree of symmetry between the two women than between either of them and the unnamed man. This also suggests that ethnicity may not be an important factor at this social level, since both women have markedly similar burials costing roughly the same price. At this time, during the 18th Dynasty at Deir el Medina, among the less affluent and lower-status individuals found in the Eastern Necropolis, neither sex nor ethnicity appears to be the formative structuring principle for determining tomb wealth. In terms of sex at least, this is the opposite of the situation present in the higher status, elite cemetery on the other side of the village. The Western Necropolis undoubtedly had more expensive tombs (both in the 18th and 19th Dynasties) and yet this was where women were under-represented and their burials were considerably poorer than those of their male counterparts.

## Satre and the Other Woman? (Tomb 1388)

This tomb is another example of a double burial in the Eastern Necropolis from the first half of the 18th Dynasty; however, both individuals were female (figure 5.6). Satre, a young woman, about 1.62 m tall with black hair to her shoulders, was buried with an expression of intense suffering on her face – something which is quite difficult to explain given burial preparations (see Bruyère 1937a: 191). The unnamed woman next to her, in an almost identical coffin, was also quite young, about 1.6 m tall with long, black, braided hair. Both women seem to have been of similar age, had good teeth, and received the same kind of wrapping. However, the unnamed female was basically skeletal and in a much poorer condition than Satre. It is not possible to determine who was buried first, but the casket coffin of Satre is positioned closer to the south wall of the vault. Tomb provisions scattered in the vault almost encircle both coffins. One might suggest tentatively that the goods placed in the narrow gap of about 20 cm between Satre's coffin and the south wall were intended for her, while

**Figure 5.6** The 18th Dynasty tomb contents of tomb 1388 from the Eastern Necropolis. The coffin of the unnamed female is at the front and that of Satre is behind (courtesy of the IFAO, Cairo)

those in the north corner were associated with the other woman. This is purely speculative due to the cramped nature of the vault, and may not represent any meaningful association. Since it is possible to identify specific items from Bruyère's numbered recording, I separate the goods into the two possible associations, but I do not draw firm conclusions from them. The other goods are ascribed to Satre and her unnamed companion on the basis of inscriptions or of placement on the body or within the coffin (see box 5.5).

Unfortunately, there is no stated affiliation for these women, either traceable by name or from coffin inscriptions. Satre's name is attested only in her coffin decoration. The women could have been sisters, cousins, companions, wives of the same husband, or mother and daughter, buried at different times. The latter two possibilities are rather unlikely: while such occurrences may have been common, there is not a great deal of documented data for double burials of women. Our natural assumption when a male and female are buried together is to assume marriage, yet no such relationship of intimacy is ever postulated for the burial of same-sex individuals (for example, Bietti

---

**Box 5.5**   Contents of tomb 1388

| Goods belonging to Satre | Price in deben |
| --- | --- |
| Decorated casket coffin | 40 |
| Shroud for coffin | 50 |
| Bracelet of beads, carnelian, stone | 10 |
| Carnelian scarab in gold | 40 |
| 1 ring with 2 scarabs | 4 |
| *Total* | *144 deben* |

| Goods belonging to unnamed female | Price in deben |
| --- | --- |
| Decorated casket coffin | 40 |
| Shroud for coffin | 50 |
| Green faience scarab | 10 |
| Carnelian scarab | 10 |
| Faience kohl vase | 2 |
| Bastet vase in faience | 2 |
| Basket | 3 |
| Alabaster kohl vase | 2 |

| Ebony stibium | 1 |
|---|---|
| *Total* | *120 deben* |

| *Goods possibly associated with Satre* | *Price in deben* |
|---|---|
| 5 baskets | 15 |
| 11 small vases with resin or wax | 110 |
| Persea fruit | 1 |
| Grain, dom nuts, raisins | 2 |
| Alabaster kohl vase | 2 |
| Ebony stibium | 1 |
| Bread | 1 |
| 1 ceramic vase, empty | 1 |
| 7 bowls with nuts, bread, fruit, veg. | 14 |
| *Total* | *147 deben* |

| *Goods possibly associated with unnamed female* | *Price in deben* |
|---|---|
| Branches of persea | 1 |
| 3 baskets | 9 |
| Bronze razor | 3 |
| Leather sandals | 4 |
| Raisins, figs, meat, grain | 10 |
| 2 pieces of cloth | 30 |
| 6 small vases with wax, grease, honey | 60 |
| Bracelet with beads | 5 |
| Ring of beads | 2 |
| 4 empty vases | 4 |
| 4 flower pots with bread and food | 8 |
| 10 small empty vases | 10 |
| 3 small decorated vases | 6 |
| 6 plates with food | 6 |
| 1 small vase with beer | 1 |
| 1 bowl with food | 1 |
| 1 large beer amphora | 2 |
| 1 foreign vase | 2 |
| *Total* | *164 deben* |

Sestieri 1992: 179). To point this out is not to propose that women such as these were lesbians, but simply to underscore the normative heterosexist narratives we constantly create in our historical interpretations. For example, because Bruyère found pieces of light-coloured hair placed in one of the containers he was at pains to suggest that a male may once have been present in the tomb. First, there is no evidence to suggest that the hair belonged to a male. Secondly, human hair was often placed as a memento in New Kingdom tombs, both at Deir el Medina and in the tomb of Tutankhamun. So Bruyère's thesis seems to be more a reflection of the desire to construct a normative scenario than to interpret the tomb as it stands. Thirdly, there was no evidence that this tomb had been pillaged at any time, as Bruyère himself noted, unlike others in the Eastern Necropolis. The tomb was found intact. There was perhaps enough room for a third coffin, though this would have made the vault space significantly more cramped than the majority of comparable burials. In sum, in order to interpret the tomb as anything other than the burial of two women, one would have to construct a rather elaborate scenario and go against the evidence at hand.

Aside from the question of a putative male counterpart, these women had somewhat similar burials that appear to have cost much the same, although the items themselves vary according to individual. Satre's burial (except wrapping) cost 144 deben, while her companion's cost 120 deben. Satre had more jewellery, some with elements of gold. Her companion had little jewellery, but her coffin contained more items, such as stone and faience vessels and items of make-up. The overall uniformity is similarly found in the associated burial assemblage, which fell approximately into two spatial areas, as noted above. The goods surrounding the coffin of Satre totalled 147 deben, and those at the side and front of the other female totalled 164 deben. Some of the items are the same, but there is a fair degree of variation. While the exact prices in deben cannot be reliably calculated, the relative values of the two groups should be taken as fairly secure. Thus, the total cost of specific individually associated artefacts, plus the loosely associated ones, were roughly equal for both women. This typifies the broadly egalitarian treatment of individuals we have already witnessed in the Eastern Necropolis. Lastly, women who lived on the fringes of kin groups, by choice or through divorce or widowhood, had few options for burial. There is no reason to deny their close relationships with other women. There are certainly texts (see McDowell 1999: 41, 43) that demonstrate women's charity to each other in hard times. These friendships were evidently vital relationships in terms of an individual's well-being, both emotionally and financially, especially in the domestic sphere. The threat of homelessness was ever present, and texts from Deir el Medina show that women might inherit meagre huts to ameliorate this situation in later life. As women grew older their prospects were very different from men, and we should not rule out the possibility that women might reside together both in life and for eternity.

## Ramesside Individuals in the Western Necropolis

So far, the burials examined and costed have been restricted to the 18th Dynasty, from the Western Necropolis (tombs 1159A and 1352) and the Eastern Necropolis (tombs 1370, 1382, 1388). It has emerged that there were marked differences in burial patterns between east and west, especially in the treatment of age and sex. Thus status and wealth determined in the first instance how age and sex relations were to be structured and reflected through the burial of individuals. On a gross level, the wealthier a man became in the 18th Dynasty at Deir el Medina, the more likely he was to have greater relative wealth in comparison with his wife or offspring. Conversely, for individuals who were less wealthy and had somewhat lower status, differences on the basis of age, sex, ethnicity and even marital status were minor. Age was perhaps the strongest determinant for differences in burial cost, particularly if one was pre-pubescent. After puberty individuals appear to have been treated similarly.

It is now expedient to determine the situation for the Ramesside Period and if the archaeological evidence can illustrate changing social phenomena. Elsewhere I have argued that the Ramesside Period at Deir el Medina reflects a new social awareness among the inhabitants, with changes in monumental structures, tomb decoration, religious ideology, emphasis in burial assemblages, number of individuals interred and bodily preparations (Meskell 1999). Unlike the tombs of the Eastern Necropolis in the 18th Dynasty, Ramesside tombs were large and multi-vaulted with massive superstructures consisting of pyramids, decorated chapels and courtyards. The inner vaults were stone-cut and elaborately painted. The burial of individuals effectively ceased at this time and the Eastern Necropolis fell out of use altogether. The Western Necropolis became the prime location for burial. Familial relations were highlighted and generations of family members (and extended family) were buried together. Such a marked intra-site change must have had social ramifications for both living and dead members of the community. I now consider whether burial wealth exemplifies social change. The single most informative tomb of this time is that of Sennedjem. Beautifully decorated and now open to the public, this tomb clearly demonstrates the radical shift of the Ramesside Period. I devote most attention to it because, while similar examples have been investigated (Meskell 1997a), the disturbed condition of many of them makes their description less compelling.

## Sennedjem, Iyneferti and their Lineage (Tomb 1)

Sennedjem belonged to the Deir el Medina community during the 19th Dynasty. His tomb complex consists of a large courtyard with two chapels and a total of three solar pyramids (see figure 5.7). The decorated chapels feature the children of Sennedjem, primarily his sons Khons and Khabekhenet. The vaults were opened by Gaston Maspero and precious items were subsequently distributed overseas to Moscow, Copenhagen, Berlin and Madrid (Janssen 1975: 210). Bruyère re-excavated and published this communal tomb and it is possible to glean valuable information from the extant burial data (Daressy 1920, 1928; Toda 1920). Twenty bodies were reported as being present in the tomb: twelve males, four females, one unsexed body, and three infants, one of whom was designated as female. Two of the unnamed neonates were placed in yellow painted boxes. Approximately 115 goods can be ascribed to male individuals, 21 to females, while only five could be considered as shared, in the sense that they name both male and female individuals (see box 5.6).

Bruyère (1926: 190–2) claimed that these bodies represent three generations, and this is borne out by the genealogical data. It is possible that more bodies were contained in the tomb and some were in very poor condition. This fits with the pattern of burial wealth demonstrated in box 5.6. The immediate family, particularly the males, had the lion's share of funerary wealth, whereas some of the extended members of the family had relatively poor burial provision. The profile of the data suggests that not all of the material was recorded. For example, Mesu does not appear to have a coffin of any type, yet he had an offering table and a handful of shabtis. Even if certain artefacts for various individuals are missing, the marked relative ratios of tomb goods will remain. Sennedjem, Khons and Iyneferti had disproportionately expensive burials, particularly

**Figure 5.7** Restored 19th Dynasty pyramid tomb of Sennedjem (tomb 1), Western Necropolis (photograph by the author)

Sennedjem. Costings are restricted only to inscribed goods (Valbelle 1985: 297). It is impossible to establish anything meaningful from the actual assemblage since exact positions were not recorded. The unattributed items consisted largely of ceramics and furniture.

Although women were quite well represented in tomb 1, they were far from equal in number to their male counterparts. More men were buried within the tomb, and subsequently more men were named, and more male inscribed goods were present. Moreover, male burials tended to cost more than those of their female relatives. Even if some

**Box 5.6** Contents of tomb 1

| Goods belonging to Sennedjem (male) | Price in deben |
| --- | --- |
| Chair of Sennedjem | 20 |
| 2 elaborate coffins | 190 |
| 2 funerary masks | 70 |
| 3 pectorals | 120 |
| Canopic casket | 20 |
| Shabtis of different materials | 9 |
| 4 shabti coffins | 20 |
| Catafalque/sledge | 60 |
| 6 canes | 24 |
| Small table | 15 |
| Stool | 8 |
| Wooden baton | 2 |
| 4 large stone statues | 60 |
| 3 stone statues | 45 |
| 12 amphorae with wine etc. | 360 |
| Cubit measure | 6 |
| Builder's grid | 6 |
| 2 builder's tools | 12 |
| *Total* | *1047 deben* |

| Goods belonging to Iyneferti (female) | Price in deben |
| --- | --- |
| 2 elaborate coffins | 190 |
| 1 funerary mask | 35 |
| 1 canopic casket | 20 |
| 4 shabtis of different materials | 4 |
| 6 boxes | 60 |
| 2 stools | 16 |
| *Total* | *325 deben* |

| Goods belonging to Khons (male) | Price in deben |
| --- | --- |
| Catafalque/sledge | 60 |
| 2 elaborate coffins | 190 |
| 1 funerary mask | 35 |
| 1 pectoral | 40 |
| 1 canopic casket | 20 |

| 13 shabtis of different materials | 13 |
|---|---|
| 1 shabti box | 5 |
| 4 boxes | 40 |
| 3 canes | 12 |

| Total | 415 deben |
|---|---|

| Goods belonging to Tamaket (female) | Price in deben |
|---|---|
| 2 elaborate coffins | 190 |
| 1 canopic casket | 20 |
| 4 shabtis of different materials | 4 |

| Total | 214 deben |
|---|---|

| Goods belonging to Isis (female) | Price in deben |
|---|---|
| 1 decorated coffin | 95 |
| 1 canopic casket | 20 |
| 1 box | 10 |

| Total | 125 deben |
|---|---|

| Goods belonging to Ramose (male) | Price in deben |
|---|---|
| 1 decorated coffin | 95 |
| 1 shabti box | 5 |
| 3 shabtis of different materials | 3 |
| 1 box | 10 |

| Total | 113 deben |
|---|---|

| Goods belonging to Parahotep (male) | Price in deben |
|---|---|
| 1 decorated coffin | 95 |
| 1 shabti | 1 |

| Total | 96 deben |
|---|---|

| Goods belonging to Tashesen (female) | Price in deben |
|---|---|
| 1 decorated coffin | 95 |
| 1 shabti | 1 |

| Total | 96 deben |
|---|---|

| Goods belonging to Khabekhenet (male) | Price in deben |
|---|---|
| 1 canopic casket | 20 |
| 2 shabti boxes | 10 |
| 2 shabtis | 2 |
| 6 boxes | 60 |
| Total | 92 deben |

| Goods belonging to Hathor (female) | Price in deben |
|---|---|
| 1 decorated child's coffin | 40 |
| Total | 40 deben |

| Goods belonging to Mesu (male) | Price in deben |
|---|---|
| 5 shabtis of different materials | 5 |
| 2 tables of offerings | 30 |
| Total | 35 deben |

| Goods belonging to Paramenekhu (male) | Price in deben |
|---|---|
| 1 shabti box | 5 |
| Total | 5 deben |

| Goods belonging to Hotepu (male) | Price in deben |
|---|---|
| 1 shabti | 1 |
| Total | 1 deben |

| Goods belonging to Amenakhu (male) | Price in deben |
|---|---|
| 1 shabti | 1 |
| Total | 1 deben |

goods are missing from this supposedly intact tomb, it would be hard to argue that the loss was selective and focused upon the burials of women. The difference between the totals of men's and women's burials is approximately 1,000 deben. Furthermore, there is a significant disparity between the burials of husband and wife, with Sennedjem's burial totalling at least 1,047 deben, while Iyneferti's was around 325 deben. Ramesside tombs have more occupants and tend to include a host of family members (both nuclear and extended), meaning a substantial increase in the representation of women and children, from the 18th to the 19th Dynasty. Despite the increased numbers of women and children, their relative wealth is still comparatively low. For example, Sennedjem's son Khons appears to have had a more expensive burial than his mother Iyneferti. The reason why the other son, Khabekhenet, has a rather unimpressive total is due to the fact that he was not in the end buried in the tomb. He constructed his own elaborate tomb complex next door to that of his father, tomb 2. Only a handful of goods bearing his name were in the tomb. Perhaps these represented funerary offerings to his deceased parents.

This pattern of greater male wealth, at the expense of female family members, seems to have remained fixed in the Western Necropolis for the 18th, 19th and 20th Dynasties. While this forms the general pattern, it is important to remember that individuals transcended these implicit rules as is evident from tomb 1352 of Setau, Taat and others. Here, at the end of the 18th Dynasty, an unnamed female far outstripped her male companion in burial wealth. These deviations from the norm were the product of individual and individual circumstances. Such slippages between society and individual are potentially the most informative about social relationships and social dynamics. Case studies like these impel us to rethink the reductive strategies that Giddens, Bourdieu and even Foucault might instigate. They also make clear the relevance of Egyptian data to interrogate top-down approaches to social life.

At Deir el Medina, while more individuals, both male and female, were represented in the Ramesside tombs, the ratio of male items to female remained high. Male wealth was still far in advance of that of women. In the tomb of Qaha (Bruyère 1933: 71–122) male wealth totalled 315 deben, whereas female goods equalled 240 deben, with 90 deben of shared items. In Nakhtamun's tomb (Bruyère 1926: 113–78), the inscribed goods of men totalled 136 deben, while those of women's only 35.5 deben. Male goods remaining in the tomb of Thothermaktwf (Bruyère 1930: 70–80) totalled 237.4 deben, but female wealth was only 30.1 deben. Unlike the intact 18th Dynasty tombs examined previously, these tomb groups had been reduced due to robbery, but losses through theft cannot account for the predominance of male wealth in the funerary sphere. We see this repeated in the Ramesside context. In an extreme case, Amenwia's tomb 356 had 165 deben in male inscribed artefacts and none that could be ascribed to women (Bruyère 1929: 76–93). This does not mean that women were not buried in the tomb, but rather that their burials were less expensive and less detectable due to the lack of named goods. It could also reflect a reduction in the inclusion of named personal items of women – their furniture, toilet sets, boxes, statues and so on. Such a situation would accord with changes already described for the end of the 18th Dynasty. In addition, the pattern suggests that magical items and those relating to funerary ritual (statues, stelae, canopic jars, shabtis) were produced less for women – and certainly children – than for men. This would have had serious consequences in terms of the afterlife. Given the knowledge of ideologies and practices surrounding the body in death, women and children would not have had access to the godly bodies to which men could aspire. Without the accoutrements of death and enhanced bodily status, there would have been significant difference in afterlife experiences. Thus, social inequalities must have extended into the hereafter, assuring men their traditional primacy and relegating many women and children to obscurity.

## Statistical Conclusions

Statistical interpretations bear out the significant degree of variation among tombs at the site. The tombs do not cluster in a meaningful way. While general patterning can be deduced from surveying all 18th Dynasty burials, and then all Ramesside ones as subsets of the total, this method should be balanced by a finer level of analysis that examines specific tombs and the individual burials within them. Both levels of analysis are necessary to provide a more accurate, sensitive picture of social life and experience. I have shown that it is possible to deduce general patterns concerning age, sex and status from the mortuary data. The 18th Dynasty burials in the Eastern Necropolis have burials for men and women that were egalitarian in terms of expense. There were exceptions, however, and on occasion women had more expensive burials than men. In the 18th Dynasty Western Necropolis, wealthier individuals spent more, often very much more, on the burials of males than females. Here, too, some examples did not fit this general pattern, such as the tomb of Setau (1352). For the Ramesside Period, women, children and extended family members are far better attested than for the 18th Dynasty, but this bodily representation was not generally matched by funerary expenditure on women and children. In some cases, such as that of Qaha (tomb 360), the disparity between husband and wife is not as marked as others, notably Sennedjem (tomb 1). In the latter tomb, father and son received the majority of the funerary wealth. However, other, presumably lesser, relatives of both sexes received much the same in terms of cost. Females such as Isis and Tashesen and the males Ramose and Parahotep all had approximately the same funerary wealth, of around 100 deben. One level down, the young girl Hathor's burial cost much the same as those of the males Mesu, Peramenakhtw and Hotepu, all being under 40 deben. There is no simple equation here based on sex: a high-ranking female would normally have a wealthier burial than a male servant. Within different status groups, the age and sex of an individual could take on different levels of importance, being the source of economic inequality in wealthier contexts like the Western Necropolis, and not an issue at all for the lower-status individuals in the Eastern Necropolis. I suggest that patterns of social difference were fluid, rather than monolithic structures.

The Deir el Medina data reinforce the problems associated with the search for representativeness in archaeological theorizing and illustrate the need for more nuanced cross-cutting examinations. In light of the interpretations presented here, nomothetic analyses based on large categorizations will fall short. It is important to examine individual tombs in context, and the individual burials within them. Only at this level can one discover where the constituents of difference intersect and which aspects are integral in the construction of self for eternity. Layered on this are concepts of embodiment and enculturation; that is, how various groups were socialized, experienced themselves during life and were prepared for the afterlife. The richness of the material data at Deir el Medina affords social analysis at this level. In this study two approaches to the archaeological data of the village have been adopted to illustrate the potential for an archaeology of individuals. First, it is possible to target specific artefacts that express social meaning and negotiations, whether it be the desire for magical intervention or personal troubles revolving around fertility and children. Secondly, contextual analyses of specific tombs and individual burials can provide a social profile for those individuals and for the social relations reflected in the mortuary sphere. Clearly, the addition of the textual record to the material would provide an even more compelling narrative and this is feasible to some degree for the Ramesside members of the community. Since hardly any texts about the community in the 18th Dynasty survive, we are left with the archaeological data for that period. It is to be hoped that the value of reconstructing an archaeological past in addition to a textual one is something that Egyptologists can recognize.

## Embedding Ancient Individuals

Evidence from Deir el Medina illustrates that a contextual analysis of mortuary data can provide a meaningful framework from which to conduct an archaeology of individuals, as well as social interaction and intentionality. Accessing individuals in a historical context appears to be an easier enterprise than for prehistoric scenarios, yet it also yields more checks, less flexibility, and more contradictions. Much of the mortuary evidence at Deir el Medina is not surrounded by textual data, but can only be set against a general Egyptian cultural framework. We have substantial information concerning Egyptian notions of the body, self and death, coupled with emotional attestations of fear and grief at facing death (see chapter 3): this dimension of lived experience should be explored further. We should also re-centre the emotive dimension when dealing with the issue of death and burial (Tarlow 1992, 1999; Meskell 1994a). Archaeologists still remain locked in the language of objectivity and exclude the subjective experience of the present and of the past. One should not mask the 'emotional force of bereavement by reducing funerary ritual to orderly routine' (Rosaldo 1986: 186). In this context, the Egyptians said: 'none returns from there to tell their conditions, to tell their state, to reassure us, until we attain the place where they have gone.'[17] There is a marked disjuncture between Egyptian feelings of confidence and uncertainty when facing death, and this is evidenced clearly in Ramesside Deir el Medina.

The evidence from Deir el Medina highlights a considerable dissonance between evocations of love among individuals and the real differences of material culture and bodily preparation in the mortuary sphere. Since the Egyptians prepared through much of their lives for this momentous transition, the tomb data also shed light on their living experiences. Although we might possess love poems from Deir el Medina, and these close attachments were real and compelling, these texts present a picture that is often at odds with the materiality of social relations we see evidenced in the tombs. Such poetry forms a specific genre, one that perhaps reduces difference and falls into established styles. It is likely that these letters were written by men and that corresponding accounts and sentiments from women are sadly absent, even if some poems feature a woman's point of view. The sexual love expressed in this poetry is thus a male construction: 'My heart thrills, my arms stretch out to embrace her. My heart is carefree in its place, like a red-fish in its fish-pond. Oh night, you are mine forever, since (my) mistress has come to me.'[18] Concomitantly, the archaeology of the settlement site and the tombs highlights the importance and high-profile nature of men's lives, at the expense of their female counterparts. The representation of women in the domestic context, in terms of named individuals, is exceedingly poor in comparison with men (Meskell 1998f: 221). The invisibility of beloved wives and children in material terms seems at odds with the documented importance of expressions of love, as embodied in literary lyrics: 'It is love of her that makes me strong! She shall cast a water spell for me. I see my heart's love standing right before my face!'[19] These intimate relations operated on different levels, among which were emotional ties between individuals, sexed inequalities at particular class levels, and social norms and expectations in the cultural realm. A multi-dimensional analysis might present a range of different vignettes, yet this complex picture may be closer to the elaborate contradictions of reality, both as they existed in the past and as they do in the present. According to feminists and postmodernists alike, disjuncture and fragmentation characterize our own cultural climate. This may, in fact, represent nothing new.

Like the modern sociological accounts of the individual highlighted at the outset, accounts of intimacy and relationships in pre-modern societies are severely limited and ethnocentric. According to Jamieson's (1998) account, people in the past were bound together by necessity and tradition. Life was characterized by a lack of privacy or desire for it. Empathy between individuals was lacking given the highly stratified and gendered nature of social relations. Love and care between parents and children and partners was generally tempered by those same social and sexed boundaries. Marrying and having children were economic arrangements in which men were perceived as owning both women and children, a view sanctioned by law, religion and community regulations (Jamieson 1998: 17). While we might acknowledge, for example, that the concept of romantic love is relatively modern, or that the concept of childhood as a sacred sphere is also a recent, Western construction, this cannot negate variability in other cultures both past and present. Pre-modern societies cannot be treated as a monolithic entity *in toto* and cultures are not subject to social stasis, despite the fact that archaeologists may not have the tools to expose shifting social relations. In our own society, within a few generations, there have been quantum changes in concepts of the emotional self, relationships and family structures. Clearly, it is easier for us to see cultural variability and disjuncture in our own society than to recognize the same qualities in past cultures.

## Conclusion

Some sentiments in the above narrative are likely to be valid for ancient as well as modern contexts. However, the data from New Kingdom Egypt challenge most ethnocentric claims, providing evidence for a complex array of intimate relations, some based on community or economic pressures and others seemingly based on love and passion. These relations are attested through letters to loved ones, in life and in death. Moreover, no marriage ceremony existed in Egypt; a couple set up house together to seal their union (Toivari 1998). There appear to have been no sanctions against sexual relations before achieving this state. Separation was also common and had economic ramifications for both parties. Moreover, we do not have a monopoly of love for children, as is shown in the Egyptian desire to bear children, adoptions of children, and the treatment of infants in burial. Yet this does not mean that their category of childhood matched our own. I have argued that children are often depicted in sexual scenarios and may have been perceived in a way similar to adults, being expected to work, and play. Unlike the position in modern societies, children did not form the centre of family interactions (Strathern 1992; Jamieson 1998: 26–9). While we may value individuality and choice above all else, this does not mean that these issues were unknown to other groups and that they existed in oppressive, inflexible social systems. Egypt is a case in point, and if a similar level of data were available for other ancient civilizations, would we be less likely to generalize so readily? In many respects I have attempted to answer Susan Kus's (1992, 1998) call for a truly anthropological archaeology, and for greater emphasis on the sensuous qualities of human experience. It is to be hoped that this re-centres human agency, choice and volition, rather than imposing narrow models of oppression, singular narratives and rigid social constructionism.

In asking why we still treat ancient people as other, in a manner from which anthropologists have long since disentangled themselves,

I would turn to Foucault (1972: 9). In Foucauldian terms, modern groups use historical narratives to embed themselves at the civilized end of the social continuum. It is no wonder that we have sought to privilege our own position by separating ourselves and our social practices from those of pre-modern groups. However, as Western European history so painfully reminds us, we are not free from the oppression of women and sexual minorities, the exploitation of specific racial and class groups, and the economic and sexual exploitation of very young children. We should also acknowledge that the depth of feelings between individuals is not necessarily borne out or reflected in material or social spheres. Thus, Egyptian men and women experienced social inequalities and material differences while simultaneously claiming real equality of feeling in emotional terms (Meskell 1998c: 377). We need to challenge the idea that in Egyptian society, for example, there was a unitary reason for entering into a marriage (our closest equivalent term). For the lower and middle classes, the reasons were not necessarily economic or due to family machinations; mutual affection could have been a central motive. As in Egypt, so in our own society, there was a host of reasons for people to enter into partnerships and as many reasons for dissolving the union. In his discussion of the Hellenistic world, Foucault stated (1986: 75) that marriage was 'a voluntary agreement entered into by the partners, who pledged themselves personally'. The same could be said of New Kingdom Egypt.

# Epilogue

People from bygone ages seem infinitely remote from us. We do not feel justified in ascribing to them any underlying intentions beyond those they formally express; we are amazed when we come upon a sentiment more or less akin to what we feel today . . . .

Marcel Proust, *Remembrance of Things Past*

I hope to have demonstrated that the archaeology of Deir el Medina offers a unique opportunity to examine the complex interrelationships between social factors such as status, wealth, sex, age and ethnicity as they are played out in the material culture of specific tombs and among members of the community. From textual records we know that the inhabitants of the village ranged from wealthy architects and craftsmen and their families to lower class servants or slaves, providing a diverse spectrum of wealth and status from which to draw life histories. Moreover, it is one of the few archaeological case studies where one can test whether sex is the primary structuring principle for social inequality. My analysis suggests that other factors were more significant for social negotiations, specifically age and status, and aims to reinstate the individual and individual agency, rather than resorting to the nomothetic analyses which have characterized archaeological discourse. From this perspective, it is possible to see how social factors intersect and become hierarchically organized at an individual level. By combining a rich archaeological context with recent theoretical developments in archaeology and the social sciences, it should be possible to bridge the gap between the diverse fields of Egyptology and archaeology.

In New Kingdom Deir el Medina the burials of children, couples, family groups and generations – sometimes named individuals with written histories – illustrate how constructions of self and social relations were embodied. I have discussed how Egyptian views of corporeality, personhood and emotion were resolved and reinforced materially in the face of death, as well as being mediated by factors such as age and status. Rarely have such social aspects of life been considered from an archaeological perspective that can shed light on areas not discussed in the texts, such as social structure or the creation of personalized funerary assemblages. In tomb 8 we see the close association of Kha to the reigning pharaoh and the impressive gifts bestowed upon him; in tomb 1370, the woman Madja seems to have been a village seer or magician; in 1352, Setau and Taat retained magical items associated with childlessness or infant mortality relating to their own personal experience; in 1379, the woman Ibentitina appears to have been a foreigner introduced and integrated into the community, as may have been the woman Nubiyiti in 1382. The site provides a unique opportunity to examine the recursive creation of society and selves, from large-scale social process to individual choices and presentations of selfhood.

I have advocated a dialectic approach that moves between contemporary social theory and archaeological data. Given the wealth of Deir el Medina data it is possible to go beyond descriptive archaeology to consider social process, materiality and individual agency. As set out in chapter 1, I propose that a balance should be struck between individualizing and communal strategies. Archaeology's concern has always been with representativeness, seeking to uncover generalizing practices and behaviours rather than individual embodied responses. That approach cannot facilitate an archaeology of difference. We must qualify these assumptions by recognizing that the relationship between individuals and society is far more complex and infinitely variable than can be explained by a simple, uni-dimensional deductive model. The evidence from Deir el Medina, a historic milieu with multi-levelled data, challenges previous assumptions and suggests that we can construct an archaeology of individuals and their social relations.

## Implications for a Social Archaeology

Throughout this book I have made reference to a host of issues and concepts now topical in the social sciences: sex and gender, the body, social inequality, difference, the individual, power, the quest for representativeness, structure and agency, as well as death and the emotive dimension. The theoretical position I advocate here, concerning many of these themes has already been applied to a variety of Egyptian and

Mediterranean material (Meskell 1994a, 1996a, 1998a,c; Knapp and Meskell 1997). The archaeological contexts covered in those publications are both prehistoric and historic; none is problem free. As Clive Gamble (1998) has demonstrated, prehistory should not be dismissed as an impossible domain of investigation in terms of individual action and agency. My results suggest that complex societies, such as Egypt, with a wealth of cultural information may provide a more meaningful framework from which to conduct an archaeology of individuals. The cultural material lessens the tendency to project our categories and notions on to ancient cultures. Material and documentary data reveal their own internal tensions, sometimes supporting, and other times contradicting, one another. The two data sets must be employed dialectically, and we should not expect to produce seamless narratives; rather, they should reflect the contingencies and disjunctures of social systems.

I have also interrogated some of the privileged categories that have become central in Western discourse, notably those of sex and gender. From the outset I have embraced a third wave feminist approach, arguing that the binary construction of sex:gender is not appropriate in all archaeological contexts. In Egypt it may be expedient to talk in terms of sex rather than gender, since this is perhaps closer to what the Egyptians experienced. I would not make explicit claims for third sex individuals in this particular context. Language creates discourses and knowledge and it is better to situate our studies within the relevant cultural context than to impose our own. In a study focusing on prehistoric Cypriot figurines, I have argued that the traditional sexual dyad (male and female) may not be appropriate in all representational terms (Knapp and Meskell 1997). It depends entirely upon the cultural context. It has also been possible to investigate Egyptian notions of sexuality and to confirm that they differed significantly from our own. Textual data suggest that sexual practices were fluid rather than categorical, although the material correlates of such information prove more difficult to locate.

In addition, I have critiqued gender archaeology for its continuation of Western Cartesian categories and its preoccupation with *women* as if they constituted a uniform and universal group. Women are not synonymous with gender, and our studies should be opened out to include men, children and other groups. To assume unity on the basis of biology is to fall prey to a universalizing tendency that cannot encompass the totality of human experience. It also privileges specific forms of difference in a canonical way: the enterprise is thus nomothetic, rather than idiographic. We cannot assume that sexed difference is the immediate structuring principle from which all others disseminate since all the major axes of difference, race, class, ethnicity, sexuality and religion, intersect with sex in ways that proffer a multiplicity of subject positions that need to be examined contextually within any discourse (McNay 1992; Moore 1994: 57). Deir el Medina has proved a convincing testing ground for highlighting the complexity of social inequality and the limitations of positioning sex as the single, primary vector of difference. For example, poorer women were buried with the same expenditure as their male counterparts, and sometimes even exceeded it. By contrast, wealthier women tended to have substantially less than their male partners. Archaeologists of gender must move beyond the identification of women, especially those who draw on ethnographic, iconographic or royal/elite data. Rather we should look toward an archaeology of difference. Judith Butler (1993: 168) has called for exploration of the historical contexts where the constituents of difference are singled out or converge with other factors. Archaeology is well placed to uncover and interpret this information.

In terms of persons, bodies and selves, the textual record informs us that the Egyptians perceived themselves as multi-faceted individuals whose own embodiment transcended death. They were concerned with questions that surfaced in later European philosophy, about being and non-being, about the meaning of death, the constitution of the body, the nature of the cosmos and humanity, and about the basis of human society. We are fortunate to have this cultural information, which we should apply critically to the archaeological record. For those who are engaged in contemporary debates, the material offers evidence to challenge social theorists who propound that the individual is a post-Enlightenment bourgeois concept and that the modern body is essentially different from that of ancient times due to the intervention of technology. Here we are talking about matters of scale, and definitional changes rather than absolute differences, given that the Egyptians had complex ideologies about selfhood and sophisticated practices surrounding the body in death.

Part of the problem with much recent social archaeology in Britain revolves around the application of dense post-structuralist theory (Gosden 1992) to the scant remains of prehistoric architecture and material culture. Much of this interesting work fails to mesh appropriate data adequately with continental philosophy. Bruce Trigger (1998: 2) also imputes to archaeologists a fascination with exotic theory, the danger being that 'archaeologists will fall under the influence of philosophies that do not match the needs or practice of their research, with a consequent wasting of valuable time and effort.' We need to examine the scales of relevance between our data sets and the social theory we apply to them, especially in terms of embodiment and being. While archaeologists naturally wish to engage with extrinsic social theory, it seems imperative to choose appropriate archaeological materials. One has to ask whether doing a particular style of theory or interpreting our data meaningfully is more important. Since most archaeologists will never be grand theorists, as the lack of independent archaeological theory has demonstrated, we may do well to concentrate on doing a better interpretive archaeology.

Throughout this volume there has been a implicit cry for a more grounded archaeology, not at the expense of theory, but rather for its more appropriate integration. This is not a reactionary programmatic statement to curtail the hard-won freedoms of archaeological theorizing, which is a welcome departure from the scientific positivist tyranny of the New Archaeology. As shown, I see great insights to be gleaned from many social theorists, but the reason why these theorists seem so exciting lies in the recognition that their ideas can impact on archaeological data, that they can illuminate in ways that I had not previously encountered. They are not within the present text simply because Butler or Foucault have become buzz words, or to illustrate my intellectual heritage: they are included because they have changed the way I conceive of the data. But the data came first; and when simple theories of oppression and domination fell short, something more nuanced and sophisticated had to be apprehended. This explanation might seem simplistic, but it is related to the concept of radical empiricism, coined by Michael Jackson (1989: 148). Attempting to bypass the dualistic choice of subject or object, theory or practice, thought or feeling, Jackson calls for a grounded experience of actual events, objects and interpersonal relationships while acknowledging the probabilities of coterminous junctions and slippages. Because the Egyptian data are so rich, they have a voice of their own, and should be allowed to speak to us, to suggest narratives that may or may not fit with a particular fashionable theory. Trigger (1998: 18) has gone so far as to say that accessing belief systems from written records or oral traditions 'counts far more than any cross-cultural generalization or any amount of non-textual archaeological evidence'. As an anonymous commentator remarked at the Interpretive Archaeology Conference in 1991, 'the central problem in archaeology has ceased to be a lack of theoretical tools, but is now a lack of people who are skilled in using the tools to create interesting and valuable accounts of the past' (quoted in Hodder et al. 1995: 231).

This volume also presents a range of arguments that are intended to deflect the influence of Foucauldian archaeology, with its emphasis on power at the expense of the individual, agency and choice. As I have shown, there are inherent problems with the uncritical adoption of extreme forms of social constructionism that privilege impersonal forces such as *culture*, *discourse* or *power*, in which these terms occupy the grammatical site of the subject after the 'human' has been dislodged from its place. Most constructionist positions are essentially deterministic and evacuate or displace human agency (Butler 1993: 9). It may prove expedient to review, if not dispense with, these constructed categories, which serve to universalize the generalities of human experience rather than (re)construct or (re)place individual persons. The villagers of Deir el Medina testify to their own social mobility, through merit, favouritism, bribery, crime or adoption. A slave girl becomes pregnant to a sculptor, a well-to-do man of the village, and instantly he ensures that she will be provided for. Her social standing is irrevocably changed (Toivari in progress). The man Hesysunebef was once a slave, but was later adopted by his master and became a member of the team of workmen, eventually attaining the notable rank of deputy. He expressed his devotion to his adoptive parents by naming a son and a daughter after them and by dedicating a stela to his father (McDowell 1999: 50). The young boy Paneb was adopted by the benevolent chief workman Neferhotep whom he later attacked in the village. Paneb became so powerful and corrupt that a number of his more serious crimes seem to have gone unpunished because of his social connections (Černý 1929). These narratives reveal that social rules were not so inflexible as to impede the movement of individuals. A balance must be struck between structure and agency, between communal and individualizing strategies.

## Archaeology and Foucault's Concept of History

Dispersed throughout this study are various critiques of Michel Foucault's writings, notably his discussions of power and the inscribed body, though much of the polemic addressed is filtered through archaeology's disciplinary adoption of Foucauldian theories. Foucault's work is undoubtedly problematic, yet significantly more criticism must be levelled at archaeologists who employ a simplistic (and decontextualized) overlaying of his work. One body of Foucauldian theory, which seems to have direct potential in a rather understated way, is his notion of history. Expounded ironically in *The Archaeol-*

*ogy of Knowledge* (1972), this has received comparatively little attention (but see Tilley 1990).

Historians, and by implication archaeologists, have been primarily concerned with revealing stable structures and processes, with continuity being the optimum goal rather than disjuncture. Foucault talked of a past passion for linear successions being overthrown by ever more levels of analysis, each with its own discontinuities and patterns. He oscillated between a gloomy picture of the fruitless search for total history or cultural totality, and the optimism that we have embarked on a new enterprise focused on displacements and transformations: 'In short, the history of thought, of knowledge, of philosophy, of literature seems to be seeking, and discovering more and more discontinuities, whereas history itself appears to be abandoning the irruption of events in favour of stable structures' (Foucault 1972: 6). This is similar to Derrida's statement that '[i]f the word history did not in and of itself convey the motif of the final repression of difference, one could say that only differences can be "historical" from the outset and in each of their aspects' (1983: 11). One could see this as being an extension of postmodern thought with its predilection for rupture and fragmentation. I argue that such a predilection goes beyond heuristic posturing and is, in fact, a more adequate representation of our knowledge of the past. As I have argued in chapters 4 and 5, we should seek different levels of analysis and not expect them to cohere neatly, but rather to present a host of interpretive pictures of individuals and their experiences. Textual information, personal accounts, settlement archaeology and funerary data might all represent different experiences of and in the past. Disjuncture need not be negative or contradictory and variability need not be smoothed over for the sake of a mistaken unity that may lend spurious weight to a convincing argument.

Foucault deconstructs our own disciplinary practices when he notes our treatment of the documentary (or material) record, how we organize, divide, distribute and order the text. Historical discourse tries to define within that material unities, totalities, series and relations (1972: 6–7). This is almost unavoidably archaeology's project, as it has been my own to some degree in this volume. Difference and individual variability have also been central themes. There is always a tension between the two, yet the full potential of operating between both levels has yet to be fully explored within the field. To be relevant and meaningful, our studies need to contribute to general understandings, while to be true to our data we must reveal the contingencies and contradictions that characterize human behaviour. In view of this, the desire for cultural totality might well be abandoned as I contended in chapter 1.

Moving out from this notion of history, Foucault indirectly articulated the processes by which history is operationalized in our society, focusing again on the notion of discontinuity. I read him as saying that it is this very difference between the past and ourselves which acts as a positional device for us to recreate history and construct ourselves simultaneously. This is particularly germane to the discussions of sex, gender and sexualities I outlined in chapter 2. Foucault stated (1972: 9) that the notion of discontinuity is a paradoxical one since it is both an instrument and an object of research. The historical enterprise individualizes different domains only through comparison and serves to locate the author in the process. Foucault's histories reflect a self-referential concept of knowledge.

I would take this paradox further to suggest that scholars constantly move back and forth between familiarity with the past and awareness of its very strangeness. Archaeology, in this perspective, becomes a strategic enterprise. Michel de Certeau plays with a similar concept in his discussion of the body, which is another major theme of this book. He states, that '[t]he opacity of the body in movement, gesticulating, walking, taking its pleasure, is what indefinitely organises a *here* in relation to an *abroad*, a "familiarity" in relation to a "foreignness"' (1984: 130). The interplay between connections of similarity and strangeness is particularly observable with the study of ancient Egypt, though this is seldom acknowledged (but see Parkinson 1997). Deir el Medina has been suburbanized and colonized largely because of our documentary knowledge of the site. We know many of the villagers' names, their genealogies, and some sensational events which touched their lives. But we always have to be careful, not complacent. Texts suggest a link of commonality between cultures because translation flattens out cultural difference. The material data from the site present a stranger picture, one that could be seen as often at odds with the texts. Everyday life, ritual practices and cultural norms all lie beyond our experience. Yet because the data sets are so rich we can tack back and forth between different levels of data and move closer towards the ancient Egyptians.

Egyptologists have an illusion of familiarity with the Ramesside community of Deir el Medina, whom we *know* through the villagers' prolific documentary output. By contrast, we can only make contact with the 18th Dynasty villagers materially, through their bodies, their relationships to other individuals interred with them, their funerary goods (most taken from life) and the tombs themselves. This mode of approach acts as a potential distancing device, reminding us that their daily and ritual lives were remote from us. The 18th Dynasty tombs in the Western, and particularly Eastern, Necropoleis demonstrate how individuals were represented within tombs. Men, women and children were buried in a variety of ways taking into account their status, wealth, age, sex, ethnicity and marital status – all those factors separated by commas, as Butler comments (1993: 168). Each determinant of difference intersects in multiple ways with other social dimensions. Social personae and life histories are also reflected in these burials. We can examine how class and status might primarily structure the presentation of self, after which other differences might be displayed in degrees of intensity – whether it be age, sex, marital status or even ethnicity, which seems to have been smoothed over in the mortuary sphere. This is the value of a third wave feminist approach. We all experience ourselves as a constellation of fluid identities in an embodied way, as has always been the case. The body constitutes the locus of identity, self and agency. The person as bodily presence is the locus – and the pretext – of action. So in all these musings it is important to re-centre the body in social experience (Hastrup 1995), especially in an Egyptian cultural milieu. In sum, an archaeology of individuals necessarily fluctuates back and forth between the familiarity and strangeness of the past and thus serves to situate ourselves in the process. From this perspective, archaeology becomes a relevant social science that says something about culture, selves and difference both in antiquity and in a contemporary setting.

## The Relevance of a Social Archaeology

Archaeological and historical discourse might then have important social implications. Foucault demonstrated that the present becomes visible only through juxtaposition with the past. Foucault's concept of genealogy reminds us that current meanings are not necessarily obvious, harmless or coherent and this is further undermined by demonstrating that radically different meanings existed in the past. Genealogy erodes the coherence of present belief or normative systems, such as concepts of sex, sexuality, the body, personhood and difference. Yet old meanings are not completely erased by new ones: there is no *tabula rasa* in the social realm. As Foucault stated (1977b: 146): 'we should not be deceived into thinking that this heritage is an acquisition, a possession that grows and solidifies; rather it is an unstable assemblage of faults, fissures, and heterogeneous layers that threaten the fragile inheritor from within or from underneath.' Given this knowledge, social categories and social dynamics should be seen as temporal and mutable – and there is always the potential for creating new epistemes. In this book concepts of difference, and by extension of sameness (Moore 1994: 1), have been central. Many of the themes resonate with contemporary society and social issues (difference, sex, the body and selfhood); this study illustrates how past cultures have constituted and reconciled these ideas in very different ways. Acknowledging difference, variability and contingency reflects a more responsible attitude to the past, but is also an empowering recognition for future change.

Inspired largely by the works of writers like Richard Rorty and Cornel West, I would suggest that the insights of our theorizing might have a notable social impact. Ancient data can add significant dimensionality to contemporary issues and debates. They can expose inequalities in the past and demonstrate the fluidity of those hierarchies of difference that produce a social totality. The pragmatism West (1995: 227) subscribes to actively opposes racism, patriarchy, homophobia and economic injustice. While this stance might seem largely theoretical, it can be put into practice in our scholarly work, even that of archaeology. In essence, there is a commitment to highlighting all elements of social difference. As Nancy Fraser notes, feminist struggles are not simply conducted along sexed lines, they are 'also traversed by other, intersecting axes of stratification and power, including class, "race"/ethnicity, sexuality, nationality, and age – a fact that vastly complicates the feminist project' (1995: 159). Fraser also calls for summary accounts of the overall study of gender power and gender struggle – something archaeology is well placed to provide.

Rorty's recent work on feminism is also in keeping with the third wave position. He suggests that under the influence of Deweyan pragmatism, feminists would free themselves from the demand for a general theory of oppression – a way of seeing oppression on the basis of race, class, sexual preference and gender – a sentiment already critiqued at the beginning of this book. He sees this move as also circumventing the associated problems of universalism, essentialism and ahistorical representations (Rorty 1995: 130). In this way prophetic feminists could envisage a society where male–female distinctions are no longer of much interest and a better set of social constructs will be created and with them a new and better sort of human being (Rorty 1995: 140). This harks back to Foucault, who also referred to the possibility for a new economy of power relations emerging in our time.

We should look to the interstices, since new ways of thinking always arise in the spaces between the concepts of the old episteme (Hekman 1990: 172). Perhaps through the creation of these discourses of difference, which permeate our studies of the past, we might effect positive changes in our own society.

Evidence from the past prompts us to question the constricting binaries we have created, like those of sex and gender, and allows us the scope to consider a more open, flexible way of seeing. Linking agendas to uncover difference and variability, past and present, can only be an edifying step forward that should highlight the intrinsic relevance of the discipline. Archaeology needs to engage more critically and relevantly with developments in anthropology, sociology, feminist theory, postcolonial studies, literary theory and cultural studies – and to communicate our findings to interdisciplinary audiences where possible. In my experience, other social disciplines are particularly open to, and interested in, archaeological findings and theorizing. Archaeology is not simply the hermetic study of the past and its people for their own sake. Rather, it should position itself in the social field where it can contribute to the issues, crises and questions of contemporary society. From an archaeology of Egypt through the millennia, we can see how people of the past negotiated social issues, how they struggled with issues of class and wealth, how they rose through the ranks by their own merit, how sexual difference was reconciled, and how a multi-cultural society functioned. Egyptian archaeology from pharaonic to Christian times sheds light on all these issues which impact on our own lives. We might even learn from those moments in history and see that our definitions and categories are not immutable. Archaeology can thus enter into current social debates with some authority. Archaeological interpretations will prove relevant because of their cross-cultural perspective and the substantial temporal depth of human history they provide. In the words of John Dewey (1916: 62), 'it is better for philosophy to err in active participation in the living struggles and issues of its own age and times than to maintain an immune monastic impeccability, without relevancy and bearing in the generating ideas of its contemporary present.' This pragmatic approach could truly stimulate archaeology to engage in current issues of cultural difference, and thereby to position itself as a necessary field within the social sciences.

# Notes

1   Translation from Robert Ritner (1993: 103).
2   Taken from Coffin Text Spell 173 (CT III, 47–59); translation from Kadish (1979: 205).
3   Middle Kingdom Egyptian text, 'The Dialogue of a Man and his Soul', translated by R. B. Parkinson (1991: 132).
4   TT is the designation given to the numbered Theban tombs.
5   Translated by Andrea McDowell (1999: 38).
6   O. Louvre 698, vv. 12–22, translation from Andrea McDowell (1999: 106–7); see also (Frandsen 1992).
7   Translation from Zandee (1960: 60).
8   From the Litany of Re (Hornung 1992: 173–4).
9   From the papyrus P. DeM 4–5 (McDowell 1999: 30).
10  Translated by R. B. Parkinson (1991: 45).
11  Taken from R. B. Parkinson's (1997: 254) translation of the Middle Kingdom text, The Teachings of Ptahhotep. It was a well-known didactic text in the New Kingdom, and known at Deir el Medina.
12  NN indicates the name of a specific individual that was inserted into a standardized text.
13  From the Tale of Sinuhe, translated by R. B. Parkinson (1997: 36).
14  The Egyptians used a barter system in which everything had a value expressed in various units. These units had a value in weights of silver, copper/bronze or in volumes of grain. At Deir el Medina the unit was most commonly the 'deben'. For example, a man commissions a coffin to be made for a total of 24.5 deben of notional copper. The buyer has to accrue a set of commodities that total 24.5 deben and does so with a pig (5 deben), 2 goats (4 deben), 2 sycamore logs (2 deben) and copper scrap (13.5), totalling 24.5 deben (Kemp 1989: 250, after Janssen 1975: 10).
15  O. DM 439 dated to the 20th Dynasty, translated by Edward Wente (1990: 148).
16  Translated by Miriam Lichtheim (1976: 138).
17  The Harper's Song from the tomb of King Intef, translated by R. B. Parkinson (1995: 194–5).

18  From the Cairo Love Songs, found written on a vase from Deir el
    Medina, dated to the 19th or 20th Dynasty and translated by Andrea
    McDowell (1999: 154).
19  Translation taken from Andrea McDowell (1999: 154).

# References

Abu-Lughod, L. 1993: Islam and the gendered discourse of death, *International Journal of Middle Eastern Studies* 25: 187–205.

Adelson, L. A. 1993: *Making Bodies, Making History: Feminism and German Identity*. Lincoln, University of Nebraska Press.

Alcoff, L. 1997: Cultural feminism versus post-structuralism: the identity crisis in feminist theory. In L. Nicholson (ed.), *The Second Wave: a Reader in Feminist Theory*. New York, Routledge, pp. 330–55.

Alexander, C. M. 1998: The political economy of the Turkish Sugar Corporation. Unpublished PhD thesis, Department of Anthropology, Cambridge.

Anderson, I. 1995: Bodies, disease and the problem of Foucault, *Social Analysis: Journal of Social and Cultural Practice: Persons, Bodies, Selves, Emotions* (37): 67–81.

Andrén, A. 1998: *Between Artifacts and Texts: Historical Archaeology in Global Perspective*. New York, Plenum Press.

Andrews, C. 1994: *Amulets of Ancient Egypt*. London, British Museum Press.

Anthes, R. 1943: Die Deutschen Grabungen auf der Westseite von Theben in den Jahren 1911–1913, *Mitteilungen des Deutschen Instituts für Ägyptische Altertumskunde in Kairo* 12 (1): 1–72.

Ariès, P. 1962: *Centuries of Childhood*. New York, Knopf.

Armon-Jones, C. 1986: The thesis of constructionism. In R. Harré (ed.), *The Social Construction of Emotions*. Oxford, Basil Blackwell, pp. 32–56.

Atiya, N. 1984: *Khul-Khal: Five Egyptian Women Tell their Stories*. Cairo, American University in Cairo Press.

Attir, M. O. 1985: Ideology, value changes, and women's social position in Libyan society. In E. W. Fernea (ed.), *Women and the Family in the Middle East: New Voices of Change*. Austin, University of Texas Press, pp. 121–33.

Babcock, B. 1993: At home, no women are storytellers: ceramic creativity and the politics of discourse in a Cochiti pueblo. In S. Lavie, K. Narayan and R. Rosaldo (eds), *Creativity/Anthropology*. Cornell, Cornell University Press, pp. 70–99.

Bagnall, R. S. and Frier, B. W. 1994: *The Demography of Roman Egypt.* Cambridge, Cambridge University Pres.

Bahrani, Z. 1996: The Hellenization of Ishtar: nudity, fetishism, and the production of cultural differentiation in ancient art, *The Oxford Art Journal* 19 (2): 3–16.

Bailey, D. W. 1994: Reading prehistoric figurines as individuals, *World Archaeology* 25 (3): 321–31.

Baines, J. 1985: Egyptian twins, *Orientalia* 54: 461–82.

Baines, J. 1988: Literacy, social organisation, and the archaeological record: the case of early Egypt. In J. Gledhill, B. Bender and M. T. Larsen (eds), *State and Society: the Emergence and Development of Social Hierarchy and Political Centralization.* London, Unwin Hyman, pp. 192–214.

Baines, J. 1991: Society, morality, and religious practice. In B. E. Shafer (ed.), *Religion in Ancient Egypt.* London, Routledge, pp. 123–200.

Baines, J. 1996: Contextualizing Egyptian representations of society and ethnicity. In J. S. Cooper and G. M. Schwartz (eds), *The Study of the Ancient Near East in the 21st Century.* Winona Lake IN, Eisenbrauns, pp. 339–84.

Baines, J. and Lacovara, P. 1996: Death, the dead and burial in ancient Egyptian Society, Paper delivered at the American Research Centre in Egypt Meeting, New York.

Bamberger, J. 1974: The myth of matriarchy: why men rule in primitive society. In M. Z. Rosaldo and L. Lamphere (eds), *Woman, Culture and Society.* Stanford, Stanford University Press, pp. 262–80.

Bard, K. A. 1994: *From Farmers to Pharaohs: Mortuary Evidence for the Rise of Social Complexity in Egypt.* Sheffield, Sheffield Academic Press.

Barrett, J. C. 1988: Fields of discourse: reconstituting a social archaeology, *Critique of Anthropology* 7 (3): 5–16.

Barrett, J. C. 1994: *Fragments from Antiquity: an Archaeology of Social Life in Britain, 2900–1200 BC.* Oxford, Blackwell.

Bauman, Z. 1992: Survival as a social construct, *Theory Culture and Society* 9 (1): 1–36.

Bauman, Z. 1995: Sociology and postmodernity. In P. Joyce (ed.), *Class.* Oxford, Oxford University Press, pp. 74–83.

Baumeister, R. F. 1986: *Identity: Cultural Change and the Struggle for Self.* New York, Oxford University Press.

Beaudry, M. C., Cook, L. J. and Mrozowski, S. A. 1991: Artifacts and active voices: material culture as social discourse. In R. H. McGuire and R. Paynter (eds), *The Archaeology of Inequality.* Oxford, Blackwell, pp. 150–91.

de Beauvoir, S. 1972: *The Second Sex.* Harmondsworth, Penguin.

Behrens, P. 1982: Phallus, *Lexikon der Ägyptologie* 4: 1018–20.

Bell, M. R. 1982: Preliminary report on the Mycenaean pottery from Deir el Medina (1979–1980), *Annales du Service des Antiquities de Egypte* 68: 143–63.

Benhabib, S. 1995: Feminism and postmodernism: an uneasy alliance. In S. Benhabib, J. Butler, J. Cornell, N. Fraser and L. Nicholson (eds), *Feminist Contentions: a Philosophical Exchange*. New York, Routledge, pp. 17–34.

Berger, M., Wallis, B. and Watson, S. (eds) 1995: *Constructing Masculinity*. New York, Routledge.

Berthelot, J. M. 1991: Sociological discourse and the body. In M. Featherstone, M. Hepworth and B. S. Turner (eds), *The Body: Social Process and Cultural Theory*. London, Sage, pp. 390–404.

Bhabha, H. K. 1994: *The Location of Culture*. London, Routledge.

Bierbrier, M. L. 1982: *The Tomb-builders of the Pharaohs*. London, British Museum Press.

Bierbrier, M. L. 1990: A Deir el Medina jigsaw. In S. I. Groll (ed.), *Studies in Egyptology Presented to Miriam Lichtheim*, vol. I. Jerusalem, Magnes Press, pp. 63–70.

Bietti Sestieri, A. M. 1992: *The Iron Age Community of Osteria dell'Osa: a Study of Socio-political Development in Tyrrhenian Italy*. Cambridge, Cambridge University Press.

Black, J. 1998: Taking the sex out of sexuality: Foucault's failed history. In D. H. J. Larmour, P. A. Miller and C. Platter (eds), *Rethinking Sexuality: Foucault and Classical Antiquity*. Princeton, NJ, Princeton University Press, pp. 42–60.

Blake, E. 1999: Identity-mapping in the Sardinian Bronze Age, *European Journal of Archaeology* 2 (1): 55–75.

Bloch, M. 1982: Death, women and power. In M. Bloch and J. Parry (eds), *Death and the Regeneration of Life*. Cambridge, Cambridge University Press, pp. 211–30.

Bloch, M. and Parry, J. 1982a: Introduction: death and the regeneration of life. In M. Bloch and J. Parry (eds), *Death and the Regeneration of Life*. Cambridge, Cambridge University Press, pp. 1–44.

Bloch, M. and Parry, J. (eds) 1982b: *Death and the Regeneration of Life*. Cambridge, Cambridge University Press.

Bolshakov, A. O. 1997: *Man and his Double in Egyptian Ideology of the Old Kingdom*. Wiesbaden, Harrassowitz.

Bonnet, C. and Valbelle, D. 1976: Le village de Deir el Médineh, *Bulletin de l'Institut Français d'Archéologie Orientale* 76: 317–42.

Bordo, S. 1993: *Unbearable Weight: Feminism, Western Culture and the Body*. London, University of California Press.

Borghouts, J. F. 1982: Divine intervention in ancient Egypt and its manifestation *(b3w)*. In R. J. Demarée and J. J. Janssen (eds), *Gleanings from Deir el Medina*. Leiden, Nederlands Instituut voor het Nabije Oosten, pp. 1–70.

Borghouts, J. F. 1994: Magical practices among the villagers. In L. H. Lesko (ed.), *Pharaoh's Workers: the Villagers of Deir el Medina*. New York, Cornell University Press, pp. 119–30.

Bourdieu, P. 1977: *Outline of a Theory of Practice*. Cambridge, Cambridge University Press.

Bourdieu, P. 1998: *Practical Reason: On the Theory of Action*. Cambridge, Polity Press.

Boyaval, B. 1977: Tableau général des indications d'âge de l'Égypte gréco-romaine, *Chronique d'Égypte* 52 (103): 345–51.

Braidotti, R. 1991: *Patterns of Dissonance: a Study of Women in Contemporary Philosophy*. Cambridge, Polity Press.

Broch-Due, V., Rudie, I. and Bleie, T. (eds) 1993: *Carved Flesh, Cast Selves: Gendered Symbols and Social Practices*. London, Berg.

Brod, H. and Kaufman, M. (eds) 1994: *Theorising Masculinities*. Thousand Oaks, CA, Sage.

Brown, J. A. 1981: The search for rank in prehistoric burials. In R. Chapman, I. Kinnes and K. Randsborg (eds), *The Archaeology of Death*. Cambridge, Cambridge University Press, pp. 25–37.

Brumbach, H. J. and Jarvenpa, R. 1997: Woman the hunter: ethnoarchaeological lessons from Chipewyan life-cycle dynamics. In C. Claassen and R. A. Joyce (eds), *Women in Prehistory: North America and Mesoamerica*. Philadelphia, University of Pennsylvania Press, pp. 17–32.

Brumfiel, E. M. 1987: Comments [on Earle and Preucel 1987], *Current Anthropology* 28: 513–14.

Brumfiel, E. M. 1992: Distinguished lecture in archaeology: breaking and entering the ecosystem – gender, class, and faction steal the show, *American Anthropologist* 94: 551–67.

Brunner, H. 1977: Herz, *Lexikon der Ägyptologie* 2: 1158–68.

Bruyère, B. 1924: *Rapport sur les Fouilles de Deir el Médineh (1922–1923), Première Partie*. Cairo, Imprimerie de l'Institut Français d'Archéologie Orientale.

Bruyère, B. 1925: *Rapport sur les Fouilles de Deir el Médineh (1923–1924), Deuxième Partie*. Cairo, Imprimerie de l'Institut Français d'Archéologie Orientale.

Bruyère, B. 1926: *Rapport sur les Fouilles de Deir el Médineh (1924–1925), Troisième Partie*. Cairo, Imprimerie de l'Institut Français d'Archéologie Orientale.

Bruyère, B. 1927: *Rapport sur les Fouilles de Deir el Médineh (1926), Troisième Partie*. Cairo, Imprimerie de l'Institut Français d'Archéologie Orientale.

Bruyère, B. 1928: *Rapport sur les Fouilles de Deir el Médineh (1927), Deuxième Partie*. Cairo, Imprimerie de l'Institut Français d'Archéologie Orientale.

Bruyère, B. 1929: *Rapport sur les Fouilles de Deir el Médineh (1928), Deuxième Partie*. Cairo, Imprimerie de l'Institut Français d'Archéologie Orientale.

Bruyère, B. 1930: *Rapport sur les Fouilles de Deir el Médineh (1929), Deuxième Partie*. Cairo, Imprimerie de l'Institut Français d'Archéologie Orientale.

Bruyère, B. 1933: *Rapport sur les Fouilles de Deir el Médineh (1930),*

*Troisième Partie*. Cairo, Imprimerie de l'Institut Français d'Archéologie Orientale.

Bruyère, B. 1937a: *Rapport sur les Fouilles de Deir el Médineh (1934–1935), Deuxième Partie FIFAO 15*. Cairo, Imprimerie de l'Institut Français d'Archéologie Orientale.

Bruyère, B. 1937b: *Rapport sur les Fouilles de Deir el Médineh (1933–1934), Première Partie FIFAO 14*. Cairo, Imprimerie de l'Institut Français d'Archéologie Orientale.

Bruyère, B. 1939: *Rapport sur les Fouilles de Deir el Médineh (1934–1935), Troisième Partie FIFAO 16*. Cairo, Imprimerie de l'Institut Français d'Archéologie Orientale.

Bruyère, B. 1948: *Rapport sur les Fouilles de Deir el Médineh (1935–1940), Quatrième Partie FIFAO 20/1*. Cairo, Imprimerie de l'Institut Français d'Archéologie Orientale.

Bruyère, B. 1952: *Rapport sur les Fouilles de Deir el Médineh (1945–1946 and 1946–1947), FIFAO 22*. Cairo, Imprimerie de l'Institut Français d'Archéologie Orientale.

Bruyère, B. 1953: *Rapport sur les Fouilles de Deir el Médineh (1948–1951), Première Partie FIFAO 26*. Cairo, Imprimerie de l'Institut Français d'Archéologie Orientale.

Bruyère, B. and Kuentz, C. 1926: *Tombes thébaines: la nécropole de Deir el Medinéh*. Cairo, Mémoires l'Institut Français D'Archéologie Orientale.

Burke, P. 1997: Representations of the self from Petrarch to Descartes. In R. Porter (ed.), *Rewriting the Self: Histories from the Renaissance to the Present*. London, Routledge, pp. 17–28.

Butler, J. 1990a: *Gender Trouble: Feminism and the Subversion of Identity*. New York, Routledge.

Butler, J. 1990b: Gender trouble, feminist theory, and psychoanalytic discourse. In L. J. Nicholson (ed.), *Feminism/Postmodernism*. New York, Routledge, pp. 324–40.

Butler, J. 1993: *Bodies that Matter: on the Discursive Limits of 'Sex'*. New York, Routledge.

Butler, J. 1995: Contingent foundations: feminism and the question of 'postmodernism'. In S. Benhabib, J. Butler, J. Cornell, N. Fraser and L. Nicholson (eds), *Feminist Contentions: a Philosophical Exchange*. New York, Routledge, pp. 35–57.

Butler, J. 1997a: *Excitable Speech*. New York, Routledge.

Butler, J. 1997b: *The Psychic Life of Power: Theories in Subjection*. Stanford, Stanford University Press.

Cannon, A. 1989: The historical dimension in mortuary expressions of status and sentiment, *Current Anthropology* 30 (4): 437–58.

Carr, C. 1995: Mortuary practices: their social, philosophical-religious, circumstantial, and physical determinants, *Journal of Archaeological Method and Theory* 2 (2): 105–200.

Carrithers, M. 1985: An alternative social history of the self. In M. Carrithers, S. Collins and S. Lukes (eds), *The Category of the Person: Anthropology, Philosophy, History.* Cambridge, Cambridge University Press, pp. 234–56.

Černý, J. 1929: Papyrus Salt 124 (Brit. Mus. 10055), *Journal of Egyptian Archaeology* 15: 243–58.

Černý, J. 1945: The will of Naunakhte and related documents, *Journal of Egyptian Archaeology* 31: 29–53.

Černý, J. 1973: *A Community of Workmen at Thebes in the Ramesside Period.* Cairo, BdE 50, Institut Français d'Archéologie Orientale.

de Certeau, M. 1984: *The Practice of Everyday Life.* Berkeley, CA, University of California Press.

Chapman, R. and Randsborg, K. 1981: Approaches to the archaeology of death. In R. Chapman, I. Kinnes and K. Randsborg (eds), *The Archaeology of Death.* Cambridge, Cambridge University Press, pp. 1–24.

Cixous, H. and Clement, C. 1986: *The Newly Born Woman.* Minneapolis, University of Minnesota Press.

Claassen, C. 1997: Changing venue: women's lives in prehistoric North America. In C. Claassen and R. A. Joyce (eds), *Women in Prehistory: North America and Mesoamerica.* Philadelphia, University of Pennsylvania Press, pp. 65–87.

Cohen, A. P. 1994: *Self Consciousness: an Alternative Anthropology of Identity.* London, Routledge.

Cohen, D. and Saller, R. 1994: Foucault on sexuality in Greco-Roman antiquity. In J. Goldstein (ed.), *Foucault and the Writing of History.* Oxford, Blackwell, pp. 35–59.

Collier, J. F. and Yanagisako, S. J. (eds) 1987: *Gender and Kinship: Essays Toward a Unified Analysis.* Stanford, Stanford University Press.

Collins, P. H. 1997: Defining black feminist thought. In L. Nicholson (ed.), *The Second Wave: a Reader in Feminist Theory.* New York, Routledge, pp. 241–59.

Combahee River Collective 1997: A black feminist statement. In L. Nicholson (ed.), *The Second Wave: a Reader in Feminist Theory.* New York, Routledge, pp. 63–70.

Conkey, M. W. and Gero, J. M. 1997: Programme to practice: gender and feminism in archaeology, *Annual Review of Anthropology* 26: 411–37.

Conkey, M. W. and Tringham, R. E. 1995: Archaeology and the Goddess: exploring the contours of feminist archaeology. In D. C. Stanton and A. J. Stewart (eds), *Feminisms in the Academy.* Ann Arbor, University of Michigan, pp. 199–247.

Connell, R. W. 1995: *Masculinities.* Sydney, Allen and Unwin.

Cornwall, A. and Lindisfarne, N. (eds) 1994: *Dislocating Masculinity: Comparative Ethnographies.* London, Routledge.

Cowgill, G. L. 1993: Distinguished lecture in archaeology: beyond criticising New Archaeology, *American Anthropologist* 95 (3): 551–73.

Craib, I. 1992: *Anthony Giddens*. London, Routledge.

Crompton, R. 1995: The development of classical inheritance. In P. Joyce (ed.), *Class*. Oxford, Oxford University Press, pp. 43–55.

Crossley, N. 1996: Body-subject/body-power: agency, inscription and control in Foucault and Merleau-Ponty, *Body and Society* 2 (2): 99–116.

Cullen, T. 1996: Contributions to feminism in archaeology, *American Journal of Archaeology* 100: 409–14.

Curto, S. and Mancini, M. 1968: News of Kha' and Meryt, *Journal of Egyptian Archaeology* 54: 77–81.

Daressy, G. 1920: Note sur l'article précédent, *Annales du Service des Antiquités de l'Egypte* 20: 159–60.

Daressy, G. 1928: La trouvaille de Sen-nezem: objets séparés de l'ensemble, *Annales du Service des Antiquités de l'Egypte* 28: 7–11.

D'Auria, S., Lacovara, P. and Roehrig, C. H. (eds) 1988: *Mummies and Magic: the Funerary Arts of Ancient Egypt*. Boston and Dallas, Boston Museum of Fine Arts and Dallas Museum of Art.

Delaney, C. 1995: Untangling the meanings of hair in Turkish society. In H. Eilberg-Schwartz and W. Doniger (eds), *Off with her Head: the Denial of Woman's Identity in Myth, Religion and Culture*. Berkeley, CA, University of California Press, pp. 53–75.

De Lauretis, T. (ed.) 1984: *Alice Doesn't: Feminism, Semiotics, Cinema*. Bloomington, Ind., Indiana University Press.

De Lauretis, T. (ed.) 1986: *Feminist Studies/Critical Studies*. London, Macmillan.

De Lauretis, T. (ed.) 1987: *Technologies of Gender: Essays on Theory, Film and Fiction*. Bloomingdale, Ind., Indiana University Press.

Deleuze, G. and Guattari, F. 1987: *A Thousand Plateaus: Capitalism and Schizophrenia*. Minneapolis, University of Minnesota Press.

De Mause, L. (ed.) 1974: *The History of Childhood*. New York, Psychohistory Press.

Derchain, P. 1975: La perruque et le cristal, *Studien zur Altägyptischen Kultur* 2: 55–74.

Derrida, J. 1978: *Writing and Difference*. Chicago, University of Chicago Press.

Derrida, J. 1981: *Positions*. Chicago, University of Chicago Press.

Derrida, J. 1983: *Margins of Philosophy*. London, Harvester Press.

Derrida, J. 1987: *The Post Card: from Socrates to Freud and Beyond*. Chicago, University of Chicago Press.

Dewey, J. 1916: Education as growth. In J. Dewey (ed.), *Democracy and Education*. New York, Macmillan, pp. 49–62.

Diamond, I. and Quinby, L. (eds) 1988: *Feminism and Foucault: Reflections on Resistance*. Boston, Northeastern University Press.

Douglas, M. 1966: *Purity and Danger: an Analysis of the Concepts of Pollution and Taboo*. London, Routledge.

duBois, P. 1988: *Sowing the Body: Psychoanalysis and Ancient Representations of Women*. Chicago, Chicago University Press.

duBois, P. 1998: The subject in antiquity after Foucault. In D. H. J. Larmour, P. A. Miller and C. Platter (eds), *Rethinking Sexuality: Foucault and Classical Antiquity*. Princeton, NJ, Princeton University Press, pp. 85–103.

Dumont, L. 1986: *Essays on Individualism: Modern Ideology in Anthropological Perspective*. Chicago, University of Chicago Press.

Eilberg-Schwartz, H. and Doniger, W. (eds) 1995: *Off with her Head: the Denial of Women's Identity in Myth, Religion and Culture*. Berkeley, CA, University of California Press.

Eisler, R. 1991: The goddess of nature and spirituality: an ecomanifesto. In J. Campbell and C. Musés (eds), *In All her Names: Explorations of the Feminine in Divinity*. New York, HarperCollins, pp. 3–23.

Eisler, R. 1995: *Sacred Pleasure: Sex, Myth and the Politics of the Body*. New York, HarperCollins.

Ekins, R. and King, D. (eds) 1996: *Blending Genders: Social Aspects of Cross-dressing and Sex Changing*. London, Routledge.

Elam, D. 1994: *Feminism and Deconstruction: Ms. en Abyme*. London, Routledge.

Engelstad, E. 1991: Images of power and contradiction: feminist theory and post-processual archaeology, *Antiquity* 65: 502–14.

Eriksen, T. H. 1993: *Ethnicity and Nationalism*. London, Pluto Press.

Fausto-Sterling, A. 1993: The five sexes: why male and female are not enough, *The Sciences* 33 (2): 20–5.

Feder, E. K., Rawlinson, M. C. and Zakin, E. (eds) 1997: *Derrida and Feminism: Recasting the Question of Woman*. New York, Routledge.

Feder, E. K. and Zakin, E. 1997: Flirting with the truth: Derrida's discourse with 'woman' and wenches. In E. K. Feder, M. C. Rawlinson and E. Zakin (ed.), *Derrida and Feminism: Recasting the Question of Woman*. New York, Routledge, pp. 21–51.

Feher, M., Naddaff, R. and Tazi, N. (eds) 1989: *Fragments for a History of the Human Body*. New York, Zone.

Fenster, T. 1994: Preface: why men? In C. A. Lees (ed.), *Medieval Masculinities*. Minneapolis, University of Minnesota Press, pp. ix–xii.

Feucht, E. 1995: *Das Kind im alten Ägypten*. Frankfurt/New York, Campus.

Flax, J. 1987: Postmodernism and gender relations in feminist theory, *Signs* 12 (4): 621–43.

Foster, J. L. 1992: *Love Songs of the New Kingdom*. Austin, University of Texas Press.

Fotiadis, M. 1994: What is archaeology's 'mitigated objectivisim' mitigated by? Comments on Wylie, *American Antiquity* 59 (3): 545–55.

Foucault, M. 1972: *The Archaeology of Knowledge*. London, Routledge.

Foucault, M. 1977a: *Discipline and Punish: the Birth of the Prison*. London, Penguin.

Foucault, M. 1977b: Nietzsche, genealogy and history. In D. Bouchard (ed.), *Language, Counter-Memory, Practice*. Ithaca, Cornell University Press, pp. 139–64.

Foucault, M. 1978: *The History of Sexuality*. London, Routledge.

Foucault, M. 1980: Body-power. In C. Gordon (ed.), *Power/Knowledge*. Brighton, Harvester, pp. 55–63.

Foucault, M. 1985: *The History of Sexuality: the Use of Pleasure*. London, Penguin.

Foucault, M. 1986: *The History of Sexuality: the Care of the Self*. London, Penguin.

Foucault, M. 1989a: *The Birth of the Clinic: an Archaeology of Medical Perception*. London, Routledge.

Foucault, M. 1989b: *Madness and Civilization: a History in the Age of Reason*. London, Routledge.

Fox, M. V. 1995: *The Song of Songs and the Ancient Egyptian Love Songs*. Madison, WI, University of Wisconsin.

Foxhall, L. 1994: Pandora unbound: a feminist critique of Foucault's *History of Sexuality*. In A. Cornwall and N. Lindisfarne (eds), *Dislocating Masculinity: Comparative Ethnographies*. London, Routledge, pp. 133–46.

Foxhall, L. and Salmon, J. (eds) 1998a: *Thinking Men: Masculinity and its Self-representation in the Classical Tradition*. London, Routledge.

Foxhall, L. and Salmon, J. (eds) 1998b: *When Men were Men: Masculinity, Power and Identity in Classical Antiquity*. London, Routledge.

Frandsen, P. J. 1992: The letter to Ikhtay's coffin: O. Louvre INV. No. 698. In R. J. Demarée and A. Egberts (eds), *Village Voices*. Leiden, Centre of Non-Western Studies, pp. 31–49.

Fraser, N. 1995: Pragmatism, feminism, and the linguistic turn. In S. Benhabib, J. Butler, D. Cornell and N. Fraser (eds), *Feminist Contentions: a Philosophical Exchange*. New York, Routledge, pp. 157–71.

Fuss, D. 1989: *Essentially Speaking: Feminism, Nature and Difference*. London, Routledge.

Gallop, J. 1997: 'Women' in *Spurs* and nineties feminism. In E. K. Feder, M. C. Rawlinson and E. Zakin (eds), *Derrida and Feminism: Recasting the Question of Woman*. New York, Routledge, pp. 7–19.

Gamble, C. 1986: Hunter-gatherers and the origin of states. In J. A. Hall (ed.), *States in History*. Oxford, Basil Blackwell, pp. 22–47.

Gamble, C. 1998: Palaeolithic society and the release from proximity: a network approach to intimate relations, *World Archaeology* 95 (3): 426–49.

Gatens, M. 1996: *The Imaginary Body*. Routledge, London.

Geertz, C. 1966: The impact of culture on the concept of man. In J. Platt (ed.), *New Views on the Nature of Man*. Chicago, University of Chicago Press, pp. 93–118.

Geertz, C. 1973: *The Interpretation of Culture*. New York, Basic Books.

Geertz, C. 1983. *Local Knowledge: Further Essays in Intrepretive Anthropology*. New York, Basic Books.

Gell, A. 1998: *Art and Agency: an Anthropological Theory*. Oxford, Oxford University Press.

Gero, J. M. 1991: Genderlithics: women's roles in stone tool production. In J. M. Gero and M. W. Conkey (eds), *Engendering Archaeology: Women and Prehistory*. Oxford, Blackwell, pp. 163–93.

Getty, A. 1990: *Goddess: Mother of Living Nature*. London, Thames and Hudson.

Giddens, A. 1984: *The Constitution of Society: Outline of a Theory of Structuration*. Cambridge, Polity Press.

Giddens, A. 1991: *Modernity and Self-identity: Self and Society in the Late Modern Age*. Cambridge, Polity Press.

Giddens, A. 1992: *The Transformation of Intimacy: Sexuality, Love and Eroticism in Modern Societies*. Cambridge, Polity Press.

Gilchrist, R. 1994: *Gender and Material Culture: the Archaeology of Religious Women*. London, Routledge.

Gilchrist, R. forthcoming: *Gender and Archaeology: Contesting the Past*. London, Routledge.

Goldhill, S. 1995: *Foucault's Virginity: Ancient Erotic Fiction and the History of Sexuality*. Cambridge, Cambridge Uiversity Press.

Gosden, C. 1992: Endemic doubt: is what we write right?, *Antiquity* 66: 803–8.

Gosden, C. 1994: *Social Being and Time*. Oxford, Blackwell.

Graves-Brown, P., Gamble, J. S. and Gamble, C. (eds) 1996: *Cultural Identity and Archaeology: the Construction of European Communities*. London, Routledge.

Greenberg, D. F. 1997: Transformations of homosexuality-based classifications. In R. N. Lancaster and M. di Leonardo (eds) *The Gender/Sexuality Reader: Culture, History, Political Economy*. New York, Routledge, pp. 179–93.

Grosz, E. 1994: *Volatile Bodies: toward a Corporeal Feminism*. Bloomington, Ind., Indiana University Press.

Grosz, E. 1995: *Space, Time and Perversion*. New York and London, Routledge.

Guglielmi, W. 1996: Der Gebrauch rhetorischer Stilmittel in der ägyptischen Literatur. In A. Loprieno (ed.), *Ancient Egyptian Literature: History and Forms*. Leiden, E. J. Brill, pp. 465–98.

Gutgesell, M. 1989: *Arbeiter und Pharaonen: Wirtschafts- und Sozialgeschichte im Alten Ägypten*. Hildesheim, Gerstenberg.

Gutmann, M. C. 1997: Trafficking in men: the anthropology of masculinity, *Annual Review of Anthropology* 26: 385–409.

Guyer, J. I. 1991: Female farming in anthropology and African history. In M. di Leonardo (ed.), *Gender at the Crossroads of Knowledge*. Berkeley, CA, University of California Press, pp. 257–77.

Haaland, G. and Haaland, R. 1995: Who speaks the goddess's language? Imagination and method in archaeological research, *Norwegian Archaeological Review* 28 (2): 105–21.

Hacking, I. 1995: Three parables. In R. B. Goodman (ed.), *Pragmatism: a Reader*. New York, Routledge, pp. 238–49.

Haddad, T. (ed.) 1993: *Men and Masculinities: a Critical Anthology*. Toronto, Canadian Scholars Press.

Halperin, D. 1990: *One Hundred Years of Homosexuality and Other Essays on Greek Love*. New York, Routledge.

Halperin, D. 1995: *Saint Foucault: towards a Gay Hagiography*. New York and Oxford, Oxford University Press.

Halperin, D., Winkler, J. D. and Zeitlin, F. I. (eds) 1990: *Before Sexuality: the Construction of Erotic Experience in the Ancient Greek World*. Princeton, NJ, Princeton University Press.

Hamilton, N. 1994: A fresh look at the 'Seated Gentleman' in the Pierides Foundation Museum, Republic of Cyprus, *Cambridge Archaeological Journal* 4 (2): 302–12.

Haraway, D. 1985: A manifesto for cyborgs: science, technology, and socialist feminism in the 1980s, *Socialist Review* 80: 65–107.

Haraway, D. 1991: *Simians, Cyborgs and Women: the Reinvention of Nature*. London, Free Association Press.

Haraway, D. J. 1997: *Modest_Witness@Second_Millennium.FemaleMan©_Meets_OncoMouse™*. New York, Routledge.

Harré, R. 1998: *The Singular Self: an Introduction to the Psychology of Personhood*. London, Sage.

Hastrup, K. 1995: *A Passage to Anthropology: Between Experience and Theory*. London, Routledge.

Hausman, B. L. 1995: *Changing Sex: Transsexualism, Technology and the Idea of Gender*. Durham, NC, Duke University Press.

Heald, S., Deluz, A. and Jacopin, P-Y. 1994: Introduction. In S. Heald and A. Deluz (eds), *Anthropology and Psychoanalysis: an Encounter through Culture*. London, Routledge, pp. 1–26.

Hearn, J. D. M. (ed.) 1990: *Men, Masculinities and Social Theory*. London, Unwin Hyman.

Heelas, P. 1986: Emotion talk across cultures. In R. Harré (ed.), *The Social Construction of Emotions*. London, Basil Blackwell, pp. 234–66.

Heer, D. 1968: Economic development and the fertility transition, *Daedalus* 9: 447–62.

Hekman, S. J. 1990: *Gender and Knowledge: Elements of a Postmodern Feminism*. Cambridge, Polity Press.

Herdt, G. (ed.) 1993: *Third Sex, Third Gender*. New York, Zone Books.

Hertz, R. 1960: *Death and the Right Hand*, trans. R. and C. Needham. London, Cohen and West.

Hill, E. 1998: Gender-informed archaeology: the priority of definition, the use of analogy, and the multivariate approach, *Journal of Archaeological Method and Theory* 5 (1): 99–128.

Hill, J. N. and Gunn, J. (eds) 1977: *The Individual in Prehistory: Studies of Variability in Style in Prehistoric Technologies*. New York, Academic Press.

Hodder, I. 1984: Archaeology in 1984, *Antiquity* 58: 25–32.

Hodder, I. 1987: The contextual analysis of symbolic meanings. In I. Hodder (ed.), *The Archaeology of Contextual Meanings*. Cambridge, Cambridge University Press, pp. 1–10.

Hodder, I. 1991a: Gender representation and social reality. In D. Walde and N. D. Willows (eds), *The Archaeology of Gender: Proceedings of the 22nd Annual Chacmool Conference*. Calgary, University of Calgary Archaeological Association, pp. 11–16.

Hodder, I. 1991b: *Reading the Past*. Cambridge, Cambridge University Press.

Hodder, I., Shanks, M., Alexandri, A., Buchli, V., Carman, J., Last, J. and Lucas, G. (eds) 1995: *Interpreting Archaeology: Finding Meaning in the Past*. London, Routledge.

Hollimon, S. E. 1988: Age and sex related incidence of degenerative joint disease in skeletal remains from Santa Cruz Island, California. In G. Richards (ed.), *Human Skeletal Biology: Contributions to the Understanding of California's Prehistoric Populations*. Archives of California Prehistory No. 24, Salinas, Coyote Press, pp. 69–90.

Hollimon, S. E. 1996: Sex, gender and health among the Chumash: an archaeological examination of prehistoric gender roles, *Proceedings of the Society for California Archaeology* 9: 205–8.

Hollimon, S. E. 1997: The third-gender in native California: two-spirit undertakers among the Chumash and their neighbors. In C. Claassen and R. Joyce (eds), *Women in Prehistory: North America and Mesoamerica*. Philadelphia, University of Pennsylvania Press, pp. 173–88.

Hollimon, S. E. 1998: Gender and sexuality in prehistoric Chumash society, paper delivered at the Society for American Archaeology Meetings, Seattle, WA.

Hornung, E. 1983: *Conceptions of God in Ancient Egypt: the One and the Many*. London, Routledge and Kegan Paul.

Hornung, E. 1990: *The Valley of the Kings: Horizon of Eternity*. New York, Timken.

Hornung, E. 1992: *Idea into Image: Essays on Ancient Egyptian Thought*. New York, Timken.

Hughes, A. and Witz, A. 1997: Feminism and the matter of bodies from de Beauvoir to Butler, *Body and Society* 3 (1): 47–60.

Humm, M. (ed.) 1992: *Feminisms: a Reader*. London, Harvester Wheatsheaf.

Hunt, L. (ed.) 1993: *The Invention of Pornography: Obscenity and the Origins of Modernity 1500–1800*. New York, Zone Books.

Jackson, M. 1989: *Paths Toward a Clearing: Radical Empiricism and Ethnographic Inquiry*. Bloomington, Ind., Indiana University Press.

Jacobs, S-E. 1994: Native American two-spirits, *Anthropology Newsletter*, November: 7.

Jamieson, L. 1998: *Intimacy: Personal Relationships in Modern Societies*. Cambridge, Polity Press.

Janssen, J. J. 1975: *Commodity Prices from the Ramessid Period*. Leiden, E. J. Brill.

Janssen, J. J. 1994: Debts and credit in the New Kingdom, *Journal of Egyptian Archaeology* 80: 129–36.

Janssen, J. J. and Janssen, R. M. 1990: *Growing up in Ancient Egypt*. London, Rubicon Press.

Johnson, M. 1997: *Beauty and Power: Transgendering and Cultural Transformation in the Southern Phillipines*. London, Berg.

Johnson, M. H. 1989: Conceptions of agency in archaeological interpretation, *Journal of Anthropological Archaeology* 8: 189–211.

Jones, S. 1996: *The Archaeology of Ethnicity: Constructing Identities in the Past and Present*. London, Routledge.

Joyce, R. A. 1996a: The construction of gender in Classic Maya monuments. In R. P. Wright (ed.), *Gender and Archaeology*. Philadelphia, University of Pennsylvania Press, pp. 167–95.

Joyce, R. A. 1996b: Performance and inscription: negotiating sex and gender in Classic Maya society, paper delivered at the Dumbarton Oaks Conference 'Recovering Gender in Prehispanic Mesoamerica', Washington DC.

Joyce, R. A. 1998: A Precolumbian gaze: male sexuality among the ancient Maya, paper delivered at the Society for American Archaeology Meetings, Seattle, WA.

Joyce, R. A. and Claassen, C. 1997: Women in the ancient Americas: archaeologists, gender and the making of prehistory. In C. Claassen and R. A. Joyce (eds), *Women in Prehistory: North America and Mesoamerica*. Philadelphia, University of Pennsylvania, pp. 1–14.

Kadish, G. E. 1979: The scatophagous Egyptian, *Journal of the Society for the Study of Egyptian Antiquities* 9 (4): 203–17.

Keller, C. A. 1984: How many draughtsmen named Amenhotep?, *Journal of the American Research Centre in Egypt* 21: 119–29.

Kemp, B. J. 1989: *Ancient Egypt: Anatomy of a Civilization*. London, Routledge.

Kemp, B. J. 1995: How religious were the ancient Egyptians?, *Cambridge Archaeological Journal* 5 (1): 25–54.

Knapp, A. B. 1995: Who's come a long way baby? Engendering society, engendering archaeology, paper delivered at the Third Women in Archaeology Conference, Sydney, Australia.

Knapp, A. B. and Meskell, L. M. 1997: Bodies of evidence in prehistoric Cyprus, *Cambridge Archaeological Journal* 7 (2): 183–204.

Koehler, L. 1997: Earth mothers, warriors, horticulturalists, artists and chiefs: women among the Mississippian and Mississippian-Oneota peoples AD 1000 to 1750. In C. Claassen and R. A. Joyce (eds), *Women in Prehistory: North America and Mesoamerica*. Philadelphia, University of Pennsylvania, pp. 211–26.

Kulick, D. 1997: The gender of Brazilian transgendered prostitutes, *American Anthropologist* 99 (3): 574–85.

Kus, S. 1992: Toward an archaeology of body and soul. In J-C. Gardin and C. Peebles (eds), *Representations in Archaeology*. Bloomington, Ind., Indiana University Press, pp. 168–77.

Kus, S. 1998: With a mother's [archaeological] regard: some notes on the Betsileo (Madagascar) girlhood of the daughter of an anthropologist, paper delivered at the Thinking Through the Body Conference, Lampeter, Wales.

Lancaster, R. N. 1997: Guto's performance: notes on the transvestism of everyday life. In R. N. Lancaster and M. di Leonardo (eds), *The Gender/Sexuality Reader: Culture, History, Political Economy*. New York, Routledge, pp. 559–74.

Laqueur, T. 1990: *Making Sex: Body and Gender from the Greeks to Freud*. Cambridge, MA, Harvard University Press.

Larmour, D. H. J., Miller, P. A. and Platter, C. 1998a: Introduction: situating *The History of Sexuality*. In D. H. J. Larmour, P. A. Miller and C. Platter (eds), *Rethinking Sexuality: Foucault and Classical Antiquity*. Princeton, NJ, Princeton University Press, pp. 3–41.

Larmour, D. H. J., Miller, P. A. and Platter, C. (eds) 1998b: *Rethinking Sexuality: Foucault and Classical Antiquity*. Princeton, NJ, Princeton University Press.

Laslett, P. 1995: Necessary knowledge: age and aging in the societies of the past. In D. I. Kertzer and P. Laslett (eds), *Aging in the Past: Demography, Society and Old Age*. Berkeley, CA, University of California Press, pp. 3–77.

Last, J. 1995: The nature of history. In I. Hodder, M. Shanks, A. Alexandri, V. Buchli, J. Carman, J. Last and G. Lucas (eds), *Interpreting Archaeology: Finding Meaning in the Past*. London, Routledge, pp. 141–57.

Last, J. 1998: Books of life: biography and memory in a Bronze Age barrow, *Oxford Journal of Archaeology* 17 (1): 43–53.

Lees, C. A. 1994: Men's studies, women's studies, medieval studies. In C. A. Lees (ed.), *Medieval Masculinities*. Minneapolis, University of Minnesota Press, pp. xv–xxv.

di Leonardo, M. 1991: Introduction: gender, culture, and political economy: feminist anthropology in historical perspective. In M. di Leonardo (ed.), *Gender at the Crossroads of Knowledge: Feminist Anthropology in the Postmodern Era*. Berkeley, CA, University of California Press, pp. 1–48.

di Leonardo, M. and Lancaster, R. N. 1997: Embodied meanings, carnal practices. In R. N. Lancaster and M. di Leonardo (eds), *The Gender/Sexuality Reader: Culture, History, Political Economy*. New York, Routledge, pp. 1–10.

Le Roy Ladurie, E. 1980: *Montaillou: Cathars and Catholics in a French Village 1294–1324*. London, Penguin.

Lesko, B. S. 1994: Ranks, roles and rights. In L. H. Lesko (ed.), *Pharaoh's Workers: the Villagers of Deir el Medina*. Ithaca, NY, Cornell University Press, pp. 15–39.

Lesko, B. S. 1994–5: Researching the role of women in ancient Egypt, *KMT* 5 (4): 14–23.

Lesko, L. H. 1991: Ancient Egyptian cosmogonies and cosmology. In B. E. Shafer (ed.), *Religion in Ancient Egypt*. London, Routledge, pp. 88–122.

Lesko, L. H. 1994a: Literature, literacy, and literati. In L. H. Lesko (ed.), *Pharaoh's Workers: the Villagers of Deir el Medina*. Ithaca, NY, Cornell University Press, pp. 131–44.

Lesko, L. H. (ed.) 1994b: *Pharaoh's Workers: the Villagers of Deir el Medina*. Ithaca, NY, Cornell University Press.

Lesure, R. G. 1997: Figurines and social identities in early sedentary societies of coastal Chiapas, Mexico 1550–800 BC. In C. Claassen and R. A. Joyce (eds), *Women in Prehistory: North America and Mesoamerica*. Philadelphia, University of Pennsylvania, pp. 227–48.

Lichtheim, M. 1976: *Ancient Egyptian Literature: Volume II. The New Kingdom*. Berkeley, CA, University of California Press.

Lingis, A. 1994: *Foreign Bodies*. New York, Routledge.

Lloyd, A. B. 1989: Psychology and society in the ancient Egyptian cult of the dead. In W. K. Simpson (ed.), *Religion and Philosophy in Ancient Egypt*. New Haven, Department of Near Eastern Languages and Civilizations, pp. 117–33.

Lukes, S. 1985: Conclusion. In M. Carrithers, S. Collins and S. Lukes (eds), *The Category of the Person: Anthropology, Philosophy, History*. Cambridge, Cambridge University Press, pp. 282–301.

Lutz, C. 1981: Situation-based emotion frames and the cultural construction of emotion, paper delivered at the Third Annual Conference of Cognitive Science Society, Berkeley, California.

Lyons, D. 1998: Witchcraft, gender, power and intimate relations in Mura compounds in Déla northern Cameroon, *World Archaeology* 95 (3): 344–62.

McDowell, A. G. 1992: Agricultural activity by the workmen of Deir el Medina, *Journal of Egyptian Archaeology* 78: 195–206.

McDowell, A. G. 1994: Contact with the outside world. In L. H. Lesko (ed.), *Pharaoh's Workers: the Villagers of Deir el Medina*. Ithaca, NY, Cornell University Press, pp. 41–59.

McDowell, A. G. 1999: *Village Life in Ancient Egypt: Laundry Lists and Love Songs*. Oxford, Oxford University Press.

McDowell, L. and Sharp, J. P. (eds) 1997: *Space, Gender, Knowledge: Feminist Readings*. London, Arnold.

McFarlane, A. 1981: Death and demographic transition. In S. C. Humphreys and H. King (eds), *Mortality and Immortality*. London, Academic Press, pp. 249–59.

MacKinnon, C. A. 1997: Sexuality. In L. Nicholson (ed.), *The Second Wave: a Reader in Feminist Theory*. New York, Routledge, pp. 158–80.

McNay, L. 1992: *Foucault and Feminism*. Cambridge, Polity Press.

Manniche, L. 1987: *Sexual Life in Ancient Egypt*. London and New York, Kegan Paul.

Marcus, M. I. 1993: Incorporating the body: adornment, gender, and social indentity in ancient Iran, *Cambridge Archaeological Journal* 3 (2): 157–78.

Mauss, M. 1938/1985: A category of the human mind: the notion of person; the notion of self. In M. Carrithers, S. Collins and S. Lukes (eds), *The Category of the Person*. Cambridge, Cambridge University Press, pp. 1–25.

Melhuus, M. 1993: 'I want to buy me a baby! Some reflections on gender and change in modern society. In V. Broch-Due, I. Rudie and T. Bleie (eds), *Carved Flesh, Cast Selves: Gendered Symbols and Social Practices*. London, Berg, pp. 237–55.

Merchant, C. 1995: *Earthcare: Women and the Environment*. London, Routledge.

Merck, M. (ed.) 1998: *After Diana: Irreverent Elegies*. London, Verso.

Merleau-Ponty, M. 1962: *The Phenomenology of Perception*. London, Routledge and Kegan Paul.

Meskell, L. M. 1994a: Dying young: the experience of death at Deir el Medina, *Archaeological Review from Cambridge* 13 (2): 35–45.

Meskell, L. M. 1994b: Deir el Medina in hyperreality: seeking the people of pharaonic Egypt, *Journal of Mediterranean Archaeology* 7 (2): 193–216.

Meskell, L. M. 1995: Goddesses, Gimbutas and 'New Age' archaeology, *Antiquity* 69: 74–86.

Meskell, L. M. 1996a: The somatisation of archaeology: institutions, discourses, corporeality, *Norwegian Archaeological Review* 29 (1): 1–16.

Meskell, L. M. 1996b: Review of S. Billington and M. Green (eds), *The Concept of the Goddess*, *Norwegian Archaeological Review* 29 (2): 117–20.

Meskell, L. M. 1997a: Egyptian social dynamics: the evidence of age, sex and class in domestic and mortuary contexts, unpublished PhD thesis, Department of Archaeology, Cambridge University.

Meskell, L. M. 1997b: Engendering Egypt, *Gender and History: Body and Gender in the Ancient Mediterranean* 9 (3): 557–602.

Meskell, L. M. 1998a: The irresistible body and the seduction of archaeology. In D. Montserrat (ed.), *Changing Bodies, Changing Meanings: Studies on the Human Body in Antiquity*. London, Routledge, pp. 139–61.

Meskell, L. M. 1998b: Running the gamut: gender, girls and goddesses, *American Journal of Archaeology* 102: 181–5.

Meskell, L. M. 1998c: Intimate archaeologies: the case of Kha and Merit, *World Archaeology* 29 (3): 363–79.

Meskell, L. M. 1998d: Twin peaks: the archaeologies of Çatalhöyük. In C. Morris and L. Goodison (eds), *Ancient Goddesses: the Myths and Evidence*. London, British Museum Press, pp. 46–62.

Meskell, L. M. 1998e: Oh my goddesses: archaeology, sexuality and ecofeminism, *Archaeological Dialogues*, 5 (2): 126–42.

Meskell, L. M. 1998f: An archaeology of social relations in an Egyptian village, *Journal of Archaeological Method and Theory* 5 (3): 209–43.

Meskell, L. M. 1999: The archaeologies of life and death, *American Journal of Archaeology*, 103 (2): 181–99.

Meskell, L. M. forthcoming a: Re-embedding sex: domesticity, sexuality and ritual in New Kingdom Egypt. In B. Voss and R. Schmidt (eds), *Archaeologies of Sexuality*. London, Routledge.

Meskell, L. M. forthcoming b: Embodying archaeology: theory and praxis. In T. G. Wilfong and C. E. Jones (eds), *Materials for a History of the Human Body in the Ancient Near East*. Groeningen, Styx.

Meskell, L. M. forthcoming c: The Egyptian ways of death. In M. Chesson (ed.), *Social Memory, Identity and Death: Intradisciplinary Perspectives on Mortuary Rituals*. Washington, DC, American Anthropological Association.

Metcalf, P. and Huntingdon, R. 1991: *Celebrations of Death: the Anthropology of Mortuary Ritual*. Cambridge, Cambridge University Press.

Midgley, M. 1984: Sex and personal identity: the Western individualistic tradition, *Encounter* 63 (1): 50–5.

Milde, H. 1988: 'Going out into the day': Ancient Egyptian beliefs and practices concerning death. In J. M. Bremer, T. P. van den Hout and R. Peters (eds), *Hidden Futures: Death and Immortality in Ancient Egypt, Anatolia, the Classical, Biblical and Arabic-Islamic World*. Amsterdam, University of Amsterdam Press, pp. 15–35.

Miller, D., Rowlands, M. and Tilley, C. (eds) 1989: *Domination and Resistance*. London, Allen and Unwin.

Miller, D. and Tilley, C. (eds) 1984: *Ideology, Power and Prehistory*. Cambridge, Cambridge University Press.

Mittwoch, U. 1992: Sex determination and sex reversal: genotype, phenotype, dogma and semantics, *Human Genetics* 89: 467–79.

Montserrat, D. 1993: The representation of young males in 'Fayum Portraits', *Journal of Egyptian Archaeology* 79: 215–25.

Montserrat, D. 1996: *Sex and Society in Graeco-Roman Egypt*. London, Kegan Paul International.

Montserrat, D. 1997: Death and funerals in the Roman Fayyum. In M. Bierbrier (ed.), *Portraits and Masks*. London, British Museum Press, pp. 33–44.

Montserrat, D. 1998: Unidentified human remains: mummies and the erotics of biography. In D. Montserrat (ed.), *Changing Bodies, Changing Meanings: Studies on the Human Body in Antiquity*. London, Routledge, pp. 162–212.

Montserrat, D. and Meskell, L. M. 1997: Mortuary archaeology and religious landscape at Graeco-Roman Deir el Medina, *Journal of Egyptian Archaeology* 84: 179–98.

Moore, H. 1988: *Feminism and Anthropology*. Cambridge, Polity Press.

Moore, H. 1990: Paul Ricoeur: action, meaning and text. In C. Tilley (ed.), *Reading Material Culture*. Oxford, Blackwell, pp. 85–120.

Moore, H. 1994: *A Passion for Difference*. Cambridge, Polity Press.

Moore, J. and Scott, E. (eds) 1997: *Invisible People and Processes: Writing Gender and Childhood into European Archaeology*. London, Leicester University Press.

Morris, B. 1991: *Western Conceptions of the Individual*. Oxford, Berg.

Morris, C. 1993: Hands up for the individual! The role of attribution studies in Aegean prehistory, *Cambridge Archaeological Journal* 3 (1): 41–66.

Morris, I. 1987: *Burial and Ancient Society: the Rise of the Greek City-State*. Cambridge, Cambridge University Press.

Morris, R. C. 1995: All made up: performance theory and the new anthropology of sex and gender, *Annual Review of Anthropology* 24: 567–92.

Mutén, B. (ed.) 1994: *Return of the Great Goddess*. Dublin, Gill and Macmillan.

Narayan, U. 1997: Contesting cultures: 'westernization', respect for cultures and third-world feminists. In L. Nicholson (ed.), *The Second Wave: a Reader in Feminist Theory*. New York, Routledge, pp. 396–414.

Nead, L. 1992: *The Female Nude: Art, Obscenity and Sexuality*. London, Routledge.

Nelson, S. M. 1997: *Gender in Archaeology: Analyzing Power and Prestige*. Walnut Creek, CA, Altamira Press.

New, C. 1996: Man bad, woman good? Essentialism and ecofeminisms, *New Left Review* 216: 79–93.

Nicholson, L. J. (ed.) 1990: *Feminism/Postmodernism*. New York, Routledge.

Nicholson, L. J. (ed.) 1997: *The Second Wave: a Reader in Feminist Theory*. New York, Routledge.

Nordström, H-A. 1996: The Nubian A-group: ranking funerary remains, *Norwegian Archaeological Review* 26 (1): 17–39.

Norris, C. 1992: Deconstruction, postmodernism and philosophy: Habermas on Derrida. In D. Wood (ed.), *Derrida: a Critical Reader*, Oxford, Blackwell, pp. 167–92.

Nunn, J. F. 1996: *Ancient Egyptian Medicine*. London, British Museum Press.

Osborne, R. 1998a: Men without clothes: heroic nakedness and Greek art, *Gender and History: Gender and Body in the Ancient Mediterranean* 9 (3): 80–104.

Osborne, R. 1998b: Sculpted men of Athens: masculinity and power in the field of vision. In L. Foxhall and J. Salmon (eds), *Thinking Men: Mas-*

*culinity and its Self-representation in the Classical Tradition.* London, Routledge, pp. 23–42.

O'Shea, J. M. 1984: *Mortuary Variability: an Archaeological Investigation.* Orlando, Academic Press.

Parker Pearson, M. 1982: Mortuary practices, society and ideology: an ethnoarchaeological study. In I. Hodder (ed.), *Symbolic and Structural Archaeology.* Cambridge, Cambridge University Press, pp. 99–114.

Parkinson, R. B. 1991: *Voices from Ancient Egypt.* London, British Museum Press.

Parkinson, R. B. 1995: 'Homosexual' desire and Middle Kingdom literature, *Journal of Egyptian Archaeology* 81: 57–76.

Parkinson, R. B. 1997: *The Tale of Sinuhe and other Ancient Egyptian Poems.* Oxford, Clarendon Press.

Petrie, W. M. F. 1923: *Social Life in Ancient Egypt.* London, Constable.

Pinch, G. 1993: *Votive Offerings to Hathor.* Oxford, Griffith Institute.

Pinch, G. 1994: *Magic in Ancient Egypt.* London, British Museum Press.

Pollock, S. 1991: Of priestesses, princes and poor relations: the dead in the Royal Cemetery of Ur, *Cambridge Archaeological Journal* 1 (2): 171–89.

Poole, F. J. P. 1994: Socialization, enculturation and the development of personal identity. In T. Ingold (ed.), *Companion Encyclopedia of Anthropology: Humanity, Culture and Social Life.* London, Routledge, pp. 831–60.

Porter, R. 1997: Introduction. In R. Porter (ed.), *Rewriting the Self: Histories from the Renaissance to the Present.* London, Routledge, pp. 1–14.

Prezzano, S. 1997: Warfare, women, and households: the development of Iroquois culture. In C. Claassen and R. A. Joyce (eds), *Women in Prehistory: North America and Mesoamerica.* Philadelphia, University of Pennsylvania Press, pp. 88–99.

Proust, M. 1921/1987: *Remembrance of Things Past.* London, Penguin.

Radicalesbians 1997: The woman identified woman. In L. Nicholson (ed.), *The Second Wave: a Reader in Feminist Theory.* New York, Routledge, pp. 152–7.

Rapport, N. 1997: *Transcendent Individual: Towards a Literary and Liberal Anthropology.* London, Routledge.

Richlin, A. 1998: Foucault's *History of Sexuality*: a useful theory for women? In D. H. J. Larmour, P. A. Miller and C. Platter (eds), *Rethinking Sexuality: Foucault and Classical Antiquity.* Princeton, NJ, Princeton University Press, pp. 138–70.

Ricoeur, P. 1981: *Hermeneutics and the Human Sciences.* Cambridge, Cambridge University Press.

Ringrose, K. M. 1993: Living in the shadows: eunuchs and gender in Byzantium. In G. Herdt (ed.), *Third Sex, Third Gender.* New York, Zone Books, pp. 85–109.

Ritner, R. K. 1993: *The Mechanics of Ancient Egyptian Magical Practice.* Chicago, Oriental Institute, University of Chicago.

Robins, G. 1993: *Women in Ancient Egypt.* London, British Museum Press.

Robins, G. 1994a: Some principles of compositional dominance and gender hierarchy in Egyptian art, *Journal of the American Research Center in Egypt* 31: 33–40.

Robins, G. 1994b: *Proportion and Style in Ancient Egyptian Art.* Austin, Texas University Press.

Robins, G. 1994c: Review of *Growing up in Ancient Egypt* by R. M. and J. J. Janssen (1990), *Journal of Egyptian Archaeology* 80: 232–5.

Robins, G. 1996: Dress, undress, and the representation of fertility and potency in New Kingdom Egyptian Art. In N. Boymel Kampen (ed.), *Sexuality in Ancient Art.* Cambridge, Cambridge University Press, pp. 27–40.

Romer, J. 1984: *Ancient Lives: the Story of the Pharaoh's Tombmakers.* London, Weidenfeld and Nicolson.

Rorty, R. 1995: Feminism and pragmatism. In R. B. Goodman (ed.), *Pragmatism: a Reader.* New York, Routledge, pp. 125–48.

Rosaldo, R. 1986: Grief and a headhunter's rage: on the cultural force of the emotions. In E. Brunner (ed.), *Text, Play and Story: the Construction and Reconstruction of Self and Society.* Washington, American Ethnological Society, pp. 178–95.

Rosaldo, R. 1989: *Culture and Truth: the Remaking of Social Analysis.* Boston, Beacon Press.

Ross, E. and Rapp, R. 1997: Sex and society: a research note from social history and anthropology. In R. N. Lancaster and M. di Leonardo (eds), *The Gender/Sexuality Reader: Culture, History, Political Economy.* New York, Routledge, pp. 153–68.

Roth, A. M. 1993: Fingers, stars, and the 'Opening of the Mouth': the nature and function of the *nṯrwj*-blades, *Journal of Egyptian Archaeology* 79: 57–79.

Rubin, G. 1975: The traffic in women: notes on the 'political economy' of sex. In R. R. Reiter (ed.), *Toward an Anthropology of Women.* New York, Monthly Review Press, pp. 157–210.

Russmann, E. R. 1980: The anatomy of an artistic convention: representation of the near foot in two dimensions through the New Kingdom, *BES* 2: 57–81.

Sawday, J. 1997: Self and selfhood in the seventeenth century. In R. Porter (ed.), *Rewriting the Self: Histories from the Renaissance to the Present.* London, Routledge, pp. 29–48.

Sawicki, J. 1991: *Disciplining Foucault: Feminism, Power and the Body.* New York, Routledge.

Schafer, A. J. 1995: Sex determination and its pathology on man, *Advances in Genetics* 33: 275–329.

Schiaparelli, E. 1927: *La tomba intatta dell'architetto Cha.* Turin, Museo di Antichità.

Scott, E. 1992: Images and contexts of infants and infant burials: some thoughts on some cross-cultural evidence, *Archaeological Review from Cambridge* 11 (1): 77–92.

Seager, J. 1994: *Earth Follies*. London, Routledge.

Seidler, V. J. 1989: *Rediscovering Masculinity: Reason, Language and Sexuality*. London, Routledge.

Seidler, V. J. 1997: *Man Enough: Embodying Masculinities*. London, Sage.

Shanks, M. and Tilley, C. 1982: Ideology, symbolic power and ritual communication: a reinterpretation of Neolithic mortuary practices. In I. Hodder (ed.), *The Archaeology of Contextual Meanings*. Cambridge, Cambridge University Press, pp. 129–54.

Shanks, M. and Tilley, C. 1987a: *Social Theory and Archaeology*. Cambridge, Polity Press.

Shanks, M. and Tilley, C. 1987b: *Re-constructing Archaeology: Theory and Practice*. London, Routledge.

Shilling, C. 1993: *The Body and Social Theory*. London, Sage.

Shilling, C. and Mellor, P. A. 1996: Embodiment, structuration theory and modernity: mind/body dualism and the repression of sensuality, *Body and Society* 2 (4): 1–15.

Simmel, G. 1971: *On Individuality and Social Forms*. Chicago, Chicago University Press.

Smith, S. T. 1992: Intact tombs of the Seventeenth and Eighteenth Dynasties from Thebes and the New Kingdom burial system, *Mitteilungen des Deutschen Archäologischen Instituts, Abteilung Kairo* 48: 193–231.

Somerville, S. 1997: Scientific racism and the invention of the homosexual body. In R. N. Lancaster and M. di Leonardo (eds), *The Gender/Sexuality Reader: Culture, History, Political Economy*. New York, Routledge, pp. 37–52.

Spector, J. D. 1994: *What this Awl Means: Feminist Archaeology at a Wahpeton Dakota Village*. St Paul, Minnesota Historical Society Press.

Strathern, A. J. 1996: *Body Thoughts*. Ann Arbor, University of Michigan Press.

Strathern, M. 1987: Producing difference: connections and disconnections in two New Guinea Highland kinship systems. In J. F. Collier and S. J. Yanagisako (eds), *Gender and Kinship: Essays Toward a Unified Analysis*. Stanford, Stanford University Press, pp. 271–300.

Strathern, M. 1988: *The Gender of the Gift: Problems with Women and Problems with Society in Melanesia*. Berkeley, CA, University of Califorina Press.

Strathern, M. 1992: *After Nature: English Kinship in the Late Twentieth Century*. Cambridge, Cambridge University Press.

Strickland, S. 1994: Feminism, postmodernism and difference. In K. Lennon and M. Whitford (eds), *Knowing the Difference: Feminist Perspectives in Epistemology*. London, Routledge, pp. 265–74.

Tainter, J. A. 1978: Mortuary practices and the study of prehistoric social systems, *Advances in Archaeological Method and Theory* 1: 105–41.

Talalay, L. E. 1994: A feminist boomerang: the great goddess of Greek prehistory, *Gender and History* 6: 165–83.

Tanesini, M. 1994: Whose language? In K. Lennon and M. Whitford (eds), *Knowing the Difference: Feminist Perspectives in Epistemology*. London, Routledge, pp. 203–16.

Tarlow, S. A. 1992: Each slow dusk a drawing-down of blinds, *Archaeological Review from Cambridge* 11 (1): 125–40.

Tarlow, S. A. 1999: *Bereavement and Commemoration: an Archaeology of Mortality*. Oxford, Blackwell.

Taylor, J. 1996: Patterns of colouring on ancient Egyptian coffins, from the New Kingdom to the Twenty-sixth Dynasty, paper delivered at the Colour and Painting in Ancient Egypt Conference, British Museum, London.

Taylor, T. 1996: *The Prehistory of Sex: Four Million Years of Human Sexual Culture*. London, Fourth Estate.

Thomas, J. 1989: Technologies of the self and the constitution of the subject, *Archaeological Review from Cambridge* 8 (1): 101–7.

Thomas, J. 1993: The hermeneutics of megalithic space. In C. Tilley (ed.), *Interpretive Archaeology*. Oxford, Berg, pp. 73–97.

Thomas, J. 1995: Reconciling symbolic significance with being-in-the-world. In I. Hodder, M. Shanks, A. Alexandri, V. Buchli, J. Carman, J. Last and G. Lucas (eds), *Interpreting Archaeology: Finding Meaning in the Past*. London, Routledge, pp. 210–11.

Thomas, J. 1996: *Time, Culture and Identity*. London, Routledge.

Thomas, J. 1998: Archaeology's humanism and the materiality of the body, paper delivered at the Thinking through the Body Conference, Lampeter, Wales.

Tilley, C. 1990: Foucault: towards an archaeology of archaeology. In C. Tilley (ed.), *Reading Material Culture*. London, Blackwell, pp. 281–347.

Tilley, C. 1994: *A Phenomenology of Landscape: Places, Paths and Monuments*. Oxford, Berg.

Toda, E. 1920: La découverte et l'inventaire du tombeau de Sen-Nezem, *Annales du Service des Antiquités de l'Egypte* 20: 145–58.

Toivari, J. 1998: Marriage at Deir el Medina. In C. J. Eyre (ed.), *Proceedings of the Seventh International Congress of Egyptologists*. Leuven, Uitgeverij Peeters, pp. 1157–63.

Toivari, J. in progress: The social status of women in Deir el-Medina, unpublished PhD thesis, Department of Egyptology, University of Leiden.

Tosi, M. and Roccati, A. 1972: *Stele e altre epigrafi di Deir el Medina. N. 50001–N. 50262*. Turin, Edizioni d'arte Fratelli Pozzo.

Toubia, N. F. 1985: The social and political implications of female circumcision: the case of Sudan. In E. Warnock Fernea (ed.), *Women and the Family in the Middle East: New Voices of Change*. Austin, University of Texas Press, pp. 148–59.

Tougher, S. F. 1997: Byzantine eunuchs: an overview, with special reference to their creation and origin. In L. James (ed.), *Women, Men and Eunuchs: Gender in Byzantium*. London, Routledge, pp. 168–84.

Touraine, A. 1995: Sociology and the study of society. In P. Joyce (ed.), *Class*. Oxford, Oxford University Press, pp. 83–9.

Trigger, B. G. 1998: Archaeology and epistemology: dialoguing across the Darwinian chasm, *American Journal of Archaeology* 102: 1–34.

Tringham, R. 1991: Households with faces: the challenge of gender in prehistoric architectural remains. In J. M. Gero and M. W. Conkey (eds), *Engendering Archaeology: Women and Prehistory*. Oxford, Blackwell, pp. 93–131.

Turner, B. S. 1996: *The Body and Society*. London, Sage.

Turner, V. 1967: *The Forest of Symbols*. Ithaca, NY, Cornell University Press.

Valbelle, D. 1972: Le naos de Kasa au Musée de Turin, *Bulletin de l'Institut Français d'Archéologie Orientale* 72: 179–94.

Valbelle, D. 1981: *Satis et Anoukis*. Mainz, Philipp von Zabern.

Valbelle, D. 1985: *'Les Ouvriers de la Tombe': Deir el Médineh à l'époque ramesside*. Cairo, Institut Français d'Archéologie Orientale.

Van Gennep, A. 1960: *The Rites of Passage*. Chicago, University of Chicago Press.

Walde, D. and Willows, N. D. (eds) 1991: *The Archaeology of Gender: Proceedings of the 22nd Annual Chacmool Conference*. Calgary, University of Calgary Archaeological Association.

Walker, J. H. 1996: *Studies in Ancient Egyptian Anatomical Terminology*. Warminster, Aris and Phillips.

Walker, S. 1997: Mummy portraits and Roman portraiture. In S. Walker and M. Bierbrier (eds), *Ancient Faces: Mummy Portraits from Roman Egypt*. London, British Museum Press, pp. 14–16.

Ward, W. A. 1994: Foreigners living in the village. In L. H. Lesko (ed.), *Pharaoh's Workers: the Villagers of Deir el Medina*. Ithaca, NY, Cornell University Press, pp. 61–85.

Wason, P. K. 1994: *The Archaeology of Rank*. Cambridge, Cambridge University Press.

Weeks, J. 1997: *Sexuality*. London, Routledge.

Wente, E. 1990: *Letters from Ancient Egypt*. Atlanta, Scholars Press.

West, C. 1995: Prophetic pragmatism: cultural criticism and political engagement. In R. B. Goodman (ed.), *Pragmatism: a Reader*. New York, Routledge, pp. 209–33.

Whaley, E. J. 1981: Introduction. In E. J. Whaley (ed.), *Mirrors of Mortality: Studies in the Social History of Death*. London, Europa Publications, pp. 1–14.

Wilde, O. 1913: *Intentions*. London, Methuen.

Wilfong, T. G. 1994: 'The woman of Jême': women's roles in a Coptic town in Late Antique Egypt, unpublished PhD thesis, Department of Near Eastern Languages and Civilizations, University of Chicago.

Wilfong, T. G. (ed.) 1997: *Women and Gender in Ancient Egypt: from Prehistory to Late Antiquity*. Ann Arbor, MI, Kelsey Museum of Archaeology.

Wilfong, T. G. 1998: Reading the disjointed body in Coptic: from physical modification to textual fragmentation. In D. Montserrat (ed.), *Changing Bodies, Changing Meanings: Studies on the Human Body in Antiquity*. London, Routledge, pp. 116–36.

Willems, H. 1988: *Chests of Life: a Study of the Typology and Conceptual Development of Middle Kingdom Standard Class Coffins*. Leiden, Ex Oriente Lux.

Willems, H. 1994: *The Coffin of Heqata (Cairo JdE 36418)*. Leuven, Peeters and Departement Oriëntalistiek.

Williams, B. 1993: *Shame and Necessity*. Berkeley, CA, University of California Press.

Williams, C. D. 1997: 'Another self in the case': gender, marriage and the individual in Augustan literature. In R. Porter (ed.), *Rewriting the Self: Histories from the Renaissance to the Present*. London, Routledge, pp. 97–118.

Winkler, J. J. 1990: *The Constraints of Desire: the Anthropology of Sex and Gender in Ancient Greece*. New York, Routledge.

Winter, I. J. 1996: Sex, rhetoric, and the public monument: the alluring body of Naram-Sîn of Agade. In N. B. Kampen (ed.), *Sexuality in Ancient Art: Near East, Egypt, Greece and Italy*. Cambridge, Cambridge University Press, pp. 11–26.

Wittig, M. 1980: The Straight Mind, *Feminist Issues* 1: 103–10.

Worthman, C. M. 1995: Hormones, sex and gender, *Annual Review of Anthropology* 24: 593–616.

Wright, R. A. (ed.) 1996: *Gender and Archaeology*, Philadelphia, University of Pennsylvania Press.

Wylie, A. 1991: Gender theory and the archaeological record: why is there no archaeology of gender? In J. M. Gero and M. W. Conkey (eds), *Engendering Archaeology: Women and Prehistory*. Oxford, Blackwell, pp. 31–54.

Wylie, A. 1992a: The interplay of evidential constraints and political interests: recent archaeological research on gender, *American Antiquity* 57 (1): 15–35.

Wylie, A. 1992b: Feminist theories of social power: implications for a processual archaeology, *Norwegian Archaeological Review* 25 (1): 51–68.

Yates, T. 1990: Jacques Derrida: 'There is nothing outside of the text'. In C. Tilley (ed.), *Reading Material Culture*. Oxford, Blackwell, pp. 206–80.

Yates, T. 1993: Frameworks for an archaeology of the body. In C. Tilley (ed.), *Interpretive Archaeology*. Oxford, Berg, pp. 31–72.

Yates, T. and Nordbladh, J. 1990: This perfect body, this virgin text: between sex and gender in archaeology. In I. Bapty and T. Yates (eds), *Archaeology after Structuralism*. London, Routledge, pp. 222–37.

Young, B. and Papadatou, D. 1997: Childhood death and bereavement across cultures. In C. M. Parkes, P. Laugani and B. Young (eds), *Death and Bereavement across Cultures*. London, Routledge, pp. 191–205.

Zandee, J. 1960: *Death as an Enemy According to Ancient Egyptian Conceptions*. Leiden, E. J. Brill.

Zita, J. N. 1998: *Body Talk: Philosophical Reflections on Sex and Gender*. New York, Columbia.

# Index